PENGU

WHISPERS OF HOPE

Chris Mabey is a writer, psychologist and emeritus professor at Middlesex University Business School, London.

He has held a career-long interest in how organizations develop their leaders. Initially this was with British Telecom and Rank Xerox. More recently his research and writing have turned to ethical leadership and the enigma of cultural leadership in Myanmar. He recently led an ESRC-funded Seminar Series on Ethical Leadership: Philosophical and Spiritual Approaches.

Chris has eleven academic books to his name (and twenty refereed papers), each subject to critical peer-review. One text he authored in Human Resource Management has sales of 21,500 to date.

Since marrying into a Burmese family in 1973, he has been a keen observer of Myanmar, making frequent visits with his wife and on one occasion with their four daughters.

PRAISE FOR THE BOOK

This book is intelligent, thoughtful, thorough, and threaded with lyrical expression especially around architecture, landscape, costume and food. It disseminates ideas and knowledge acquired from and inspired by a unique location, with the gravitational undertow of faith and family.

Anastasia Parkes, feature writer and author

. . . a fascinating manuscript. It's so rich in texture and colour that it is like an enigmatic painting with so many bright as well as dark shades in it leaving the viewer in awe as well as a bit sad. It also brings out things that you see as a non-Myanmar which we do not notice or are oblivious of. I think many Myanmar as well as others who are interested in our country will find your book very refreshing and vibrant as you have written in a warm, friendly way, touching vividly on many areas, of the past and the present, from an emotional as well as psychological angle.

Kyi Kyi May, former BBC Correspondent to Myanmar

. . . affecting, influential, challenging, educational, balanced and compassionate. And of course, while the boundary is that of Burma, it extends well beyond that, into some resonant place in our souls. The research is painstakingly but not loudly done. It draws upon sources sparingly, and give all credit where credit is due. This gives an air of trustworthiness, of reliability to the entire project. The mix of narrative voices – often complimentary, sometimes contradictory – brings much colour, vibrancy, immediacy to the piece.

Dr Daniel Doherty, founder of the Critical Coaching Research Group, UK

It is wonderful as a collection of personal stories, interspersed with reference to political and historical reports. I found your speculation of the position and silence of Aung San Suu Kyi helpful. The later chapters illustrating what young activists are doing were inspirational . . . Having looked for things to read about Myanmar prior to my visit a year ago, I feel confident that this book is a unique and contemporary addition to what exists.

Dr Clare Rigg, Senior Lecturer, University of Liverpool

The plight of the many minority peoples in Myanmar today is heart-rending yet, apart from the ethnic cleansing of the Rohingya, it is rarely publicised. Also perplexing is the public stance of Aung San Suu Kyi. In a gently probing manner, Dr. Mabey exposes the roots of these and other vexing issues. In this rare and revealing book, the conundrums of modern Myanmar are animated by a string of unusual encounters, family connections and intimate observations.

The Baroness Cox, Founder and CEO Humanitarian Aid Relief Trust

The history of Burma is encapsulated in this brief piece of work, done with a lightness of touch . . . Aung San Sui Kyi's observation that the Burmese realise that "one's destiny is decided entirely by one's actions" is borne out by these lovingly crafted vignettes of expats and Burmese people from all walks of life: their resilient spirit permeates the exquisitely crafted tale. This is a deeply intimate yet eternally universal story about family, survival, culture, nourishment, memory, courage, and love – all unfurled before the pitiless and uncaring gaze of politics, governments, edicts, laws and military juntas. Ultimately it is a tour de force of how we lose ourselves and then find ourselves.

Dr Christine Eastman, School of Business, Middlesex University

Whispers of Hope is a memoir of Burma/Myanmar with a difference as only Chris Mabey (a renowned academic in Leadership studies and a devoted Christian) and his family can tell it. The story begins with the author's telling of his meeting with a beautiful Burmese girl in England and falling for the warmth of her family. As the story unfolds, the author delicately weaves together the conversations about Burma he had with the family members and the people he met in the country and his reflections on the changes in Burma. This family memoir gives an insight into the real lives of Burmese people and their culture and history. It will be of interest to anyone who is intrigued by the paradoxes of early and modern Myanmar.

Linda Hsiu-Yun Hsieh, Associate Professor at
Birmingham University Business School

WHISPERS OF HOPE

A FAMILY MEMOIR OF MYANMAR

CHRIS MABEY

PENGUIN BOOKS

An imprint of Penguin Random House

PENGUIN BOOKS

USA | Canada | UK | Ireland | Australia
New Zealand | India | South Africa | China | Southeast Asia

Penguin Books is part of the Penguin Random House group of companies
whose addresses can be found at global.penguinrandomhouse.com

Published by Penguin Random House SEA Pte Ltd
9, Changi South Street 3, Level 08-01,
Singapore 486361

First published in Penguin Books by Penguin Random House SEA 2021

Copyright © Chris Mabey 2021

ISBN 9789814954259

Typeset in Adobe Caslon Pro by Manipal Technologies Limited, Manipal

www.penguin.sg

With love to April,
from whom I am still learning

CONTENTS

SECTION 3: HOPE

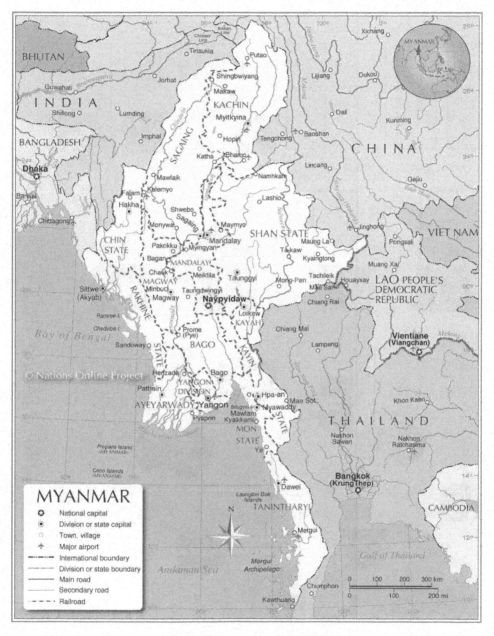

Source: UN Cartographic Section
With permission from the United Nations Map No. 4168 Rev. 3 June 2012

APRIL'S FAMILY TREE

- Findlay Francis, Anglo-Indian
- Daw Seri Nyunt, Shan
- U Thar Yike, Mon Chieftan
- ?
- Henry Yarde, 1860
- Martha Mah Thit, 1862
- Maung Maung Gyi
- Lady-in-waiting to Queen Supayalat

- Henry Francis 1893
- Thar Kyu 1893
- Frederick Yarde 1894
- Khin Khin Nu 1904

- m. 1918
- m. 1923

- Austin Horace Francis 1917
- Uncle Abu
- Auntie Jessie
- Margaret Yarde 1927

- Morris: April's cousin

- m. 1948
- Gay b.1954
- April Francis b.1950
- Elizabeth b.1948

PREFACE

This is a fascinating manuscript. It is so rich in texture and colour that it is like an enigmatic painting with so many bright and dark shades, leaving the viewer in awe as well as a bit sad. It also brings out the things you see as a non-Myanmar which we do not notice or are oblivious of.

After reading *Whispers of Hope*, I was left with a mixture of feelings about my motherland. It's hard to describe it. Was I agonizing about the past? I don't know. Am I feeling sad about all the things happening at present and/or am I worried about the future of our beloved country? It's quite akin to what the author has written about his dear wife's treasured jewels from Burma which were lost in the English sea. Some of the most cherished things of the past are irretrievable and yet we cling on to them in our memories. I wonder if people from similar backgrounds and similar fates have the same feelings? Readers who have lived here and loved the country of Burma will naturally feel nostalgic when they come across episodes in this book that remind of wistful encounters from the past. Readers who have never been to Burma but have jotted down the country's name on their bucket list, will be enticed to go and see for themselves, to check whether the author has romanticized it too much. I'll leave it for the reader to find out themselves.

As a Myanmar, it is thrilling to read the conversations the author had with the Burmese people of different generations and

varied backgrounds: the aunt who remembers in minute detail about
the time when General Aung San was assassinated seventy years
ago; the young Chin national who wants to save money to own a
business, open a restaurant ten years from now and then teach the
younger generation how to cook and bake, on top of teaching them
about 'Jesus' love'; the soul-searching journey that the author and his
wife embarked upon in their twenties, as followers of a new cult-like
movement from California, was also intriguing and I think people
with open minds from all religious denominations will find it heart-
warming. It's equally moving to know that someone from a farming
background is now working for the Mines Advisory Group, helping
people affected by land mines. There are so many positive stories
as well as heart-rending ones: the story of the beautiful bungalow
that had seen happier times being deserted in the Shan states, the
author's family on a trip in search of a half-remembered holiday
home, or making friends with the restaurant owner in Sandoway
and so on.

This book is a treasure trove of many precious gems. The
reader can pick and choose whatever he or she fancies and can gain
some insight into a mysterious albeit charming country. Still in a
conundrum, its people are waiting for much longed for peace, unity
and prosperity among the many diverse groups that form the Republic
of the Union of Myanmar. For those who want to understand the
political situation of Myanmar in a nutshell, the chapters entitled
'Some Burn-Up' and 'Letting Go' offer an overall account of the
past decades. For myself, like a schoolgirl turning the pages, I am
fascinated to read about people and what they experienced in the
good old days and how they struggled during the harrowing times
after Burma gained independence.

I think many Myanmar nationals, as well as others who are
interested in our country, will find this book very refreshing and
vibrant: an eye-opening, tongue-tingling, mind-stretching, spirit-
enriching experience. It is written in a warm, friendly way, touching
vividly on many areas of the past and the present, from emotional

as well as psychological angles. This is what we might expect of a professor of psychology but he also writes as someone who grows to love Myanmar through the love of his life, a precious gem of Burma, whom he met and married nearly half a century ago.

Kyi Kyi May
Head of Burmese Service (retired) BBC World,
Shwe GonDine, Yangon

September 2020

PROLOGUE

The radio crackled with the news that Dag Hammarskjold had died in a plane crash over Africa. For some reason, that strange-sounding name stayed with me. He was described as the Secretary General of the United Nations, whatever that was. Not yet a teenager, I knew nothing about the UN, nor about the awful follies of the Second World War and the subsequent attempts to foster international peace. I had no inkling that in other countries children of my age were desperately poor, prone to disease and without schools. Geopolitics in the 1960s may have been in the balance, but I only knew that whenever I pulled on my school's gold and green football shirt I felt warm pride, far removed from something they called the Cold War. Distant nations may have been using technology to devise weapons of mass destruction, but I was more gripped by the technology behind the moon landing which we watched on our first black-and-white TV set. I do recall that Hammarskjold was succeeded by someone with an equally unusual name: U Thant. A name I would by chance unearth half a century later.

It must have been a few years before this that I came across a very old copy of the *National Geographic Magazine*, dated July 1930. I found it in a pile of *Rupert Bear* comics and *Eagle* annuals in the box-room at my grandmother's house. An article on Burma caught my attention. I'm not sure the country name registered at the time but the stories and photos of elephants logging teak in the forests were entrancing. It took me to another world. For an hour or so, I sat oblivious to the melancholy tick of the grandfather clock on the landing, to the lazy buzz of summer flies. There was something magical about the slightly quaint description of this imperial outpost with photos of elephants wading into forest pools:

> 'their heavy saddles . . . are padded with several layers of an astringent bark to prevent galling the back. The breast straps, plaited out of bark rope by the riders themselves are well-dressed with pig's fat from Chicago.'

From the fading yellow pages emerged the wonderful journey of the lumber once the elephants had hauled it to the creek beds. As the monsoon rains fell steadily, blinding sheets from an overladen sky, the water level rose and the logs began to jostle as they floated. Then moving merrily, they crashed together with a sound like thunder that could be heard above the roar of the water, borne by the flood to the big river. From here they were caught and made into rafts of about 125 logs apiece in the charge of four or five men. The description transported me down that river. For all the unfamiliarity with the scene, I was on those rafts and part of the lumberjack adventure. Once on the broad, lazy reaches of the Irrawaddy, the logs drifted and were steered by launches through the busy shipping lanes beyond Rangoon. At the mills, five, six or seven months after leaving the forest, they found themselves safely behind the booms waiting for the saws. Bandsaws working under electric power ripped them into planks for shipbuilders throughout the world.

I loved my trips to the local Odeon cinema as a child. Sinking into the plush crimson seats, I watched one of my first war films in the late 1950s. It was *Bridge on the River Kwai*. The Japanese had invaded Burma and needed better communications to support their troops. Two labour forces, one based in Siam (now Thailand) and the other in Burma, worked from opposite ends of the line towards the centre. Despite a huge loss of life, the railway was never connected.

Most of the details passed me by but the early technicolour images stayed with me. The film fired my fascination for this part of the world.

With all these magical moments infused in my memory, I guess I was subliminally prepared for the encounter with Burma which came when I was sixteen. I found myself welcomed into a very different home to my own. A gentle, no-airs-and-graces, unconditional embrace at the table of a Burmese family. Possibly the only non-English household in the sleepy English village where I lived. One of their three daughters enchanted my heart, but it took a few months for my innate shyness to melt enough for me to ask April out for a date.

Feeling very grown-up, I took her to the beach at Winchelsea. It boasts a two-mile stretch of sea wall. Esplanade is too fine a word. It has neither the jaunty thrills and amusement arcades of neighbouring Hastings nor the cobbled streets and picture-postcard appeal of nearby Rye. I had spent many holidays on this part of the Sussex coast as a boy. My dad would park our two-tone Austin Cambridge at the sea wall. Peter, my older brother, and I would clamber up the steps with towels, picnic box, wind-break, cricket bats to survey the beach beyond: a strip of tarmac, then pebbles with a few sandy patches and mud at low tide. As kids, we were dispatched to 'bag' a breakwater. Not difficult as few holidaymakers had yet discovered this out-of-the-way resort.

It started as a carefree day—April in her checked gingham skirt and tie-dyed top, the beach to ourselves. The salty air brought back boyhood memories of endless cricket games and crabbing at low tide. I was not to know it would backfire. Looking back on that day, I wish I had never gently cajoled her into the sea, which even in the height of summer, shocked her delicate disposition. For someone more used to the balmy waters of the Bay of Bengal, this was torture and she was soon out again. As she huddled in a beach towel she discovered that her two rings, an emerald and a lustrous moon sapphire, had slipped from her fingers. Among the few precious possessions she had brought with her from her homeland four years before, they had now been claimed by the muddy waters of the English Channel. Of course, we searched, scrabbling desperately at the stones. We waited till the tide had turned and searched again, but we knew in our hearts that the fine gems were forever gone. April looked out silently at the churning surf and let it pass, knowing that some things can never be recovered.

Fortunately for me, this was not the end of my hopes for winning her heart. As time passed I realized that I had fallen in love not only with a Burmese girl but also with a Burmese way of life. The warmth of her family home, the tantalizing tastes that came from their kitchen, the disarming beauty of a daughter with a far-off look from a distant land. But was I becoming seduced by the exoticism, rocked by the romance of difference? And was I in love with the idea, a misty-eyed image of Burma rather than Burma itself? As time went by I discovered a very much less enticing picture of modern Myanmar. A story of a country wrapped in pathos. A lost empire ruled from Ava and Mandalay. Racist rule by Britain followed by an unending secretive and brutal regime. A record of atrocious human rights and Aung San Suu Kyi's tarnished reputation. I began to find much of the cultural heritage of Myanmar as a nation to have disappeared from view, scattered and ground underfoot by the relentless march of military boots.

Unlike the gems forever lost in the English sea, I wondered whether the bejewelled and serene resilience of Burma could ever be retrieved. Could any hope for the country be found among its upcoming millennials? It seemed, a miracle was needed. And what of the two of us, what would become of our early romance? The enigmatic Orient coming up against the coded rationalities of the West. Much of what I held dear was being challenged by the conundrums of her conflicted country.

SECTION ONE

EARLY ROMANCE

'I have no family link with Burma. No distant relative ever toured the country . . . but for ten years that chance visit haunted me. In those seven days the Burmese cast a spell over me, winding themselves into my heart, and leaving behind an ache, a gnawing hunger.'

Rory Maclean, *Under the Dragon* (2008: 2)

CHAPTER ONE

(1852–1936) FIRST IMPRESSIONS

The breathtaking view of the imperious Kanchenjunga mountains, their snowy peaks tinged rose-pink in the setting sun, did little to diminish the heartbreak. April was inconsolable and cried for days. The teachers called her older sister Elizabeth to come and sit with her in class. Being packed off to boarding school for an unbroken stint of nine months was hard at the age of eight. The hugs from her parents at Rangoon International Airport before boarding the Thai Airways flight to Calcutta were all too brief. After an overnight stay at the Great Western, there was a further short hop by a plane that took them to the foot of the Himalayas. Meeting up with the other far-flung kids and catching the narrow gauge railway to Mount Hermon School in Darjeeling, eased the pain of parting. As the steam train began its faithful climb—zig-zagging through the forests—there was an excited chatter, later a little subdued as the air began to cool and the snow-capped peaks came into view. Each child lost in their private world. Their names were on a class list, they were assigned a bed in the dormitory but, as they unpacked for the new term, their hearts were elsewhere.

Each year, April and Elizabeth were away at the school. Their parents, Austin and Margaret, felt this a sacrifice worth making because the education was far better than what was available in Burma in the 1950s. April spoke Burmese at home when she was a young girl. In time, the awkwardness thawed, the English language came and friendships were forged. There was serene Muna with long limbs and dark eyes beneath a fringe. Several half-terms were spent with her family in Kalimpong, high in the Himalayan hills of Nepal. Kenlong from Thailand was another classmate. She arrived at the start of term with her overstuffed suitcase. The latest US-made clothes, petticoat dresses, and shiny leather shoes spilled onto the bed.

'Help yourself,' she said to April.

'Oh, really!' Being something of a tomboy, April didn't sample the frilly stuff, but there were other clothes she tried. She ran her nimble fingers over the textures and noticed the warp and weft of different fabrics. Even at this early age, April showed an interest in design. Then there was Tenzing, a Tibetan and relative of the Dalai Lama. He was also a special playmate. But one day he was no longer in class. He and his family were whisked off to a safe haven in Switzerland.

Just as the annual stint at Mount Hermon was becoming more of an adventure and less of an ordeal, the political situation worsened back home in Burma. For a decade since January 1948, the country enjoyed independence from the British. But now the Anti-Fascist People's Freedom League headed by Prime Minister U Nu was beginning to fall apart. They had to rely on hard-core leftist support in parliament while the minority people-groups from the uplands of Burma, especially the Karens, were pressing for self-rule. As rumours of coups and counter-coups swirled around the streets of Rangoon, General Ne Win, now head of the Burmese army, was steadily assembling an efficient military machine.

Foreigner groups packed their belongings and left. Businesses and industries throughout Burma were nationalized. Austin found himself at a desk job back in Rangoon and Margaret took a secretarial position at the United Nations. There was no choice but to move the girls back to schools in Burma. First to classrooms at Maymyo, just north of Mandalay, and then to St Joseph's convent in Rangoon.

But the education for their three girls was looking dire. In xenophobic pique, Ne Win ordered the removal of English from the curriculum. This 'theft' was to last for thirty years, leaving a generation of Burmese relying on the occasional pirated films and books for exposure to the English language. It also exacerbated Burma's international isolation. With the military presence on the streets becoming more menacing, Austin and Margaret began to gather documents necessary to leave the country. One day while Margaret and the children waited for the domestic ferry across to Syriam, secret police brusquely quizzed her for papers. This harassment was the final straw. With the emigration window closing fast, ex-patriate friends like Jack Strain found temporary employers for them in London, which meant they were able to secure visas to enter Britain.

In January 1964, a month before the Beatles flew to New York for their first US tour, a Pan American Boeing 707 from Rangoon touched down at Heathrow, via Delhi and Zurich. Among the passengers, out stepped Margaret, a glamorous lady in her late 30s with Eurasian looks. Following her down the steps, their breath freezing in the chilly air, were two of her daughters, April, aged thirteen and Gay, four years younger. A new beginning for the Francis family. Austin stayed behind in Rangoon with their eldest daughter Elizabeth. They followed a few months later when she had finished her GCE exams. Very English names and distant English connections, but for all that, this was a huge step for a Burmese couple to make in their late thirties and mid-forties. They surrendered their passports on entry, so there was no turning back. Apart from some heirloom jewellery and shipped items of furniture, they departed with just £100 each in their pockets, leaving all their possessions and most of the wider family behind in Burma.

For April, this was a bewildering time. Before and after arriving in England she endured a blur of six different schools in five years. Fractured friendships, disrupted studies, and a family in upheaval. A teenager learning to trust only a precious few and not to dream

April, Gay, Auntie Rosie, Margaret and Elizabeth at Stratford, 1964

too much. As friends chatted on the way to school and gathered in
the playground, it was a different English language from the more
formal textbook grammar April knew. It was easy to feel alone, but
fortunately, the occasional teacher or classmate eased the transitions.
People who showed love to the outsider in their midst.

'School dinners were a novelty,' April said of that time, 'things
like toad in the hole and steamed puddings; I loved them. Back in
Burma, my school days were very different. Up at 6 a.m. for the
driver to take me to train at the swimming pool. The sun would rise
on my first length of the Olympic-size pool. My coach at the Kokine
Lakes club was very sad when I said we were leaving Burma, as I was
in line for the national swimming team. My sisters would come in
the car with breakfast which I ate on the way to school. We were
home by 1 p.m. for the main family meal.'

Later in life, April enjoyed nothing more than potting little plants,
nurturing them to flower in the spring. For her, the befriending of
young shoots, the sacred silence, her fingers in the damp soil, is prayer.

'For that, I thank my Biology teacher,' April recalls. 'When
other sixth formers were sitting around in the common room at

lunchtime, discussing their latest dates and holidays, I would be at her side in the school greenhouse watching her propagate plants.'

Oblivious to all this, I was working hard at the Boys' Grammar on the other side of the main road in Tunbridge Wells. It just seemed the right thing to do. To pass exams, to excel at sports, to keep my head down. Rarely did the conformity of it all occur to me. Placating my parents, impressing my peers, keeping everyone happy became an end in itself. It was tiring but it kept me out of trouble. Well, most of the time.

While April was moving countries, my family was migrating from the edgy streets of Eltham—where Boy George later came of age—to the verdant hedgerows of Crowborough. I had little influence over my choice of schooling, but for different reasons to April. My parents chose Haberdasher's Askes in New Cross. When we moved out from London, I went to Skinners School. Both funded by medieval guilds, posh hatmakers followed by furtraders.

By now it was the winter of 1967. Snow a foot deep crept into the village overnight, as generously as a prince. The angled roofs and jutting chimney pots smoothed like icing, the branches of trees bowed low and all early morning sounds muffled in awe. Still, the Christmas parcels needed to be delivered. Toys from distant aunts, mysterious packages in brown paper and string, bulging envelopes with exotic stamps from foreign shores. The postroom was full of students, back from college to earn some spending money. They trudged out from the sorting office making first impressions in drifts of snow.

Spotting a slight, duffle-coated figure struggling beneath her heavy hessian sack, Peter slid alongside and offered to help. He had noticed her Eastern features as they bagged up their rounds earlier. Vietnamese or possibly Malaysian? Unusual in this sleepy Sussex village.

So it was on Christmas Eve that my older brother boasted of Elizabeth, his new girlfriend, their footprints converging in the snow. He returned to spin a spicy story of a Burmese family.

'You must come to meet them,' he said.

'Why?'

'She has younger sisters.'

'So?'

'You wait till you see April.'

On that slender promise, a few days later I was at his side approaching the Francis household. Before we reached the front door, the unfamiliar but enticing fragrance of curry greeted us. Then a living room of brown faces and big grins and a beer thrust in my direction by April's father, Austin. It was an icy night, they were warm and comfy watching TV. The prospect of coming out with us was far from appealing. Eventually, wrapped in scarves and woolly hats, the sisters joined us at the Blue Anchor pub on Beacon Hill. The barman refused to serve alcohol to Elizabeth because she looked underage and, of course, April was only sixteen. It was nearly four years since the family's arrival from the stifling heat of Rangoon.

After this inauspicious introduction, I often caught sight of April on the school bus. She sat at the back of the lower deck, frequently the late bus, usually alone and avoiding eye contact. Later she told me it was to get away from the boys who delighted in calling her 'passion flower' and other less savoury names. Being the only girl of colour she was an obvious target for middle-class lads from the grammar school who had a lot to learn. I was secretly smitten, but it was several months later before I gingerly invited her out to a cheese and wine party. We swapped family stories and shared our vinyl favourites over a glass of Blue Nun. I waxed lyrical about Dylan and Donovan. She hummed the harmonies of the Everly Brothers.

I do hope 'the sun *will* shine some more' and 'the moon *will* rise in the sky', I thought to myself.

Happily, they did. After two or three dates, our first kiss under the orange orb of the street light on Jefferies Way unsteadied my normality. My first *real* girlfriend. I was ambushed by love. We could so easily have slid past each other like characters in different movies. Through my friendship with April I was also stepping across a threshold to a distant and unanticipated world: the royal connections of her great grandparents in Mandalay; her illustrious Buddhist grandparents growing up in a period of relative ease under the British rule. While many countries were recovering from global war and reeling from financial collapse, the 1920s and 1930s saw Burma gather importance as a hub of trade and commerce. Rangoon University become a sought-after place of learning in South East Asia. But it was a divided country and most nationals saw themselves as on the receiving end of colonial superiority. I knew none of this at the time as I found myself drawn towards—and into—a Burmese family. Nor, as the cultural barriers dissolved between April and I, did I have any inkling of the chequered and less-than-comfortable relationship between Britain and Burma.

For centuries the Court of Ava, across the Irrawaddy from Mandalay, held sway over the Burmese empire. A dynasty of warrior kings succeeded in not only galvanizing the disparate people-groups but ruled over vast tracts of South East Asia. In the early 1800s, however, Burma came up against another empire. The British, in the form of the East India Company. It was expanding eastwards from India in search of lucrative spoils. King Bagyidaw and the Burmese armed forces were defeated and agreed to surrender a large chunk of their territories. The provinces of Manipur, Arakan, Tenasserim, all slid into British control, along with a huge indemnity. The royal treasury was virtually bankrupted and from this point, the Burmese empire began to unravel. Another war with Britain followed in the 1850s. King Mindon was forced to relinquish more of his diminished empire: this time the British annexed lower Burma including Rangoon.

Margaret's paternal great-grandfather had pearl blue eyes and the name of Walter Yarde, a common surname in Devon. He served as a military pharmacist and when he was in his twenties, he and his brother received orders to join a ship bound for India which is where their battalion was to be stationed. It was during the Second Anglo–Burmese War in 1852 that Walter was drafted to neighbouring

Burma and rose to the rank of major. Subsequently he fell in love
with a Burmese lady in Monywa, in central Burma. Although rural
churchyards, huddled on the dreamy hillsides of Devon, are replete
with Yarde gravestones, Walter never returned home. For a while
there was a street near Inya lake in Rangoon named after the family,
but it's long since been renamed by the military junta.

Walter's son was named Henry Yarde. Margaret's grandfather,
one of three children, attended the English St John's College in
Rangoon, going on to become an apothecary like his father. At the
age of twenty-three in 1883, Henry married Martha Ma That, two
years his senior. They went on to have seven children. Margaret's
father, Frederick Yarde was the fourth, born in 1894. Burma was now
a province of India, with a British governor served by a whole raft
of divisional commissioners in their pith helmets and sand-coloured
uniforms. Many, like Frederick, benefitted from the improved
infrastructure and educational opportunities that opened up at home
and overseas. But although there was a good deal of autonomy under
colonial rule there was also a growing appetite for nationalism based
on the Buddhist faith of Burmese-speaking people, especially in
Rangoon where discrimination was rife. European-only clubs and
British officers routinely taking Burmese mistresses didn't help.

On her mother's side, Margaret's ancestry was pure Burmese
and centred on Mandalay, historically the jewel of Burma's far-flung
empire. It was here that the royal family lived in the splendour of a
glass palace, so called because of the gemstones, sapphires, jade, and
rubies encrusted into the pillars of the king's quarters. A moat, with
minitowers guarded by golden lion statues at each corner, surrounded
the ornate palace. Looking down from Mandalay Pagoda on the hill
above, 365 small, white pagodas, or *stupas*, could be counted within
the one kilometre square. One dwelling for each concubine, so it was
rumoured in days gone by.

'My maternal great grandfather,' Margaret told me on one of my
early boyfriend visits, 'was Thandawsint U Po Oh. The first part of
the name signifies a royal title in Old Burmese. He was a minister

in King Thibaw's court and his daughter was a lady-in-waiting to Queen Supayalat.'

In 1885 a British gunboat advanced up the Irrawaddy. It was met with no resistance and King Thibaw capitulated. An anti-climactic end to centuries of proud monarchy. It conjured a pitiful sight for the Mandalay crowd to see their king and his family taken to exile in India. Having lost his royal patronage, U Po Oh nevertheless stayed on in Mandalay and started a printing press and newspaper, among the first in Burma.

'One of their sons was Maung Maung Gyi, my grandfather,' said Margaret. 'I remember him with a droopy moustache. He used to wear a pink silk longyi, a sarong for men, long hair and a traditional royal turban.' Apparently, he met his first, cheroot-smoking wife at the palace.

'I don't know how they fell in love,' Margaret mentioned on another occasion, 'they didn't go out together in those days. He was a Buddhist and had two wives. My step-grandmother lived in another house. Khin Khin Nu, my mother, was born in 1904.' Although always more factual than romantic, mention of her mother brought a warm smile to Margaret's face. These, it seemed, were halcyon days of yore for the family. 'At the Buddhist Light Festival, we used to make all these stars and decorations with coloured paper and thinly-cut bamboo with candles inside to light up. For three days the houses were illuminated and we made all kinds of sweets, some from coconut. And when people came to visit we ate together, and played with the sparklers and crackers.'

'Of course, eating was a big part. We tucked into *mohinga*, a noodle broth, and *le-pet*, a kind of pickled tea, followed by various sweetmeats. As dusk fell the air was thick with the smell of cooking and melting candle wax and the shrieks of excited children. Each town, each quarter, or even each road tried to surpass each other in their streetlighting.'

Perhaps Frederick and Khin Khin met at one of these neighbourhood celebrations, followed by secret trysts under acacia trees at dusk. Whatever the circumstances, in 1923 they were wed, although sadly their marriage was to last only fourteen years. Margaret's parents made a dashing couple. Her father Frederick was tall and suave with full lips and gentle features, his dark furrowed brow shielded deep-set eyes speaking kindness. A no-nonsense yet empathic demeanour well-suited to his medical profession, which he continued in the family tradition. Unmistakably Burmese, he nevertheless retained something of his grandfather's Anglo heritage. Her mother, Khin Khin Nu, with a rounded face, fair complexion, and large oval eyes, was arresting in her beauty.

Margaret was two when her father had to leave for the UK for further studies. He studied at the Royal College Hospital at Paddington in gynaecology and took an apartment nearby. He came back to Burma when Margaret was five.

Margaret's parents Frederick Yarde & Khin Khin Nu
with brothers Walter and Peter, c 1933

'I didn't recognize him at all,' she recalled. 'There was a ship carrying the Indian royal family coming into Rangoon harbour, this had to dock first before the ship from England could disembark. We all waited at the quayside. Then he came and I was quite frightened. I wouldn't go to him and he tried to coax me with all the toys, but it took me a while to get used to him. I don't remember seeing photos of him while he was away, but he used to send postcards from each port that he called at. My grandfather, who lived with us, used to help us put them on the map.

'Walter, my elder brother, and I were very close to my mother. She was a Buddhist. She was very clever with her hands, always hand-painting the silk longyi and embroidering them with little pearls for her older sisters. The best satin came from China or Paris—slipper satin—long crepe scarves, the bottom part painted the same as the longyi. She was pure Burmese, her mother died when she was very young.'

Margaret was unusually passionate as she revisited these memories. It was as if another person was coming alive, someone who had slept for a long time. She didn't hug easily, her kiss of greeting barely brushed one's cheek, and apart from items of jewellery handed down the family line, there was nothing sentimental about her. Yet her love ran deep. Typically, she would stay quiet for much of the conversation but missed nothing. Very occasionally her composure dissolved as she shed a tear or convulsed in sobbing laughter.

From snippets of conversation with April and her parents, from the private history of earlier generations, the mysterious faces in sepia photos, the aromas of strange spices, an enchanting story began to unfold. Recollections of life in Burma that spanned sixty years and more. Later I was to hear about the swagger of Burma Boys in wartime Calcutta from her mother and nostalgic dreams from her father. The twists and turns of mid-century politics in Rangoon related in forensic detail by April's aunt, Jessie. But at this early point, as a naïve newcomer, I revelled in the romanticism of this far-off land, in these characters from a bygone age. A country which in the sixteenth century ruled much of South Asia from the imperial court where a succession of powerful monarchs asserted themselves. Then, at the end of the nineteenth century, humbled to become an outpost of the British empire. Throughout all this, it was a land swathed in natural beauty, blessed with precious gems, bordered by impenetrable mountain ranges and deep forests concealing wild elephants and Bengal tigers. Simple villages of bamboo huts and golden pagodas, unsullied by package tours. And from what I gleaned, it was inhabited by people of unmistakable poise and serenity, who always seem to be smiling.

Here I was in a Sussex village, just a cycle ride away. A credulous teenager falling for the warmth of a Burmese family and the charms of their middle daughter. First impressions may be unreliable and misleading but they are often magical. Like my brother Peter's footprints in the snow that Christmas a year earlier: the fun of making them, the surprise of finding them.

'What,' I thought to myself, 'is there *not* to love about Burma?'

CHAPTER TWO

(1936–45) AUSTIN AND MARGARET

When we were dating I used to spend more time in April's home than in my own. One day, Margaret and Austin were in the kitchen making *buthi kyaw*—golden brown fritters. Margaret was chopping marrow into thin fingers while Austin was preparing the batter, mixing in the rice flour, garlic powder, and ground ginger. They work silently side by side, unhurried—as one in a familiar task. As I wandered in, they readily absorbed me into their culinary ritual.

'The traditional ingredient is bottle gourd or *buthi*,' Austin told me, 'but you can use marrow or even courgette.' He took down a new bowl and started mashing overripe banana ready for some fritters to follow.

Methodically, Margaret ensured each vegetable stick was covered evenly in batter before dunking them into the sizzling groundnut oil. She told her stories of Myanmar in a similarly deliberate way, starting with plain events and then dressing them with tasty detail. As she worked, the conversation turned to Mandalay.

'Mandalay had an old-world feel in those days,' she said, speaking of her childhood. 'Sometimes we caught the train from Rangoon. It rattled through the night to arrive early morning. The seats were hard and the windows were open to the mosquitoes. At each stop, vendors appeared out of the dark, clustering at the windows with snacks and kettles of steaming green tea. Sticky rice in banana leaf parcels was my favourite.'

April and I looked at each other. It was one of the childhood delicacies April missed.

'I used to go and spend the day with my friends, Olga and Marjorie Brown,' Margaret said. 'They had a big house near Mandalay Hill. It was there that the news came that my father was posted to Myitkyina, way up in the Kachin State, not far from the Chinese border.'

As I got to know Margaret, I was impressed by her dynamism. She exuded relaxed hospitality, but not far from the surface was a fierce independence. She took certain matters seriously. Little things like common courtesy and big things like education. She was determined that her daughters received good schooling. She also staunchly defended 'Anglos', Anglo-Burmese and Anglo-Indians. We were all at a party on one occasion, when the host launched into ill-chosen remarks about mixed-race folk. I think the phrase he used was 'half-castes'.

'What do you know?' she exclaimed like a riled tiger. 'You should never talk about Anglos in that way.' The normally ebullient host fell silent and the matter was over. No grudges, no simmering uneasiness, just a matter of getting things right. Of course, there are no 'castes' in Burma anyway. How, I wondered, had life events fashioned her strong character?

The groundnut oil in the wok was bubbling expectantly. Margaret let me help deep-fry the *buthi kyaw*, two or three at a time, till they were golden brown, each with a crispy batter shell. Placed on kitchen roll to remove excess fat, the savoury fritters were now ready. With the tamarind dip in hand it wasn't long before the plate was emptied. The serious preparation, the slow cooking, the eating, and chatting were joyous, almost a sacrament. As we cleared away the dishes, Margaret sat back and dabbed her face with a tissue. Something stirred her memory.

'I was ten and in the fourth standard. I was very happy, I was looking forward to being a boarder. They had long lists of uniform; my mother gave most to the tailors to make them up, but she sewed

April's mother Margaret, c 1960

in all my name tags.' The details were lodged precisely in Margaret's mind. 'On 4 October 1936, on a Saturday, she was to take me to school. My father was away but because my mother was ill my grandfather had to take me. He loved that.

'He was dressed in a long black Bangkok *pasoe* and a *gambaung*, a silk headdress. He looked very smart and took me in a horse-drawn carriage called "gharry". I was worried, I knew there was something wrong with my mother. She wasn't coming down to eat and told me to bring a little bit of rice—just one spoon—and some dried salt fish. I used to get it from the kitchen and put two spoons of rice thinking that if she ate more she would get better. At the same time, I was excited about going to school. My brother Walter had already gone to Rangoon and had lots of stories about the fun he was having as a boarder.'

Often subdued or preoccupied with cooking, I was struck by how absorbed Margaret was in this recollection. This was unambiguously her moment and nothing would deter her now from relating her story.

'Mother told me Phay Phay, my grandfather, would come to see me on his return from Myitkyina. He didn't look very happy. Looking back on it now, he probably knew I might not see her again. She stayed upstairs in her room, she didn't come down to wish me goodbye. From the gharry, I looked up at her window and saw her face. She waved and that was the last time I saw her alive.

'The English matron, Miss Cooper, was there with her spaniel. She ticked everything off as I unpacked my trunk. It was all in order . . . my mother had packed everything so well. On Monday my father came and explained that she had been taken to hospital. I was so happy to be at school, I didn't want to spoil it. I never thought my mother was going to leave us, that it was death on the way. He brought a big tin of assorted biscuits and said he had to go to Rangoon to take his medical exams. That afternoon I sent her a letter with one of the girls. I wrote how I missed her and was so sorry that she was not well. She got the letter. When she died the nurses found it under her pillow.'

The pathos of that moment was profound. Although understated, I sensed this was a pivotal moment in Margaret's life. The unbridled anticipation of a new school term blotted out by an unthinkable loss. A loving family torn asunder by grief. An uncertain future for the four children until the arrival of a stepmother who, though, was never able to fill the gap.

With little prompting, it seemed important to Margaret to relate her story, to let us into her private world. In each of the English towns and villages where she and Austin spent the second half of their lives, many folk were drawn to the warmth of their hospitality, but only a few got close to Margaret. It was almost as though, after the initial welcome . . . the guests were left in the hall, wondering who was at home. I have often wondered whether this was a way of protecting herself against further disappointment. One thing is for sure, Margaret's loss helped to forge a strong maternal bond with her daughters, a steely determination to see them succeed in life.

April's father, Austin, was a perfect foil for Margaret. Relaxed, unperturbed, like a rock smoothed by a constant torrent of water. Better to romanticize about retirement than get agitated by current events, to tend his roses rather than moan about life's thorns. His great-grandfather was originally from southern India and practised pharmacy. His grandfather, Findlay, became postmaster, at an out-of-the-way trading port on the Salween river and a hub for smugglers from nearby Thailand. He fell in love and married Daw Sen Nyunt who was the sister of the headman of several Shan villages. By the 1920s, Burma was a thriving trading partner with many commercial enterprises in the West, and their son, Harry Archibald Francis, became a department manager for Finlay Fleming, agents for Burmah Oil. The company also imported textiles and Drakes whiskey. Harry, though fond of his cigars, was himself a teetotaller. He married Daw Thin Kyu from a Mon family (an ethnic group in the south of Burma), whose great grandfather was a Mon tribal chieftain. Their first child Austin was born later the same year, 1918.

April's father Austin Francis, c 1950

Austin and his five younger siblings were the product of a rich mix of bloodlines, a family with a penchant for quintessentially English names, and a whiff of royal lineage. Although it must be admitted that with so many people-groups in Burma, each with their history of semi-autonomous jurisdiction, to have a connection with local royalty was not rare. Austin rarely talked about his early years, and when he did, the stories were brief and more sketchy than those of April's mother. It wasn't that he was reluctant to chat or guarded about anything, rather just content to let sleeping dogs lie. However, one evening when I was dropping April off following a date at the cinema, Austin invited me in as he always did. As he was relaxing, scotch in hand, he told us that, being the oldest, he was the most revered by his father, but it was his mother who was the most influential in his life.

'She liked me very much,' he said, giving a little laugh. 'She used to give me pep talks . . . although it went in one ear and out the other. She wanted me to marry a distant relation and introduced me to several second and third cousins. I wanted to go into business. My dream was to set up a rice mill. But that didn't happen.'

The Second World War changed a good deal for Austin, for Margaret's family, and set the country of Burma on a new course. Austin's university education was cut short. He joined the British–Indian Army, and with the invasion of the Japanese, he evacuated under General Gracey from north-western Burma into India. There he was trained as a commando in Karachi, picked up some Hindi language, and was sent to patrol the East Pakistan–Burma border. Based in Chittagong, he often spent his leave in Calcutta with many other Burmese evacuees.

Margaret and her younger sister Jessie were forced to evacuate their home in Maymyo, a town up in the hills a couple of hours drive beyond Mandalay. Being cooler than the Irrawaddy plain, Maymyo was a favoured spot during the British regime and took on the appearance of a peaceful English town, with timbered houses, rose gardens and well-kept parklands. We learnt more about this period many decades later, when visiting Aunty Jessie.

'The Governor went there for the summer along with the British contingent.' Jessie told us. 'In the evening the officers would dress up in their military attire for dinner even if they were eating on their own.'

But all the ceremonial comforts were soon to be shattered. At 10 a.m. on 23 December 1941, the first Japanese air raid took place over Rangoon. Burma was to become one of the bloodiest theatres of the Second World War. As Japanese troops pushed northwards, Frederick was anxious to get his children away to safety. They left their rented house in Maymyo in a hurry to head for the comparative safety of the Chin Hills.

'We left the car in the garage. A three-year-old Austin. The furniture and piano, all the photos were left behind, along with the porcelain and glass. Mother's lovely embroidered clothes. The only thing they had time to pack was some silverware and jewellery. We gave the key to our driver to look after the house.'

Once Jessie was in her stride, there was no stopping her. The memories came in quick succession. As a seven-year-old at the time, the whole thing seemed to be more of an adventure than an ordeal.

'It all happened so quickly. We got the train from Maymyo to Mandalay. At Mandalay station, lots of clothes in big baskets got mixed up. We never saw them again. We managed to clamber aboard a train to Monwya, where grandfather was from. We spent one night there, then caught the ferry, a flat-bottomed sampan with a little bamboo shelter over the back. This took us up the Chindit river to Kalaywa and Kalaymyo. There was forest on both sides and we could see the Indians fleeing through the trees on either side. That night we slept in a village. We went into one of the houses. They had made fresh chicken curry and rice.

'Our father had made arrangements. He met us at Kalaymyo with three horses and forty mules and coolies that belonged to the hospital where he had been visiting Chin people. I was seven. The Chin coolies had long baskets and at first, they carried me and my young stepbrother. Margaret rode on a horse, but it was treacherous.

Especially going across the suspension bridges. The horses walked close to the edge because they were afraid of falling stones from the mountainside.'

Again, Jessie was making it sound like an exciting vacation.

'After a week of trekking, we reached father's bungalow at Falam. We were in the Chin Hills for a year. A lot of Anglo-Burmese officers who got away from Burma joined the British Army. They used to come and have whiskey with my father by the fireplace. I would wander around the bungalow on the mountainside. The rhododendrons were in bloom and also the big white wild orchids and the rare blue ones. The birds were beautiful, bright yellow and vibrant red. That's where I started learning to knit. We made knitting needles from bamboo.'

Then news came that broke in on this rural idyll. The Japanese continued to advance. 'When they got closer, my father said we'd better get across to India. So, we trekked over the Patkoi mountains to Ainjaw, then by train to Calcutta.'

I later learned that this was a treacherous journey covered by thousands of refugees in 1942–43. It meant traversing high mountain ranges, deep valleys, and raging torrents—especially for those who evacuated in the monsoon season. The death toll, from dysentery and disease, was high, with many corpses stranded in the mud along the way. Margaret showed us a book called *White Butterflies*, where an acquaintance describes his family's ordeal:

'It was devilishly hot and the air was still, so still that the smell of death lay like a shroud over the whole area. The first thing that greeted us was a corpse in the middle of the track. I shall never forget the sight of this body, even though I had already seen hundreds. It was covered in what appeared to be a white sheet. As we stepped carefully around it, our movement appeared to disturb the shroud. Then we saw a cloud of white butterflies rise up with whirring, humming sound, exposing the bloated, shiny corpse of an Indian refugee . . . the butterflies must have been drawing on the juices secreted from the skin.'

It is difficult to imagine how Margaret as a fifteen-year-old and her younger sister, Jessie coped with the horrors they saw. Typically, they related their escape to us in a matter-of-fact manner. Perhaps referring us to this book was a way of keeping the nightmares at bay.

Frederick's second wife, daughters Margaret and Jessie, and younger brother Peter with their three younger step-brothers took a more northerly route. It was no less arduous and gruesome, but at least they had their father with them. He made sure they were provided for and, as a doctor knowledgeable about dysentery and cholera, he insisted they drink from cans of evaporated milk and not local rivers.

'When we finally made it to India,' said Jessie, with no hint of sentimentality, 'we stayed with a Burmese family and then got our own flat. Father got a job in West Bengal as Burma was closed till 1946. The countryside was ravaged and famine relief was a number one priority.' On account of his Karen wife, Frederick was suspected of sympathizing with the Karen rebellion and imprisoned for a while when he returned to Burma. When released, he continued his medical practice and lived out his days in Toungoo.

When the War ended, Margaret went back to the family home in Maymyo. 'The house was no more, it was bombed out,' she said, registering no emotion, 'everything was gone. As I went past the Maymyo Lakes, I noticed the driver's wife coming along in our mother's clothes.'

What, I wondered, was Austin doing at this time? Rarely forthcoming on his own exploits, I gathered he returned with the 17th Indian Division— the *Black Cats*—to the Arakan beaches under the overall command of General Slim. 'I was responsible for training a platoon of commandos,' Austin said, 'to make secret missions behind enemy lines. It was our job to signal the all-clear to British ships based in the Indian Ocean to land the troops.

'The Japanese were advancing through the jungles of north-west Burma. They wanted to take the mountain roads as a gateway to the plains of India.' Austin opened up a map book to point to the route which most of the refugees had taken just two years before. 'Our job was to keep Slim's troops supplied. They had to hold Imphal and Kohima, towns close to the border with Burma, at all costs.

'Just before the monsoon rains, in mid-May, we heard that fighting had intensified. It was all about the hill town of Kohima, surrounded by tea plantations. Later the whole story came out. The battle centred on the strip of ground comprising the gardens and bungalow of the British Deputy Commissioner. There were huge casualties on both sides, but eventually the allied forces held on.'

That the fate of war-torn Burma should ultimately be determined—in part at least—by cross-fire over a tennis court might be considered bizarre were it not so brutal. Once the allied forces had reinforcements from the 2nd Battalion Dorsetshire Regiment, the Japanese were on the back foot. They had run out of time, supplies, and ammunition. It was a remarkable and decisive turnaround.

For all his interrupted education, escapades behind enemy lines, and family sadness, one good thing came from the War for April's father. While on leave in Calcutta he met his future wife. In those days Austin's broad shoulders and handsome square jaw set him up well for boxing, a sport he pursued. However, his face was too kind and his demeanour too genial for a boxing ring or, for that matter, commando missions. In her late teens, Margaret already possessed a dusky and serene beauty. With the loss of her mother at ten and ensuing family dislocation, as well as the harrowing trek out of north-west Burma into India just a couple of years before, she was no fickle bride-to-be, ready to be swept off her feet. However, those around the couple looked on and saw the love kindle between this somewhat bashful, big-hearted soldier and the feisty student with the looks of a princess. They all knew well before their engagement that they were destined for each other.

As April's boyfriend, I was treated to many Burmese and Indian meals by Austin and Margaret. The exquisite aromas and flavours of these dinners were matched by the flow of conversation about days gone by. On one occasion, out came her speciality, Maharani

Austin and Margaret's wedding, Taunggyi, 8th March 1947

Chicken, gently fried in ghee with desiccated almonds, coconut, garam masala and ground cardamoms. As we dipped *pouris* into the delicious sauce, Margaret began to reminisce about India:

'Austin was in the Army based in Calcutta in 1943–44' Margaret said. 'We were all refugees from occupied Burma. We were in the same class as lots of Parsee girls, Indians from Bombay.

'I was eighteen when we met up again. I went over to the Browns one day to see them. They were like sisters. In Calcutta in those days it was quite safe—ten minutes' walk from my place and sometimes we would get a rickshaw. Austin was there with the other Burma boys from the Army.

'The balcony was wide and we would sit there in the cool and talk. He came in and all I could see was his teeth and those awful khaki shorts; he was very slim and smiling away. I don't know why he was smiling at me. I got quite annoyed . . . I don't know who had been saying anything to him about me.'

Margaret was chuckling at this point. These were poignant moments she was describing with an undertow of humour at Austin's expense. 'He said let's go to the Indian Coffee House. Well, he had to take us all . . . Olga, Marjorie, and Megan, they all bullied him. We thought "boys on leave with lots of money. Let's go for a good coffee, fresh iced coffee, and ice cream cake. Any size".'

We all laughed, including Austin, who knew what was coming of course.

'We met a second time when Austin took my aunts and me in a taxi to get tickets at Howrah station. He took us all out for dinner at a nice restaurant in Park Lane. The way he ate was quite refined, like an Anglo-Burmese. Then Aunty Rosie asked Austin over for lunch and I invited my friends as I didn't want to be alone with him. Shirley, Cathy, and Maisie came over. Maisie was my best friend from a huge house in Calcutta with a big room for the Sabbath. They were business people and one of her sisters was the best seamstress in Calcutta . . . she made my wedding dress. I lost touch because we had a robbery at Chauk and my handbag was stolen with my address book. I was so sad.'

By this point, I was drowning in an avalanche of aunts and acquaintances, but it seemed necessary for Margaret to report the build-up. It was like all the stage scenery needed to be in place for the punchlines to be delivered.

'Austin was the only boy there and he was so shy. The girls all pulled his leg. Auntie Rosie remarked that he didn't know whether he was putting the chicken or the noodles in his mouth. All clean fun.'

More laughter and knowing looks all round.

'After that, he sent me gifts and a photo of himself. Auntie Rosie remarked that he's only a sergeant. Then a grey leather handbag. I shall never forget that it was filled with lipstick, rouge, and powder . . . all very hard to get. It was so generous.'

This was the closest I ever saw Margaret come to a verbal expression of love. It was as if for someone robbed of her mother at ten and starved of kindness for long periods since, Austin's thoughtfulness and generosity was all the more precious.

'In 1945 he came for Christmas. That was when he wrote and proposed to me. He went to the Calcutta Newmarket and bought me a real snakeskin handbag, it was very expensive. ₹35. I bought him a little scarf for ₹12. He still won't throw it away. He washes it and keeps it. We got engaged when we returned to Burma in 1946.'

As these memories were gently unwrapped, without drama, I was struck by Margaret's reference to that handbag and scarf. Emblems of love and loyalty that April's parents had kept private and brought with them from Burma. To specify their value seemed odd. Perhaps it was part of Margaret's eye for facts. But evidently, it was not their price tag that mattered, rather the fond memories they evoked. The highly charged connection to carefree, love-soaked times in Calcutta and to the post-war days back in Burma that had promised so much.

However, there was something I missed at the time. Here we were, April and me, currently gliding along on echoed happiness a full generation later. A similar exchange, not so much of material presents, rather the giving of ourselves to each other, falling into the lovely unknown. The clue I failed to register when hearing Margaret's story was the significance of homeland. It was as if April had started with everything. Back home with her family, her bond with nannies in Lashio and Chauk, and with grandparents and the generations before them. Then, one by one, most of those she held dear had been taken from her. Wrenched from her parents for long periods at Mount Hermon in India, lots of goodbyes to newly made schoolfriends for a fifth time in a row, a one-way ticket out of Rangoon. Was it any surprise that April was, emotionally at least, looking backwards? *I must protect myself from more loss. I cannot take any more abandonment.* For me, it was different, almost the opposite. It was, as if, I started with nothing (or very little) in my 'handbag' and was, as a restless teenager, seeking something but not sure what. *There must be more to life than this. Some adventure up ahead?*

Then, with minimum fuss, with few false starts, we caught hold of each other as soulmates, like passengers on a busy platform. To kiss was to taste honey, to embrace was to melt into each other, but we were heading in different directions. How long could we hold onto each other before the call of 'home' for April (not so much the country but the people and things she'd cherished there) and the yearning for future purpose for me, would pull us apart?

CHAPTER THREE

(1947–64) JESSIE AND THE POST-WAR YEARS

Margaret's younger sister, Aunty Jessie, now lives in Aarhus in Denmark, and is our last oral link with her generation. With high cheekbones and still-black hair pulled back into a neat bun, she retains her striking good looks. She lives in the same house that she and her husband, Tage, built when their children were young. A generous plot of mature trees and gardens, it blends seamlessly into their well-heeled suburb. Once inside, the shelves and display cabinets are full of photographs, lacquerware, Burmese silverware, and oil paintings—some by Jessie. The atmosphere speaks of a very different heritage to those of her Danish neighbours and friends.

April and I have visited many times. Each time we hear new stories from the past and sometimes the old ones retold. As she sits knitting or embroidering, Jessie's recall for her early years in Burma nearly eighty years ago, is captivating.

At the time of her mother Khin Khin Nu's death, she was just three. When her father Frederick Yarde later remarried in 1939—to a Karen nurse named Amy—she had less trouble adapting to the new home regime than Margaret. Nevertheless, as a civil surgeon, their father moved every three years and they saw little of him. Jessie was packed off to boarding school a lot of the time, starting in Maymyo at St Michael's where she was taught by Anglican nuns.

When Frederick was posted to the Chin Hills, Jessie was sent to La Martiniere school in Calcutta.

With the help of her English teacher, Miss King, who was also the principal, Jessie achieved very good marks in her Senior Cambridge exams. Later, April reminded me that British exam boards still held sway at this time. 'You have to remember that, at this time, the history that was taught was the British version of events in Burma.'

The war effort had drained the British Treasury. Far-flung territories like Burma receded in importance. Although I'd heard how the Francis family had fared during this period, I knew very little about political events in Rangoon. Once in full flow and fortified by her lunchtime glass of white wine, Aunty Jessie was once again able to give us a ringside view of events as they unfolded in the capital.

'Following the War, Burma was in a sorry state. Probably more so than anywhere else in Asia. First, we were overrun by the Japanese. Then they were pushed back by the British. The towns and countryside were bombed down . . . ports and bridges, power stations and factories flattened, oil wells and mines. So much was destroyed.

'Aung San was a pure Burman and called himself the leader of the people, part of the ruling class of Burmese. After the Second World War, he started negotiating independence. He found himself pushing at an open door. The British government was reeling financially.'

I had seen photographs from 1947 showing the diminutive figure of General Aung San, in a wide lapelled greatcoat and tall military peaked cap outside Downing Street in London. He has a serene half-smile rather than a look of triumph, while Clement Atlee, Britain's Prime Minister at the time, looks a relieved man behind his stiff upper lip.

'Back in Rangoon,' Jessie recalled as if it were yesterday, 'there was a rival group among the Burmese led by U Saw, who was a minister during the British regime. He was not part of the famous

Thirty Comrades like Ne Win and Aung San who'd gone to be trained by the Japanese during the war.

'It was a Saturday in July 1947, around noon. I was standing with my school friend, Mary Saw, the daughter of U Saw on the school balcony. "Jessie," she said in a hushed voice, "Aung San has been shot along with the whole cabinet, the whole secretariat". We were both quiet. We didn't know what to say. Then she added: "I'm sure we will have to go to the funeral".'

Apparently, a few days before this, U Saw was being driven in his limousine and he was shot, but the bullet just grazed his forehead. He immediately suspected one of Aung San's people because they were rivals. 'There is a Burmese saying,' Jessie said, '"if one is good to you, then you must show gratitude ten times over" . . . and it also applies in reverse!' Well, U Saw retaliated. He arranged for three or four men disguised in khaki uniforms as guards to get into the parliament buildings.'

April and I have since been to look over the concrete wall at the nondescript secretariat off Dalhousie Street in Rangoon. It was chilling to think of the assassin shooting all the would-be cabinet members and Aung San with a machine gun.

'Everybody knew everybody in Rangoon. Immediately they went to U Saw's house and on Saturday evening he was arrested. I was thirteen and head prefect. Mary was two years older than me but my classmate. I remember she was very refined. She was taken from school the next day, it was a Sunday. U Saw was hanged after court proceedings . . . apparently, he confessed. I've not seen Mary or her family since.

'There was a big state funeral.' Jessie was enjoying her role as historical reporter. 'Ten girls from the boarding school, including me, went to lay wreaths on the coffins of Aung San and the others at the Shwedagon Pagoda Road. They were regarded as heroes because they were shot.'

Jessie filled us in on the events that followed. 'U Nu took leadership and in January 1948 Burma got full independence. Many thought it was too early because we were still recovering from being bombed badly in the war: Rangoon, Mandalay Palace, where the Japanese had their headquarter, and the road up to Lashio and China. General Aung San had wanted the British out of Burma. It wasn't like in India where it took a lot longer or Indonesia, where they had to fight for their independence from Holland. It was very easy compared to that. A lot of Burmese officers got promoted after the British left. Ne Win became a general.'

We started to clear away the lunch plates. 'General Aung San used to speak on the radio. He regularly gave fiery speeches and was very rabid against foreigners.' Never one to mince her words, she added: 'He was not a great public orator but after the War, he gained the confidence of the people.'

'I remember framed pictures of him in public buildings and shops when I was young,' April remarked.

'Yes, he was revered as *Bogyoke,* or "General" Aung San. His wife was a Karen nurse. Aung San Su Kyi was a little girl when her father was shot.'

Auntie Jessie's recollections sparked my interest when we were back in the UK. Aung San had been part of a small group of contemporaries and friends at Rangoon University in the 1930s. Other students were U Thant, the name that had first intrigued me as a boy, and U Nu, who was a political 'survivor' and a devout Buddhist. He proved to be a natural politician. Also studying at University College was Than Tun, who led the Communist insurrection, and Shu Maung, who would later become known as Ne Win. Although their political destinies were very different, by a strange quirk of fate, the history of Burma in the twentieth century could almost be told as the history of these few students.

Ne Win was involved in the struggle for Burmese independence from the British. He served as an officer in the Burma National Army, becoming the second Commander-in-Chief after Independence. Now a General, he became increasingly extreme, believing that British rule had made the Burmese weak, lazy, and ill-disciplined.

He railed against the arrogance of the British Raj but was also brutally intolerant of the minority groups in Burma now vying for 'a place at the table.'

As I learned more about these turbulent times, I was keen to discover how the Francis family were faring in post-Independence Burma. Again Jessie was happy to oblige, this time on our next visit to her home in Aarhus a year later. By now, her two children Freddie and Rosa were making their own way in life and our company gave Jessie an excuse to revisit old times.

'There were quite a few young Europeans in Rangoon at that time, including some Danish engineers working for the East Asiatic Company. They were installing air conditioning for Burma Broadcasting and at the international airport.

'It was 1955' Jessie told us, as April and I moved in closer. 'I remember one Saturday, a Burmese officer from Deradoon invited me to a movie and then to an ice cream shop . . . coconut ice cream. We sat at a table in the garden. Who was there but my old friend Sheila from Maymyo! We used to go dancing together. "Oh Jessie, it's a long time since we saw each other. This is my boyfriend, Peter. I'm so happy to see you. Where are you staying?"

'Anyway, a couple of days later a letter came from Sheila: "I don't care what you are doing, you must come with us this Saturday and meet Peter's friend. Come to YWCA". So Tage Hansen was invited. His friends warned him to be on his best behaviour: "Jessie is from royalty in Burma, you know, and her father's a doctor. She's always getting eligible bachelors. So be careful, she's from a very fine family!"'

April and I knew Uncle Tage from various family get-togethers. A tall, genial man with a gravelly voice which I always wanted to listen to. He was so knowledgeable. On our visits to Aarhus, he was always delighted to drive us around, remarking on local history and acquainting us with Danish culture. Our slow jaunts invariably ended up in the pastry shop.

It was special to hear Jessie describe their first meeting:

'I went down these big steps. He was smiling and came over to introduce himself. He was wearing a bow tie and a white long sleeve shirt. We all drove off in his VW to a Chinese restaurant at 8th Mile. After that, we went to Club 99 for a dance.

'From the first, he was very keen and we dated regularly. I kept him on a shoe-string for three months . . . ' Jessie smiled broadly, 'then he got typhoid and I realized I cared for him.'

As she pulled out some of their wedding photos, Jessie recalled an earlier incident in India: 'You know, fortune tellers always used to tell me I'd marry a foreigner. Once when we were in New Delhi, this Sikh fortuneteller said: "Come, come only ₹2 ". I thought no harm. I took two scrolls of paper. "You are going on travels, when you get back you're going to meet a foreigner, a businessman." We laughed, my Indian girlfriend and I. But it must have been fate because that's what happened.'

April's Aunty Jessie in her 20s

By now Austin had established himself as a valued manager with Burmah Oil. With their young family, he and Margaret spent enjoyable months together in Lashio, high up in the Shan State which was where April was born in 1950. It became less relaxed when Chinese insurgents started to terrorize the locals. Burmah Oil moved Austin back to the Irrawaddy basin and the shipment depot of Chauk. April's Kachin nanny came along but found the climate too hot. Despite being less than one and still crawling, April still recalls looking through the legs of her family as the nanny bade farewell. 'I was confused by the commotion. I knew something sad was happening.' Another early memory was at the funeral of her grandfather Frederick.

'As only a toddler could,' April said, 'I managed to kick off one of my shoes and it landed in the grave on top of the coffin. It was pouring with rain but Sunny, one of my half-brothers, managed to slide in to rescue it.'

Although rural, Chauk was well served by schools, a hospital, and comfortable bungalow accommodation not far from the ex-pat club.

'There was a schoolhouse in the town. Mum ran it for a while,' April gazed into the middle distance, picturing the scene. 'In the afternoons we used to go down to the Burmah Oil club. While my parents played tennis and socialized over drinks, Elizabeth and I swam in the pool. It was a huge concrete basin with diving boards and everything.'

'No supervision?'

'We just got on with it. Those were happy times. The grown-ups had fancy dress parties and put on pantomimes at Christmas. That was when the Burmah Oil fire engine was rolled into the compound with presents for all the children. Once I got a walkie-talkie doll from England for Christmas, but my favourite was a squidgy plastic dolly that could drink and wee. I loved that one and mum made clothes for it.'

Later I glimpsed this era, thanks to a jerky cine film that Austin had kept. Elizabeth and April were learning to dance the cha-cha-

cha and the jive. It was delightful to see them in their flouncy party dresses and short white socks concentrating hard as they practised on the veranda. There was no sound, but they got quite cross when the other one got their footwork wrong.

'There were scary moments too,' added April. 'One evening we heard the crack of rifle shots. Our nanny, Ma Mhay whispered to us girls to lie on the bathroom floor. It turned out some ethnic insurgents were storming through the village to create havoc, torching the police station and injuring some of their families. Fortunately, they didn't set the oil alight.'

April and her family telling their stories-of-old from Burma took me to another world. When I visited, Margaret and Austin would have changed from their work suits into their longyis. Their way of relaxing was to cook. I'd hear them in the kitchen calling out to each other in their mother tongue. '*Adaw gyi!*' Austin would exclaim, referring to his 'madam boss' in a gently mocking way. A few pieces of furniture in their modest lounge caught my eye. One was a chunky sideboard made of teak. It had a fairly beaten, reddish-brown patina with a thin black and vermillion detail around the edges. When she spoke of dinner parties back in Burma, I could visualize Margaret asking a servant to select the special plates and cutlery from its drawers, the guests picking at 'short-eats' as the local gossip got going over dry Martinis. Along with their double bed with side cabinets and teak slats (made in Rangoon in a modern 50s style), these were among the few possessions reunited with the Francis family when they arrived from Rangoon. Transported by ship across the Indian Ocean, through Port Said at the head of the newly nationalized Suez Canal and on to Southampton docks. Now, as Margaret reached into the sideboard with its lingering fragrance of sandalwood and spices, to pull out some old photo albums, she was also reaching back across time. Meanwhile April's treasured doll still sits, re-clothed and repatriated to the UK, on our bedroom chair at home.

When they were growing up, Burma had been a 'promising Asian star' with a world of opportunity at its feet. In the years following independence, the nation steadily descended into disarray. By then, Austin and Margaret had two children, with another to come, and their jobs were relatively secure. But much of the country was an unstable patchwork of rebels and government loyalists ruling with uncertain authority. Taking advantage of this political vacuum, General Ne Win and a group of young colonels were steadily building a welldrilled and efficient Burma Army in the background. The ideology, such as it was, guiding this growing assertiveness, was a Burmese version of socialism. There was a coterie of military men, backed by a huge supporting cast of soldiers, ready to take centre stage. Then, according to the Burmese historian Thant Myint-U, their moment came:

> 'In the already balmy early-morning hours of 2 March 1962, tanks and mechanized units of the Burmese Army rolled into downtown Rangoon and took over the Government House, the secretariat, the High Court . . . other Army units swept across the leafy residential neighbourhoods to the north of the Royal Lakes and arrested nearly all the top leaders: Prime Minister U Nu and five other government ministers and the chief justice were taken into custody, together with 30 Shan and Karenni chiefs.'

Several symbolic and decisive acts followed. A revolutionary council made up of Ne Win's senior lieutenants was installed, answerable only to itself. The Army took over the local government from the existing judicial courts. Freedom of the press was curtailed and Western foreign aid agencies and educational institutions were shut down, including English language centres. The entire top echelon of bureaucrats, a professional class schooled in the old colonial service, was systematically dismantled.

If anyone had any doubt about the political direction of travel, the bloodless coup of 1962, led by General Ne Win, spelled it out. All major businesses and industries were nationalized. Unqualified military men replaced experienced managers in the running of organizations, and not surprisingly, performance crashed. Industrial production fell drastically and unemployment in the cities soared. Having enjoyed fifteen years of favour as an engineer in Rangoon, Tage knew their days in Burma were numbered. He and Jessie packed their bags and departed to Denmark in 1962. At the relatively remote oil-field in Chauk, Austin and Margaret were more immune, but events in Rangoon soon caught up with Burmah Oil. Securing the necessary paperwork for the family to emigrate was a long and tortuous process for the Francis family and many like them. Two years after Jessie and Tage, they finally flew to London.

Exchanging the olive green uniforms of a junta-led Burma for the leafy suburbs of Aarhus and London might seem the comfortable option, but Jessie and Margaret, together with their young families, had to rebuild their lives from the ground up. Jessie and her husband, Tage converted their summerhouse on the outskirts of Aarhus and quickly endeared themselves to local Danes. In London, Austin, the oil company executive and ex-boxer, settled for an administrative job in Shell, punching well below his weight. Margaret found secretarial work at Burmah Oil's head office in Britannic House. If they felt it was a sacrifice, they never mentioned it.

Against this recent history of turmoil and big decisions for the family, and despite the expanse of ignorance that still existed between us, April and I were falling in love. I revelled in stories from the distant past and was restless for what was to come. April was content with the here and now. Our arguments were still soft and forgiving, like the newly mown grass on which we lay down.

'I loved the straightness of your nose, and for being tall and slim. You were very good-looking. And you were kind in those days,' April later told me when we were reflecting on those early days.

I guess this contrasted with Burmese noses which tend to be flat, thanks to their Mongolian ancestry. I'm not sure where the kindness went! As for me, raised in an English world of charades and sarcasm, I had found a rare thing: a person free of insincerity, unacquainted with guile.

'I warmed to your stillness,' I said, 'your definiteness, your creativity, and your deep, dark eyes which contained a whole mood in one look. You were always making things, upcycling stuff from charity shops. Most of your outfits were unique, run up on your mum's sewing machine. And you went on to make a fair number of wedding dresses over the years.'

For all our fascination with each other, any talk of marriage for *us* was a long way off. A friend who knew us both at the time recently wrote: 'My memories of April are very similar to how I view her today—a gentle, thoughtful, caring, wise soul who always thought before she spoke and whose opinion was worth listening to. Oh— and who loved you completely!'

In a recent visit to Aarhus, we gathered round Auntie Jessie's old photo album again. There were pictures of family gatherings from the late 1960s when she visited England. As ever the chattering crowd tucks into an Asian meal. In one picture, April wears a self-made yellow trouser suit setting off her olive complexion, and her hair is in a cute, Twiggy style, bob. Unaccountably I'm wearing a tie, a skinny suede, one I'd borrowed from my teddy-boy brother and I'm scooping curry into my mouth. 'Christopher always liked his food!' Jessie quipped.

It seems strange now, looking back at us as an unattached couple. As far as her family were concerned, I might have been the first of many boyfriends who would pass on, well fed, into the night.

CHAPTER FOUR

(1967–69) FIRST LOVE

Having first rented and then bought a house in Streatham, Austin and Margaret reckoned they could commute to London in their Ford Anglia from Crowborough, a village near the Kent–Sussex border. The Francis family fell into a routine. In the evening the parents pounded the fresh ginger and garlic for the following day, then set off at 7 a.m. After school, the girls finished the cooking, preparing the rice and vegetables for when mum and dad returned from London eleven hours later. The regime was punishing but incomparably better than what they had left behind in Rangoon. Yes, like many Burmese families, they'd benefitted from a cook and a driver, but the precariousness of day-to-day living had become unbearable.

It was in 1967 that I first visited April's home, and began to hear Austin and Margaret's backstory. Stories about their distinctive lineage, the love and affirmation they had received as children, the tough times—of personal loss and lives disrupted by the war—and the joy of finding each other in Calcutta. All this had seemed so upbeat for them as they began married life with young children, echoing a period of fragile post-Independence promise in the country at large. So hearing about the unhappy episode of their forced departure came as a shock and was beginning to sink in. Maybe my first impressions of Burma were inflated and somewhat idyllic. The nation comprised a loose federation of people-groups, each with their own language and way of life. This much was evident from Austin and Margaret's mixed heritage. It was also a nation at war with itself. Having thrown off the burden of colonial rule, deep fissures were beginning to appear, different visions for the future of Burma. And, as if the cruelties of the Second World War were not enough, in the ensuing months and years, bitter fighting flared up between the dominant Bamar people and the ethnic rebels, especially the Karen, who saw their promise of autonomous rule disappearing. There was so much more to learn, but for a while, at least all the questions were shelved as more immediate events took over.

For a few months following our first encounter engineered by my brother, April and I shyly averted gazes as I boarded the school bus. But now we sat together. Little by little I was glimpsing the secret garden of her homeland. It was a door that was only slightly ajar and I learned not to push too hard or too often.

'What was school like for you in Burma?' I asked one day.

There was a long pause, 'I have mixed memories of Mount Hermon School.'

'That's the one in Darjeeling?'

'Yes. It was awful being stuck there for so long, especially when all the other children had gone, like at half-term. Or once, when Elizabeth was ill with a heart issue and had to be taken to southern India for a medical assessment. I was so lonely.' April was looking away. I could see her wistful reflection in the bus window.

'But did it get better as time went by?'

'Yes, I made friends and sometimes stayed with them and their families in the holidays. I went with Muna to her aunt and uncle's place sometimes, it was about a day's drive through the mountains. They were Nepalese Christian doctors and worked at the hospital in Kalimpong. I used to love staying there. They had church in their house on Sundays. They were all very friendly but of course I didn't understand the language.'

'What about the school?'

Again April deflected. 'Mount Hermon was set in lush gardens, surrounded by tea plantations with the mountains beyond. In the cool of the spring mornings, we sometimes walked between the huge rhododendron bushes. We used to pick and suck nectar from the wild fuchsias and catch dewy cobwebs, sparkling like jewels.'

'How did you do that?'

'We made little "rackets" by twining twigs together in the shape of a hoop. The older children were allowed to go into Darjeeling town on Saturdays. We asked the Burmese boys what we wanted and they brought us back goodies: cream cakes from the baker, whole cucumbers to munch through and pickled mangoes to put in sandwiches. We helped ourselves to bread from the kitchens.'

I didn't find it difficult to visualize April charming the older boys in this way. I too was falling under her spell. Finally she got round to school itself:

'Being a mission school, the teachers were Christian and their example and teaching rubbed off on me in a way. I came to enjoy that school a lot. But when it came to the end of term, I was very excited when we flew back home. We'd been away for nine months. As the small plane circled the airfield in Chauk, Elizabeth and I couldn't stop chattering in anticipation of seeing our family again. We threw off our uniforms and pattered barefoot across the cool tiles, the polished teak floors of our bungalow.'

We got off the bus and walked the rain-soaked pavement to our respective schools in Tunbridge Wells. Then April broke the silence:

'Although it was sad to leave Burma, we were all looking forward to seeing England. Mum had been before but it was all new for us. Always thinking ahead, mum had taken us to the tailors in Rangoon to be measured up for skirts and jackets before we left.'

'What were they like?'

'They were very smart but hardly what teenage girls were wearing in England! And of course, it was our first experience of nylon stockings. What did we hold those up with? Suspender belts I suppose.' With that delectable thought lingering in my imagination, we parted until after school.

Our conversations put me in mind of my own primary school. I see a boy in a blazer—lost in heroic dreams—dawdling homeward along the suburban streets of Eltham, the distant foghorn of barges sounding across from the Thames. For my eighth birthday, my uncle Albert took me in his steam barge from the docks up to the Thames estuary and back. To stay up so late and be with his gang of tug-men was a real treat. I felt so grown up.

It is strange to think that at fourteen, April has her own suburban memories of south London. 'After renting in Thornton Heath for a while, our first house was a terrace on Glenister Park Road in Streatham. It was small and I don't know how all the bulky Burmese furniture fitted in. Sunday afternoons were a highlight: sitting with my sisters watching westerns like *Bonanza* with a plate of iced buns.

'I got to know the girl next door. Christine. She was a gentle, only child, and only too pleased to befriend me, the dark-skinned newcomer next door. Her father got tickets and drove us to concerts in his big black Wolseley. He worked for Tesco and got us front row for the Byrds at Fairfield Hall. Another time, I remember us screaming from the balcony at Tooting Bec when the Rolling Stones ran on stage.'

While April was finding her way with new friends in an unfamiliar country, I was on my own spiritual quest. For some reason, I also had a rich vein of Christian teachers at my school and there was no shortage of sports, social events, and cycling camps laid on. Going along to the Bible sessions on a Sunday seemed like a fair deal at the time. I got to know the religious instruction teacher quite well and one evening, I told him how my life was just not adding up. I was sixteen. Mike listened patiently and then said something which I have never forgotten.

'You know what, Chris, you are running away from God!'

Yes, in my head I was in a hurry, running if you like, and I wasn't at all sure of the direction. But to say I was fleeing God initially seemed absurd. I didn't see that coming and it struck me like a rugby tackle in the chest. In those moments, the faith of my grandmothers—one of few things the two had in common—which I had naively viewed as fanciful, must have resurfaced. As did the non-proselytizing attraction of other Christians I had met along the way. In the uncertain silence there registered an unmistakable call, deep calling unto deep, that something was missing in my life.

I hurried back home, closed the bedroom door and sat on my bed. This was definitely a non-interruptible moment. My fingers clutching the eiderdown a little too tightly, I began to speak in whispers. I felt foolish but persevered. 'God,' I said, 'if you are there, I need you.' My heartfelt groans seemed to bounce off the ceiling. What was I doing? This is ridiculous. Talking to yourself is what *old* people do. But the darkness softened, and silence was welcoming. 'Here's my life, it's over to you,' I stammered. Like a rope bridge across a ravine obscured by mist, I stepped into the unknown. How I wanted to hear a voice, to see an angel, to feel a touch. I was still the only person in the room, yet somehow I felt the answer had come. God was present. Always had been.

It felt a relief to stop trying so hard to be somebody and to simply abandon myself to my Maker. Little by little prayer became a natural thing to do and I blew the dust off my Bible. How relevant, how honest, how wise the scriptures were. It was like somebody was writing me a personal letter, somebody who knew me through and through and yet loved me with no strings attached. This was new. So much in my life up to that point had been conditional. Many years later, I tried to retrace what I felt at the time:

There is a voice I've heard since I was young,
a voice quite different from all others.
Calling my name when the world had begun,
silently singing, soft as a mother's.

Like a river, deep calling unto deep,
it cascades with no noise but real,

through the canyons of my sleep,
rousing my senses to see and feel.

. . . it echoes in the chambers of my heart
whispers love in the boudoirs of my soul.
In the science of life where I lost my art
it calls me again to make me whole.

I resist, press on and cover my ears,
a restless soul intent to roam.
But then amidst the pain and tears
I turn around and head for home.

All this was happening around the time I was getting to know April. Not in a way that I could explain to her, or to anybody else for that matter. My parents shrugged it off as a religious phase I was going through. I later discovered they had been keen church-goers, which I gather was a majority activity in 1930s Britain, and had even been involved in Christian youth work. Like April's father in Rangoon, my father's time at university was cut short by the Second World War. He ended up as a Major in the Royal Engineers under Montgomery in North Africa. His experience of recovering equipment(and charred bodies) from tanks blown up by Rommel's forces, left him understandably cynical about a benevolent God.

Meanwhile, there was the practical matter of transport to get to and from April's place. Although not a full-blown *Mod* with a motor scooter boasting multiple mirrors and gleaming chrome, I did possess a fur-hooded parka. For some historical reason, my scooter was a Lambretta-Vespa hybrid that had long lost its kick-start. When picking up April, this meant ringing her doorbell, then running alongside the scooter to jump-start it down the hill and coming back around the block for her to jump on as I came past. We got it down to a fine art.

In the days leading up to our A-levels, we spent long, sunny days together. Ostensibly to cram for the exams, although I'm not sure how much revision got done. April was studying for Zoology and Geography and I was gunning for good grades in History, Geography, and English Literature, having got an 'A' in Art a year early. Due to narrow syllabi, together with a heavy reliance on question-predicting, I ended up with an incredibly selective secondary education. I knew a lot about the War of the Roses but nothing about the Americans in Vietnam nor the British in Burma. I could recognize a glacial valley but knew nothing of wilful deforestation of ancient teak forests in Asia. I delighted in poetry by Byron and Donne (and Dylan) but was unaware of Gandhi's Salt March in India or the speeches of Martin Luther King. Perhaps most bemusing of all, I could read in Latin about Hannibal's elephants crossing the Alps, but I didn't see love coming. How is it, I often thought to myself, that such an exotic Eastern apparition should concern herself with me, a wisp of whimsy blown in by a foreign breeze? A gadfly upon a deep pool.

The true depth of that pool, April's parental and cultural heritage as well as her mysterious persona, were to take a long while to fathom. I was being introduced to Burma, a country with which I had such faint acquaintance, a dim resonance with something past. At the same time and much more privately, I was also becoming familiar with a spiritual country. Again the plaintive sounding of piano chords played in my heart, as if I somehow knew the voice which was calling. Although I had set out on the pilgrimage, the 'promised land' to which I was destined was still far off. Just as I was relying on April and her parents to furnish the details of their homeland, so my discovery of life with God was still largely mediated by others. I was sure the *place* existed, I had glimpsed what was on offer and I had met some inhabitants. They talked about a life-changing friendship with God and the equanimity they carried was enticing. But, like Burma, there was so much more for me to learn. First-hand.

Many decades on, I still hear snatches of April's younger days for the first time, like a patchwork quilt a lifetime in the making. Only now am I beginning to understand her reticence.

'I don't like talking about myself.'

'Why?'

'It's private. It's not relevant.' There is a definiteness in April's tone.

'*I* am interested. Other people are interested.'

'Are they? I don't think they understand. They switch off because they can't identify. Except perhaps those who have been to boarding school.'

'I get that.'

'Friendships don't last because you're always moving schools. You learn to become self-sufficient.'

'A way of protecting yourself?'

'Yes. I suppose I don't want to be exposed.'

'What's the fear?'

'There's no fear. It's just a fact.'

I can see this is an uncomfortable territory for April. Also, the irony of writing a book about her and her family settles on my shoulder like an ungainly bird. 'What are you doing?' the bird seems to whisper in my ear, 'making all this personal stuff so public?' I sit back, feeling slightly chastised.

'For me, it was also the language,' April says, finally, 'especially in the early days in this country. I found it difficult to express myself. I had to take English O-Level twice. It really hindered my education.'

'So you've got used to keeping your thoughts to yourself?' I say, more of a statement than question. 'The thing is, this can come across as acceptance, of not having strong views. I think a lot of people see you as a good listener, which you are, but they fail to see the real you. It's like they are dealing with the sentry at the entrance to the tent rather than the general inside.'

'Well, that's fine. After all, I am an introvert.'

CHAPTER FIVE

(1969–73) WEDDING

Apart from trying to process what was happening to us—April and her new-found country, me and my newly discovered faith—we were also figuring out what to do with our lives. Neither of us had many ideas about a career, just the next step. Cecil, my headmaster surveyed all from his dark-panelled office, the panoptic eye of my grammar school. I'd only ever been to his study for mild misdemeanours. Now that I was leaving with a fine clutch of A-levels, we were equals. Well almost. He no longer had power over me.

'What are you reading at university? Classics I hope, chap.' We were all his chaps. The fullest fountain pen comment I'd had from him on my annual reports had been: 'Stick at it, chap'.

For the first time, I saw him as a short-armed, high-handed figure. His captain's chair creaked when he leaned forward, as if he could cajole me to follow his crusty tradition of Latin and Greek. His cloaked form was silhouetted against the leaded light window. This was a pity because I could only feel, not see, the full measure of his scowl as I announced:

'Sociology at Reading, sir.'

I had more time for the other authority figure in my life. My father had wisely advised me not to rely on a new and rather suspect subject like Sociology to get into a competitive job market. So while I didn't follow his ex-military advice to polish my shoes, I

successfully interviewed for a thick sandwich course with what was
to become British Leyland. The main factory produced the classic
Austin Mini and a long line of other, very much more forgettable
models. This meant a year at the Longbridge plant, three years to
pursue my studies at Reading, and then a guaranteed job following
my fifth year back in Birmingham. I was one of the ten so-called
scholarship apprentices. All the other intake were engineers and had
an intrinsic interest in car mechanics. I had none.

'You are an experiment,' the recruiting panel said, as if to reassure
me, 'we see you going into Personnel Management.'

As for April, her interest in clothes, sewing, and the latest
trends in clothing design had gathered momentum and she'd
secured a place at the London College of Fashion on Oxford
Street. This was to follow a 'gap year' to earn some cash. So,
in ways that were prescribed before we started dating, we were
destined to go our separate directions when we left school. For
four years we lived in different places and carried on a long-
distance romance. At Reading my friendship group included many
delightful members of the opposite sex and April mixed with
a cosmopolitan collection of pattern-cutters, seamstresses, and
wannabe dress-designers at her college. For all the temptation
and distraction we remained committed to each other. The letters
piled up, my love-poems found a steady outlet, and weekend
meetings were sometimes fabulous, sometimes fraught.

April was trying out some early clothing creations. At the
wedding of her older sister Elizabeth, she wore a stunning full-
length Afghan coat over a pair of hand-crafted velvet, cadmium-
yellow knickerbockers, and knee-length suede boots. Her foray
into trousers was a little less successful. Using me as her guinea
pig for cutting patterns, the prototype pair were low-waisted and
tight, slightly short which is the fashion now but not then. They
were also devoid of pockets and not very practical. Following the
Carnaby Street trend, the second pair were also hipsters, similarly
tight and flared like loons. There was little room to spare and

April at London College of Fashion, 1970

when we sat down after the first hymn, the seams split from waist to knee. Fortunately, I had a coat with me. We didn't visit that church again.

For all my infatuation, I was guilty of taking our relationship for granted. April wasn't impressed with the fact that she was having to fit in around all my other activities. For her, this hooked deep-seated feelings of loneliness and loss, which I had not yet fully appreciated. Every now and again, she would drop a hint.

'Are you serious about us or not?' April asked quietly as we travelled back to her parents' place from London by train. It was a spring day in the first year of college.

'What do you mean?' I said, semi-hypnotized by the scenery scudding by. The back gardens of Watford: identical terraced houses, some chic, some shabby, all individualized in some way. I was always fascinated by other people's backyards. The private worlds of vegetable patches, garden furniture, and ramshackle potting sheds in full view to trainloads of commuters.

'About us.'

'The party. Yes, I think we should go'.

'Not the party. Us'. April was in my ear now, unusually insistent.

I was beginning to sense this was a serious question and turned away from the window. 'Oh, engagement and that sort of thing?' A topic that we'd skirted around before.

'Do you want to marry me?' April asked, in a fairly harsh whisper.

'Oh, gosh! Yes,' I whispered back, conscious that other passengers were tuning in. It was now *our* private world that was coming into public view.

'Good,' she said, drawing closer.

'Good,' I repeated emphatically, aware that there was a carriage full of suitors if I was to show the slightest hesitation.

So not the most glamorous of proposals. Between Hemel Hempstead and Apsley, the deed was done. We were to be married.

At the same time as promising fidelity to our blossoming relationship, I was mulling over commitments of other kinds. As an eighteen-year-old, I had turned up at factory gate E of the Austin-Morris plant at Longbridge, ready to change the world. The trouble was I did not recognize the world in front of me. Summer jobs hadn't acquainted me with the taste of grit and furnace heat of a foundry, the brain-numbing boredom of an assembly line, or the nagging moan of the factory hooter at 7.30 a.m., as if each new shift was an air-raid. Even in Birmingham, I was regarded as a soft southerner with hippy-long-hair. Clocking in my punch card and pulling on green overalls I became a faceless worker, dumb and dispensable like the milky swarf that curled off the threshing lathes. Here was a factory, a mile and a half long, employing 75,000 employees, where the vast majority had no intrinsic interest in what they were doing. Why should they, it was organized to be mindless.

It was also a work-world in which I felt I had no part. Although nothing like as momentous as Austin and Margaret's exile from

Burma, I experienced my own sense of being outside, of not belonging. For many years following their arrival in England, the Francis family possessed no passports. The local Police made yearly checks at their home. They were not physically threatened but remained under scrutiny until each member of the family secured naturalization papers and eventually, their passports. I had a passport to a career at a car plant. I just wasn't sure I wanted to go there.

So it was a year later that I arrived at Reading with many vexed questions about work, loyalties, and life. Does the workplace have to be a dispiriting, punishing place? On the personal front, my exploratory belief in God was growing but was still tentative, somewhat compartmentalized and more head than heart. I didn't see much evidence of God's presence around me in south Birmingham, except for one or two families who took me in. As for life, I was still in the woods.

In some ways, university didn't help. It was like living in two worlds. One was the upbeat and unquestioned reliance on reason. Each of my undergraduate courses, sociology, philosophy, and economics, rested on the supremacy of knowledge. Okay, their versions of knowledge weren't the same, but the common and vital tool was human intellect. Wherever I turned, there was optimism, a belief that no problems were unsolvable, that societies could be changed for the better, and a promise that with sufficient analysis and applied knowledge, there was nothing that could not be explained. What worried me was that, for all the enthusiasm, anything other than the material was dismissed. In my mind, this failed to resolve moral issues or address unsettling questions about truth and meaning.

The other world was what my lecturers called the 'sacred realm', a kind of receptacle into which belief systems, worship, and religion were unceremoniously bundled. Like a bag of dirty washing, this was deemed inherently private and derided by much social science. At best it was an anthropological feature of primitive cultures, outmoded and irrelevant to the modern age.

Of course, the choice was not presented as starkly at the time, but it hung heavy in the air and it perhaps explained the existential doubts I felt in my student days. As if the worlds of well-argued, scientifically sound reasons and well-rounded, experiential spiritual beliefs could not coexist. Indeed, could not cross-fertilize. It took a long while for me to recover from this deception.

I guess this split also described my feelings about Burma at the time. Intellectually I was becoming informed, my curiosity was being fed and the curtain on this mysterious country was gradually being lifted. But at an emotional and spiritual level, I was not yet immersed. I remained uninitiated into the ways and norms of this far-off society, my soul untouched. Only later when I was to spend time in that country was I able to bring the two—my head and my heart—together.

It's 7 a.m. on the seventh day of the seventh month, 1973. April recalls the holy day:

'I got up early on the biggest day of my life. I remember going down to the bottom of the garden of my parent's house in Apsley. The white and pink roses wafted their perfume as I passed. In days gone by, this rectangle of grass would have been a tennis court, now it is a lawn and will host the reception later in the day. Tables were partly laid with cloths, name places ready to be allocated. I thought of the guests we had invited. Glasses will be clinked, jokes jeered and anecdotes spun. But for the moment, all was hushed apart from the striped and faded marquee which flapped gently like a yacht's spinnaker on a cloudless day. I felt a slight tingle of nervousness. We were setting sail together.'

Staying over with friends Doug and Nancy in north London, I also have butterflies in my stomach and have no appetite for the American pancakes they kindly cook me for breakfast.

The next thing I remember is the church service. The minister pulls no punches in his message, relishing a captive audience, and his prayers are too long. Amidst the twirling hats and swirling nerves, I'm not taking much in and wonder how all this religious stuff is going down with my agnostic friends and family. I needn't worry

April and I get married, 7 July 1973

about my older brother Peter. Later he tells me he and our cousin Heather were sharing a spliff outside the church.

There is a beautiful Burmese 'princess' on my arm. The photographer captures us as we come out of the dark church onto the street, blinking in the bright light and then ducking as if the suspended confetti might hurt if it lands. April wears a fitted cotton dress, tapering to a slight fish tail at her feet with a silk, flower-patterned organza jacket. She made the stunning outfit herself. A white rose is in her bobbed hair. It is all still a bit unreal. Did she truly come half way around the world for us to share this day together?

At the reception two families mingle, most meeting for the first time, to celebrate a confluence of ancestral streams, an interleaving of family trees. British reserve is disarmed by the warmth of a Burmese welcome. April's two sisters glide in their longyis between clusters of guests. Elizabeth, now married to John, and her younger sister Gay, a demure bridesmaid, along with cousin Rosa from Denmark. I'm relieved that mum and dad look as though they are relaxed and enjoying themselves. It is difficult not to with Austin and Margaret as hosts. A few months before, my father, bless him, had taken me aside for a fireside chat. He wanted reassurance that his son knew what he was doing marrying an Asian bride.

April and I politely pose and smile, meet and greet, but I have the feeling of floating in a private bubble barely aware of the public gaze. Like cosmonauts on the moon's surface in slow motion with no gravity. I pause to gaze around the garden, now filling with guests. I'm impressed with my university friends, the guys have found ties and the girls have bought hats: great saucers of straw and wide-brimmed velvet swathed in purple and pink. How unusually smart they look. It is graduation day but most have preferred to join us in our celebration, rather than line up for their degree scrolls in stuffy gowns and mortarboards. In the days of sit-ins and student protests, it is a comfortable way for us to collectively snub the establishment. Strangely, and sadly, this is the last day we will all be together, as we spin off into different orbits.

The wine is still flowing and the party is still going strong as we set off down the hill in dad's white minivan which he's lent us for the honeymoon. Lipstick love messages scrawled on the side, tin cans noisily trailing behind. The whooping of well-wishers subside and the crowd waving at the front gate disappears from the rear-view mirror. I know April is looking at me in the lovely, approving way she does. We're on our own now. Exhilarating, mystifying, unnerving.

CHAPTER SIX

(1970–80) TURNAROUND

Some seasons in life turn out to be foundations to what happens later. Ostensibly, this decade had little connection to Burma other than the fact that it featured a treasured, now part-westernized Burmese female student. On another level it shaped the rest of our lives.

It was during the first year at our respective colleges in 1971 that we caught the train from Euston as two independent souls and arrived at Apsley destined to spend eternity together. This very nearly did not happen. Two events made it possible, the first serendipitous, the other momentous.

My first term at Reading was intoxicating, and I don't just mean the ready access to alcohol. More than that, the whole freedom thing was mesmerising. At the start of Freshers' Week, my parents dropped me off with my luggage at Windsor Hall, and to my shame, I didn't even invite them to my room and brew a cup of tea for them. As I covered my walls with posters, I was eager to draw a line under my cosseted youth, followed by a chastening year in Birmingham. I was ready to move on, to put innocence behind me, and squeeze the maximum from the next three years. Apart from sitting in lectures with hundreds of students, wide-eyed that our first essay deadline was a whole month away, there was the field-hockey team, soccer in the grounds of Fox Hill by the lake, marathon table-football sessions, three-day-long games of Monopoly and crowding into the Junior Common Room for *Monty Python's Flying Circus*. And that

Me with friends at Reading University, 1970

was just the day time. Where was April in all this you might ask. And so did she. Again it is a matter of chagrin that April got slightly sidelined.

One Friday afternoon in November, I had a choice: a full weekend of social and sporting activities at the university, or a dash across country to see April. I knew she was going to Kent to visit her sister and brother-in-law, Elizabeth and John. What I didn't know is that they had lined up a choir-singing male friend to take April to a concert. On the spur of the moment I hitch-hiked to London, caught the tube, and then a train to Canterbury. As I was standing at the side of the road hitching to their village, the three of them happened to pass, bouncing along in their *Citroen deux chevaux*. Stifling their collective surprise they naturally stopped to pick me up. Much later it struck me that had I not appeared that afternoon, I may have lost April for good.

Our long-distance romance revived and we went to the Christmas ball together. She wore a splendid dress she had created at her fashion college, where she was deep into pattern-cutting and experimental designs, and me in my grey 'interview' suit with a dark shirt and shiny, powder-blue tie. We danced the night away but all was not well. I knew, deep down, I had a letter to write. It was awful to compose and—in the bigger scheme of things—awesome in its consequences. I'd made a decision before university not to hide the fact that I was a Christian believer. By now I had felt the tender touch of God in my life . . . too many answered prayers, fulfilled promises, glimpses of heaven for me to doubt that God was real and, incredibly wanted my attention. Indeed I was discovering he wanted more than that, he wanted my wholehearted devotion. It all came down to some cryptic words of Jesus, puzzling yet profound: 'Unless a grain of wheat falls into the earth and dies, it remains alone. But if it dies, it bears much fruit.'

Jesus was saying to me, 'If you really let go, reckless in your love, you'll have life forever, real and eternal'. At nineteen, I was determined to take God at his word and let go. Yes, I was ready to risk everything for him. What I hadn't bargained for was such an early and searching test of my new-found resolve. Through the scriptures I was reading and advice from Christian friends, Father God made it clear to me that, much as I loved April, there really was no future in our relationship so long as she held him at bay. She was happy that I believed, had met many of my Christian friends, and was in no sense antagonistic.

'I knew about God from films like *Ben Hur* and *The Ten Commandments*,' she said of that time. 'And the staff at the Christian mission school in Darjeeling were kind and caring. But that was all on the outside.'

So here I was trying to explain my dilemma to April in a letter. That my love for God had to come before my love for her. My hand was heavy and it did seem cold-hearted even as I wrote it. I'll let April take up her side of the story . . .

'The letter from Chris ruined my Christmas, I was heartbroken. I was watching God influence my life and I was facing abandonment again. I

couldn't understand why our relationship had to end. Over the holidays our whole family went down with heavy colds, but it was stinging anger that I was wrestling with. Eventually Chris phoned. The least you can do is come and see me. To say goodbye.

Chris agreed. He admitted he'd been a coward in writing rather than talking face to face. So this is what we did for most of that first weekend in January 1971. Chris talked about God's involvement in his life, as if God was a friend and that such a friendship was only possible because of Christ's death and resurrection. And that this demanded an individual response. For the first time, it was actually making sense.

On Sunday evening we went to a church in Golders Green. I think it was a Scottish Presbyterian. Neither of us had been there before, nor since. Anyway, on this chilly night, the speaker quoted a verse in Revelation where Jesus says: "Look at me. I stand at the door and knock. If you hear me call and open the door, I'll come right in and sit down to supper with you." He was mainly addressing the young people in the church but it was like Jesus was speaking to me personally and I thought, well it's now or never. So there and then, I invited Jesus to come into my life. I didn't make any public response. Chris knew nothing of what was going on inside.

He went back to Reading. Our relationship was in limbo. But I think we both felt better for having talked things through. What happened next is difficult to put into words. It was as if I was swept along on a wave of euphoria. Jesus was so close to me. It was like being immersed in his Spirit. This person who had seemed so distant was now at the centre of my life! All the early Christian teaching I'd been exposed to, the Bible stories, the kindness of Christians I had met . . . now it all began to come together. I wanted to be sure this was real. So I didn't tell Chris for three weeks.'

When April phoned and told me, I was ecstatic, I took the call on the sixth floor, the top landing, of our hall of residence. I don't know how I got to the bottom . . . in two or three leaps, hollering as I went. Anybody I saw I seized to pass on the fantastic news. Christian friends who'd been praying and agnostic friends who'd met April. Everyone got a hug.

I have often thought about this turnaround of fortunes. Surely it was unfair of me in the first place to write such a letter. To talk about finishing a loving friendship that had started three years before, and to do so in such an abrupt manner. To turn my back on April's delightful family, when they had taken me in and shared with me private stories of Burma long ago. Then maybe some people might doubt April's motives. Surely this was just an elaborate means of keeping her man. To profess Christian belief was a sure way of breathing new life into a faltering love affair. Especially having had so many past friendships torn apart by changing schools and moving countries earlier in her life.

My interpretation is different. It is simply this. That our Heavenly Father wanted us to be together. He knew how deeply we were in love. But he also knew that for our relationship to thrive over time, we needed to be of one mind, a single heart, and a shared spirit. And for that to happen, our relationship had to 'die' and start again on a different foundation.

I'm not laying this down as a rule for others. All I know is that it was a stunning intervention on God's part. Caring enough to stop us in our tracks. 'Tough love' from on high. Akin to a father delighting in the sacrificial obedience of his children and lavishing his favour upon them. The rest of this memoir pivots on this rather exposing episode: the re-balancing of our relationship, our subsequent engagement and marriage (yes, we both enjoyed the company of close friends, but never did these usurp our commitment to each other), our joint call to pioneering charity work, our amateur attempts to raise a family, and our unanticipated reconnection to April's homeland. I believe none of this would have been possible without a shared desire to follow Jesus, to enjoy his company, 'sitting down and eating supper with us' as he promised he would. The way we related to Jesus and expressed our love for him was starkly different—and even more so now. We are in no way clones. But that difference keeps the flame of love burning.

Something else happened in that first year at university which was almost as precipitous. Amidst all the other new things and people I ran into was an unusual bunch of Christians called Campus Crusade for Christ (CCC). They were knocking on students' doors and explaining their faith to anyone who'd listen. Maybe I was looking for a cause to sign up to, but these were people I wanted to be around. They were good company, hot on theology and wanted to change the world. Without missing a beat, they told me their goal was to give every student at the university the opportunity to respond to God's call on their lives. For a new and somewhat bashful believer, this was liberating. All the restrictive religious garb systematically removed, layers of legalism cast off, the petticoats of piety tossed aside to reveal the glorious, simple truth of Jesus and the adventurous life he promises. I could see no reason not to join them in this endeavour. If God is God, we cannot keep quiet. April had a similar experience with the CCC team in London. As her enthusiasm for God overflowed, friends and family wanted to know more. Several started to follow Jesus.

Three years later, April and I were spending the first year of our marriage in Redditch and the colour was being leached from our lives. We'd bought a matchbox house on a huge housing estate. I was back at the Longbridge factory, in the fifth and final year of my thick sandwich apprenticeship, being groomed for Personnel Management. April was having no joy finding a job in fashion and settled for being assistant librarian at the University in Edgbaston.

For all the career frustrations, there was joy ahead. April was in the early days of pregnancy. The morning sickness was bad to start with and as she came through the front door after work, April would regularly throw up. It seemed to seal the conclusion that we were in the wrong place. We sat on our makeshift furniture and weighed up options.

Spurred by the excitement of seeing God change people's lives in our student years, we decided to leave house and jobs and applied to join the full-time staff of CCC. Dozens of British graduates were doing the same. It was not the 'career move' that those around us were expecting. My boss at British Leyland was surprisingly positive (I think he'd seen my head metaphorically hit my desk often enough to know I was cut out for other things). On the domestic front, my father was none too pleased that the carefully staged entry into a professional career was being rejected. April's parents were also doubtful about what it all meant. Even the church ministers we knew were suspicious of this cult-like movement from California. All eventually came round when they saw how revitalized we became, how our children loved the extended family aspect of regular conferences and how we coped financially. April's father, Austin, even started to affectionately call me a *pongyi*, the Burmese term for a monk!

We were a long way from donning Buddhist robes but a couple of aspects of staff membership were unconventional. None of the staff was salaried. We were each responsible for raising our own support (in effect, this meant asking sympathetic friends to donate a sum into our account each month). Also, it was not possible for one of a couple to join, both were either accepted or not (the rationale being that the demands were stretching, sometimes sacrificial, and it was important for both parties to be 'on board'). We were assigned to Reading University. I was back in my old haunt, this time with April, and bump, at my side.

The strategy was to go to the Students' Union or knock on doors in the halls of residence to conduct a simple survey to ascertain students' thinking about God and Jesus. These days, such a direct approach could be deemed intrusive, as undesirable proselytizing. To then go on to present those who showed interest with a factual account of life, death, and raising of God's Son might be considered arrogant. As if there were just one version of the truth, one religion. At a time when the likes of influential philosophers like Lord Bertrand Russell was writing pamphlets on 'Why I am not a Christian' (to say nothing of liberal Bishops questioning the veracity of Jesus' miracles and resurrection), surely it was daring, if not foolish, to be declaring that it was possible to know the living God. To be fair, in the early 1970s, we had very few arguments of this nature. Indeed there was an openness to discuss matters of belief and give a platform to contrary opinions that has largely evaporated from Western campuses today.

Each day April and I ventured into common rooms and student hostels. Some shut the door on our faces. Many couldn't see the relevance of Jesus at all, even if it happened to be true. 'So what?' they said. Other students were surprised at what the New Testament actually contained and decided to follow Christ. We are still in touch with some a generation or more later. One sleepy afternoon in March, we knocked on a hostel door and were invited in by Javier. He was a mature student doing a PhD in Linguistics and only too pleased to chat about faith. We subsequently got to know his family well and visited him a couple of times in Mexico.

In 2013 we received this letter from him:

'I have been waiting for this day, 24 March , to send this greetings and love. I am seventy-two years old today and I have been a Christian for thirty-six, and a blind and lost man the other earlier thirty-six. But you Chris were instrumental for the grace of the Lord to have been shed upon me; and you, dear April, were such a wonderful helper and friend collaborating to the same . . . At that time of your visit, I didn't even know there was a Christianity, a manner of being and believing that was an alternative to any other religion. I learned that from you, dear brother and sister. You took me aside and explained to me the ways of God more accurately by word and deeds.'

It was amongst you that I realized how blind and lost I had been, and it was amongst you that I was blessed by a faith in the truth of God as it was manifested in the Bible; also, I made a decision to become a Christian and to be baptized in testimony of the new life that I intended to live from then onwards. It was 1977, I may have been very much lacking in Christian experience, but the change in me was deep and the seed planted in me grew. After thirty-six years it has become whatever kind of tree I am today, still by the same blessed grace

*of God. My conversion may have been a very small start, but it came
about against the fierce and disdainful opposition that there was in me
towards all things Christian.'*

For six thrilling years after we were married, April and I were part of
a team talking to students. Conversions, like this one described by
Javier, were not unusual and kept us going when times were tough
and rebuttals were many. Meanwhile, our wider support team of
friends and churches faithfully sustained us financially. As our family
grew, we never went without a meal.

Our house, close to the university, was open much of the time.
Fellow staff, students looking for home comforts, and young mums
whom April had met, all came and went. Often they were part of
birthday parties, reading to the girls, and teaching to ride bikes on the
campus. It was a fulfilling and chaotic time when many friendships
were forged, among the most special and long-standing ones of our
lives. Thoughts of Burma were pushed to the back burner, but a
different narrative was being played out.

Although not obvious to us at the time, these years laid down
some golden maxims that would guide April and me through our
lives and reconnect us with her homeland. Planted in us was a desire
to, wherever possible, work side by side. In a business culture where
the work practises of so many organizations—including churches—
tends to segregate families, we valued the opportunity CCC gave
us to work as equals as part of a local team and wider staff family
with our children feeling very much part of it. Pursuing a common
vision lifted us above the many chafing, personal differences we
undoubtedly had. Also embedded in us was a heart for reaching out
to those uninformed about Jesus, a radical man, concerned for the
plight of marginalized people. Students seemed to be a particularly
strategic group, given their likely spheres of influence in years
to come.

On top of this, serving with the charity CCC and occasionally
attending their international conferences, opened our eyes to a needy

world. CCC's 'impossible' global mission and rubbing shoulders with staff members from other nations, stirred us to look beyond the relatively privileged shores of Britain.

We finally left CCC in 1980. However, this abiding vision continued to burn brightly for both April and me. It would be another thirty years before all the latent ingredients of this heady cocktail came together in, of all places, the city of Rangoon. First came an appetizer: a family visit to Burma in 1995–96.

CHAPTER SEVEN

(December 1995) DISTANT DRUMBEAT

It was a while before the embers of my fascination with Burma were stoked again. Having four girls in the space of nearly eight years consumed most of our energy. Occasional news about their family back in Rangoon filtered through from April's parents, but apart from a clutch of national reports covering student riots and democratic elections in the late 1980s, the newsfeeds were ominously quiet. Burma was doing a good job of isolating itself from the rest of the world.

Zoe came first. Her name means life, not simply physical but 'God-given life', which summed up our joy at her arrival. April did all the hard work but it was me who fainted at the moment she emerged into the world, after a long night of labour. Born in January 1975, it was a special moment to see my father embrace his first grandchild, just a few weeks before bronchitis took his noble life too early. Sundy Lin is a Burmese name meaning 'star shine'. We weren't to know when she was born in 1977, that she would indeed grow to look the most Burmese of our daughters. Louisa Le came next two years later. We had the name Louisa on both sides of the family, so that pleased everyone. Her second name Le signifies 'little' in Burmese, because we thought we'd come to the end on the procreation front. But then in 1982, along came our fourth, Mala Su, Burmese for 'well-being'. By then April's mother was desperate for a grandson, Elizabeth having already produced two girls. When

I broke the news of another granddaughter over the phone, to add to the five she already had, she couldn't help herself: 'Oh no!' she exclaimed again and again.

From the start April wanted to stay at home with the children to raise them with definite values. To be there when they came back from school in need of a snack, a hug or a chat, something April had sorely missed as a child boarder. In the early years we saw some delightful glimpses of our children's emergent personalities. When she was nine, Zoe announced: 'I'm going to get married when I'm 19, and I'm going to get earrings when I'm 20 . . . I don't want to marry someone with spots.' She also had a highly developed intuition: 'I know someone at school. You can tell where they're from their accents, before they even speak.'

Sundy Lin was less verbal, more self-contained. She would quietly cut the fringe from our lampshades and 'anonymously' announce her presence by peeling the wallpaper and scribbling her name on the plaster. One winter it snowed heavily and everything came to a magical halt outside. I donned her in wellingtons, duffle coat and woolly hat. As we trudged through the drifts I said: 'Oh Sundy, look at how low the branches are with all the snow, see how deep it is. Isn't it so lovely and quiet?' I shan't forget the little Paddington Bear figure beside me looking up and saying: 'Yes daddy, except when you're talking.'

As a youngster, Louisa quietly observed the vicissitudes—the ups and downs—of her older sisters and placidly trod a middle, safe path. Then, when we forgot all about her, a plaintive voice could just be heard in the melee, 'Me too!' As for Mala, at seven, she was showing an interest in life and immortality: 'Do you think I'll stay alive all my life until I die? Grandad's seventy but he's not dead.' Actually, it was a near-fatal accident of one of her school friends some years later which started her journey towards God.

For a while, April and I quietly congratulated ourselves on being a happy family. That was until hormonal rage set in and we wondered—for ten or more rollercoaster years—'what have we unleashed on the world?'

One thing the girls fondly remember is Sunday evenings. We tried to set this time aside for just us as a family: soft boiled eggs, toast fingers, and home-made cake. No TV, no phone calls, no social engagements. It was on one of these occasions, when they were in their teens, that the conversation got around to whether they felt different as they were growing up.

'I have become more conscious of being half-Burmese as I've got older,' said Zoe, who had just started sixth form. 'Visiting Grandma and Grandad, we have experienced Burmese culture through them as people. And the food they cook.'

There were 'mmms' all round at this point. Our daughters had each developed a strong liking for Burmese curries and delicacies. The highlight of the week was when we visited April's parents.

Sometimes they stayed over. Zoe stood up and mimicked an old person: 'I won't forget seeing grandad in the morning with his baggy pyjama bottoms and woolly hat . . . '

' . . . those are called *Shan-baun-bi* . . . ' said April, 'literally it means Shan pants.'

'Oh yes, he wore his woolly hat *to bed*, didn't he!' chimed in Mala, giggling. 'Is it Grandma who likes to sleep with the window open?'

'I think we can guess who wins that little battle,' said Zoe. 'Do you remember she told us all off for not saying good morning at breakfast when we came down?'

'You were fortunate growing up and going to primary school in Reading. It was a lot more multicultural there,' I said to Zoe.

'Yeah, at one time there were seventeen different nationalities in my class. Moving to Milton Keynes I had the first experience in the playground of being 'different' and was called names because of my browner skin. This wore off quickly . . . '

' . . . the insults or the skin?' I said. Predictable groans for a bad dad joke.

'I remember a friend stuck up for me on the first day.'

Louisa was often the last to speak: 'All through our lives,' she said, 'people have taken an interest in our Asian look or sometimes

Our four daughters: Louisa, Zoe, Mala Su and Sundy Lin

passers-by think we are Mediterranean. They can't pinpoint where we are from. Clearly not English through and through.' Then looking at her older sister Sundy she said, 'I remember you being asked countless times at school if you were Chinese because of the way your eyes slit across your face when you laugh.'

'Mmm,' said Sundy, 'I was forever saying that I was from Burma. I often got puzzled looks, as clearly no one had heard of Burma. I've just got used to saying it is somewhere in between India, China, and Thailand. Now we're asked about this less. Maybe it's because we blend in more.'

This was a rare insider view to the world of our daughters. We discussed it a few days later when they were all at school. As I stirred my coffee, I asked April why she said so little about her upbringing.

'You've got to understand . . . ' April said with a sigh and a pause, ' . . . what it was like for me at a young age to be cut off from my school, to leave my friends behind, and my country.'

I knew this was not easy for April, but I gently probed.

'My parents had to sign an oath before we left Burma that none of us would return for twenty years. When we first came to England I felt like an alien, that I didn't belong here.'

I squirmed inwardly at the strength of feeling April was finally expressing.

'Yes, we were gradually Anglicized. We had to make the best of it, learning to integrate. For a long while I coped. I buried the pain of leaving everything behind. But as the children grew, so did the responsibilities. Decisions about *their* upbringing and schooling, dealing with *their* insecurities.' Then, after a pause, 'It was also a time when you were away a lot with work.'

Indeed I recalled 1989–90 being a difficult time. I was particularly busy with work commitments, leaving April to pick up the pieces at home. Sometimes I was away from home most of the week. I was flying high tutoring on leadership development workshops but when I got home I had little left to give.

'That was a tipping point,' April continued. 'It was like the trauma of the past finally caught up with me. I couldn't get out of bed in the morning. Do you remember . . . Zoe used to bring me a cup of tea. Then she'd get breakfast for everybody and do the lunchboxes for her and her sisters?'

I didn't fully understand at the time, but I could see she was depressed. Fortunately one of the ministers of our church was a trained counsellor. Week by week she helped April to let go of the past.

'It was a relief to know that I *could* be weak, to express my feelings, my sadness. Giving myself permission *not* to cope. It was the first step to recovering my mental health.'

This period really opened my eyes. I could see that, once again, I had neglected our relationship. I became more acutely aware of April's fragility, when she'd been so consistently strong as a partner and mother. She had exuded calm and poise for so long, I was alarmed to see her so anxious. Recognizing it as depression was a turning point and she was gradually able to find herself again. Part of her renewed confidence led April—in 1991—to enrol for a BSc. in Psychology and subsequently to train as a counsellor.

Now that it was less raw, we were able to talk about this whole period. I could also see its significance in our decision to visit Burma as a family at the end of 1995. Having faced and grieved for past losses, April was now emotionally ready to go back.

With Burmese officials declaring 1996 as 'Visit Myanmar Year', I was curious to sample what was on offer.

'I'm not sure it's a good idea,' April said. It was never a good idea to surprise April. She needed time to ruminate and make up her own mind.

'It'll be fine,' I said, 'and it will be good for the girls.'

'You don't know the country.'

'Exactly.' For me that was a good reason for us to go. For her, the opposite.

A little more time passed and a couple of things occurred that helped my case. Austin and Margaret made their first visit back to Rangoon since leaving in 1964. And by all accounts, the reunions had been sweet and the reconnection with the past had been stirring in a mainly positive way. Also, after a brief battle with lung cancer, my mum had passed away in 1994 and left us money enough to fund an extended family trip. Knowing her fondness for the Burmese family I'd married into, I was sure she would approve of spending money in this way.

'What do you think?'

'It'll be a bit strange . . . with the family over there.' April was still not convinced.

'They will be delighted to see you . . . and us,' I said, not knowing whether this was true.

'My Burmese is very rusty'.

'We'll get by, some of them will speak English I'm sure.'

I could understand April having mixed feelings about returning after more than thirty years, but she came round. We managed to carve out time from schools—at a time when it was easier to do so—and work schedules to arrange a five-week visit spanning the Christmas holidays into January 1996. For each of us, and especially our four daughters aged thirteen to twenty, it was to be an eye-opening, tongue-tingling, mind-stretching, spirit-enriching experience. Seeds of curiosity and connection that are still with all of them today, flowering in different ways. Born as Anglo-Burmese, they were hearing the distant drumbeat of their DNA. The past catching up with their present which cannot now ever be the same again.

For me, an Englishman (with traces of French ancestors and Cornish pirates), it was different. There were no such resonances. Just the prospect of a fresh and beguiling encounter with the exotic. That was the word I used at the time but it grates a little now . . . was I labelling and over-romanticizing the 'other' just because it was different? I am not sure whether the workers in the paddy field, the orphan street sellers peddling roasted betel nuts, even the women at their lotus looms on Inle Lake, would see themselves as exotic. This trip did signal a significant shift in my perceptions of the country now rebranded Myanmar. Entranced by April and enfolded in the richly threaded stories woven by her parents, my love affair with all things Burmese was about to receive a reality check.

I still remember the blend of excitement and trepidation as we completed landing forms on carbon paper in sweaty triplicate before we disembarked. Rangoon Airport (since demoted to domestic flights only) felt like a glorified bus terminus. The December tarmac shimmered in the heat, and my throat was equally dry as we made a big step into the unknown. Just as I was beginning to have doubts about the whole thing, April pulled my sleeve. 'Look!' she said, 'over there.' And she started rattling off Burmese names. There in the arrivals section were a whole throng, twenty or more, of April's family who'd come to greet us.

Hugs and tears are not a natural part of how most Burmese interact. But today was different. It was like the prodigal had returned. April, whom they last saw when she was thirteen, had come home. Carrying cases behind her was a tall, white man and four leggy daughters. Each day aunts, uncles, and cousins descended on us bearing delicious curries as if our lives depended on us being well fed. It was humbling to be so cared for by the wider family who had stayed put in Burma with all the strictures of a military junta. Our arrival seemed like a great excuse for family get-togethers with much reminiscing about old times. For most, meat would have been a luxury and even rice was pricey. I lost track of who was married to whom and had to start sketching a family tree and writing down all the strange-sounding names.

After a week of wonderful hospitality from the extended family April seemed in good spirits and was even trying out some Burmese. Meanwhile our girls were ready to head out in search of hamburgers or pizzas. We were staying at a guesthouse near the university in Rangoon, now renamed Yangon, and while waiting for them all to get ready, I took in the morning bustle. Across the street, a man with a long yoke over his shoulders was squatting down. As he stood he raised a column of stainless steel containers to his left and right, balanced like weighing scales. His forehead glistened with sweat as he stooped under their weight. Their contents soon became apparent. Steaming soup, boiled rice, fried vegetables, and roasted meat kept warm by a charcoal fire suspended at the base of each column. As commuters gathered in ragged groups for their buses into town, many paused to stock their tiffin carriers. Lunch for later in the day.

Students in their lime green and plum purple longyis and brightly woven Shan shoulder bags passed by the lake on the way to classes. Even by 9 a.m., it was sticky hot and they shielded their heads with their note-books and parasols. I had read about the students' bravery and bloodshed on these same streets just five years before. But now that I was here, it was different. The visceral nature of that slaughter sunk in. One thing that had impressed me about the Burmese people I had met was their unhurried charm, a benign outlook that seemed to take everything in its stride. This perception did not sit easily with the warrior-king mentality of past Burma empires. Nor did it stack up with occasional populist outbursts that have peppered her more recent past, times when the cultural traits to pacify and tolerate have stretched to breaking point.

One such occasion was the general strike led by militant students, including Aung San, against the British in August 1938. Exactly fifty years later, students and workers were on the streets again. This time they were pushed to the edge by decades of economic decline and mismanagement which left the health system in a state of collapse, schools starved of resources, and spiralling living costs.

After months of sporadic protest in early 1988, the pent up fury of young people and pacifist monks finally boiled over as they risked everything by demonstrating on the streets. These uprisings, sometimes referred to as 8/8/88 because of the date on which they occurred, were met by grisly violence from the military government. Around 3,000 people were gunned down in just a matter of weeks, with many more imprisoned. The hospitals couldn't cope and even medics, unmistakable in their white uniforms, were slaughtered in cold blood. Evil unleashed. The gutters just by me had been running red with blood. Although it made international news it made none of the headlines of student protests in Tiananmen Square in China, ten months later. It is part of the sad tragedy that in a period when socialist-planned economies were in the process of being toppled in many countries, the spark of revolution that began in Burma is largely overlooked. While a new political order was replacing corrupt and tyrannical regimes elsewhere in the world, little changed in Burma.

For a while, it did look as if a radical shift had occurred and the generals would have to step aside in the face of people-power. Aung San Suu Kyi formed the National League for Democracy (NLD) and to most people's surprise won a landslide victory in hastily held elections in May 1990. Did she feel weighed down, like the breakfast man, with the scales of injustice? Whether she did or not, the government lost their nerve and, sensing chaos, refused to allow elected members to take the seats in parliament.

Like many people growing up in the West, I had known little about General Aung San or his daughter. According to the author and biographer Peter Popham, Suu's mother was no purdah wife, lurking deep indoors polishing the silver: Ma Khin Kyi was articulate, well-educated and strong-willed, heir to the Burmese tradition of robust, emancipated women. When I read this description, I couldn't help thinking of April's mother, who was a similarly formidable force when in full-flow and did not suffer fools gladly. Other parallels became apparent. Like April, Suu was also schooled in India before coming to the UK in the same year, 1964. Suu studied at Oxford and met an academic, Michael Aris. Due to the nature of his studies in far off Tibet, their romance was a long-distance one with infrequent times together and lots of love letters over a period of three years. They married in 1972, a year before April and I tied the knot, having also gone in separate directions for the preceding four years. We too have a bundle of love letters and, yes, I later became an academic. Perhaps most telling is their similarity of character. Ma Thanegi, a close friend and travelling companion of Suu in the 1990s, describes her as strong and robust. Although it took a while for it to surface, I would now use similar words to describe April. Most people who meet April encounter a warm, private, and softly spoken individual. Easily misinterpreted as a 'walkover'. To the few who know her well, she is anything but. To our children she was loving but firm and not to be messed with, imbuing in them a strong sense of right and wrong. Those soft dark eyes could also be fierce.

Suu came to prominence in 1988, having returned to Burma to care for her ailing mother. She had returned to her homeland many times over the years but this turned out to be a decisive visit, thirty years after her leaving Burma. A similar passage of time to the return April was now making with us, her family, in tow.

In 1988 the mood on the streets was volatile. Patience with the military junta was wearing thin and the country was in tumult. However, they were largely leaderless and reluctantly Aung San Suu Kyi found herself as the figurehead of protest. It was the revered status of her father Aung San that parachuted her into this role. Inspired by the non-violent campaigns of US civil rights leader Martin Luther King and India's Mahatma Gandhi, she organized rallies and travelled around the country, calling for peaceful democratic reform and free elections. The demonstrations were brutally suppressed by the Army. Suu Kyi was placed under house arrest the following year.

A decade later, I was in conversation with a Burmese national who I won't name because her views are politically sensitive. She had left Burma in the early 1960s but retained a close interest in events there:

> 'Aung San Suu Kyi came back in 1988 and started the whole farce again. She had a handful of students but no one from the Army to back her up. That was her problem. Burma is bordered by five countries. There are always problems with Bangladesh because they have floods and people pour across the border. Then we have to be very appeasing to China. We have good relations with Thailand but historically the Burmese kings were very brutal all the way down to Bangkok. The Burmese are the most disciplined in South East Asia. But they also bribe their officers, they live in big houses. One person we know, her father owns the New Horizon Travel company, invited us for lunch at their opulent quarters . . . that's why they have such loyalty. They don't dare to introduce democracy'.

I found this a telling insight and frankly not one I was anticipating. Yes, it said something about the military rule and government paranoia, but I was taken aback by her description of Aung San Suu Kyi's involvement as a 'farce'. This did not fit with what I had gleaned from the books on Burma I had read; in particular, a speech Aung San Suu Kyi made to a mass rally on the open ground to the west of the Shwedagon Pagoda in August 1988. At this time she was still new to many inside Burma, so she addressed these concerns:

> *It is true that I have lived abroad. It is also true that I am married to a foreigner. These facts have never interfered and will never interfere with or lessen my love and devotion for my country by any measure or degree. Another thing people have been saying is that I know nothing*

of Burmese politics. The trouble is I know too much. My family knows
how complicated and tricky Burmese politics can be and how much my
father had to suffer on this account . . . the present crisis is the concern of
the entire nation. I could not as my father's daughter remain indifferent
to all that is going on.'

At the time of our visit to Rangoon in December 1995, Aung San Suu Kyi had recently been released from house arrest by the government but she was choosing to stay in her house and compound in Rangoon. Two moments in the following week stand out for me. The first was when a cousin of April's took us to University Avenue on a Saturday afternoon. Suu Kyi appeared on a raised platform from behind her garden wall to address the waiting crowd. This had become a regular occurrence each week. The street was jammed with NLD supporters hours before and the atmosphere was electric. It reminded me of a football crowd just before kick-off . . . everyone caught up in a wave of expectancy and excitement. If there were government officials present, they were hopelessly outnumbered and blithely ignored. As she stood up, spontaneous applause crackled down the street and then an immediate silence, as the crowds hung onto her every word. She knew how to hold an audience. No hype. No dramatic gestures. She could almost be chatting over a garden fence. Yet her piercing dark eyes spoke of integrity, her mischievous laughter of being totally in tune with the mood of her people. With majestic poise, holding a megaphone, she spoke of the hopes for the NLD item by item. Much to everyone's amusement she also lampooned the government's weekly bulletin.

The second occasion, which followed soon after, was very special. Through the same cousin, who was an old school friend of Suu Kyi, we were able to arrange a personal meeting at her home, 54 University Avenue, on the banks of Inya Lake. This was where she had been held under house arrest, pretty much alone for five years. The family house had seen better days but, as we were signed in at the gate, we noticed the grounds were reasonably well kept. She

Aung San Suu Kyi addressing crowds from her garden 1996

and her husband Michael Aris stood under the porch to greet us. I was struck by her dignified demeanour: her shining black hair swept back with fresh flowers on one side, her vividly coloured longyi and a disarming smile, which put us immediately at ease. She had taken the opportunity in preceding months to travel up-country and gauge the mood on the streets, her first trips out of the capital for five years. We compared notes on what we had encountered in more rural areas and mentioned that our daughters were taken aback by the poor state of public toilets. Suu laughed when we told her that the girls were rating guest-house and restaurant loos out of ten.

We spoke mainly about the challenge ahead for the NLD, a political party with no experience of governing. 'Hundreds of NLD members have disappeared since 1988,' she said, 'Many have been tortured and imprisoned.'

She had been unable to see her two boys and her husband for years. But despite the battered state of her party-in-waiting, as well as the family privations she had suffered, there was no sense of rancour, no hectoring of the regime. She was positive, amazingly well informed, and brimming with determination. I do not doubt that her solitude and daily meditations as a practicing Buddhist and ardent pacifist invested her with a core of inner strength.

'A key priority for us is to get the NLD equipped to lead the country when the time comes. We have no experience of government, even in opposition. We badly need know-how and skills in basic management.'

Working as I did for the Open University Business School at the time, I promised to get some management development materials delivered to her. The fact that these were designed as distance learning courses seemed to suit the situation well, with NLD members dispersed across the country. When back in the UK, I duly dispatched the teaching material of the Effective Manager, a course that had been extremely successful in the UK. I was careful to mail the parcel under cover of neutral packaging, but I never did hear whether she had the opportunity to utilize these courses. Given that it wasn't long before she was under house arrest again and the fact that hundreds of NLD members continued to languish in jail, I suspect the moment never came. Nevertheless the fact that we had arrived during the short window when she was free to receive visitors felt like a very fortuitous and timely turn of events.

For me, Burma had always been both real yet remote, scintillating but second-hand, magical but mysterious, mediated as it was through the memories of April and her family. In this first brief encounter, I had, for the first time, come close to their native land. To taste the distinctive flavours, to breathe in the spicy smells, to hear the wit and weariness, to touch the fragile fabric of Burma. Although my senses were already sated, there was more to come. Not all of it as heart-warming.

CHAPTER EIGHT

(JANUARY 1996) OUT OF STEP

Rangoon was an adventure. Each day traversing busy streets, choked with traffic and blaring horns as well as navigating the backstreets to where April's family lived. Margaret's family lived in the Karen district near Insein, and Austin's relatives nearer to the city centre. As April talked nostalgically of her younger life, we were all itching to travel further afield. Avoiding the few package tours which steered visitors to the palatable face of Myanmar, we managed to book an internal flight to the seaside.

Our twin-propeller plane hugged the Arakan coast of north-western Burma for twenty minutes. Below us were views of an ultramarine Indian Ocean, glinting like liquid chainmail, rippling palm-fringed sands. An hour or so out of Rangoon, we were touching down on a near-deserted landing strip at Ngapali.

'This was also known as Sandoway,' April stopped and looked out to sea, shielding her eyes from the bright sun. 'We used to love coming here for holidays. See that lagoon, we used to swim there. It was quite shallow and safe because of the coral reef, perfect for snorkelling. Mmm, fresh barbequed fish for dinners.'

We rolled our bags across the single runway. 'Look at the terminus. I can't believe it.

Nothing's changed.' There was a youthful excitement in April's voice which was infectious. The anticipation was building.

The bus that took us to our hotel, slipping in and out of a tunnel of trees as we bumped along the coastal road, was a fading lime-green 1950s touring coach straight out of my childhood comic books. The windows were long gone so it was well ventilated. The six of us were joined by a jolly group of portly young men and women in grey tunics, the sun glancing off their shaven heads. It all felt a little unreal and I couldn't help feeling out of step with the time and the place. Here we were, in a Saint Trinian's bus, surrounded by what turned out to be Korean monks and nuns on a retreat, destined for beachside bungalows, recently refurbished by the military regime for a hastily arranged national 'Year of Tourism'. An attempt by a reactionary government to encourage exposure to the West. Albeit a carefully controlled exposure. Were we too early for this commercially minded overture, I wondered. By visiting, were we as tourists colluding in and assigning credibility to a suspect government? Or, on the other hand, were we way too late? Should we be leaving April's recollections alone, safely undisturbed in a treasure trove of childhood memories?

After fifteen minutes or so, we arrived at some rustic bungalows tucked amongst the palms and banana fronds. But the accommodation to which we were directed—as a part-Western family presumed to be laden with US dollars—was the two-storey chalets looking out over well-hosed gardens of poinsettia shrubs and the glinting surf beyond. To call them chalets is a bit misleading. The intricate teak carving of the balconies and the shuttered windows stood proud against the timbered walls. The rich purple of bougainvillea tumbled generously over the lacquered double doors, leading to the cool, dark interior. Here we were greeted by the sheen of seasoned floorboards and the allure of four-poster beds, draped with mosquito nets which sighed gently in the morning breeze. It wouldn't have been out of place on a movie set, except that we were still somewhat disoriented. We didn't know the plot and we hadn't learnt our lines.

It was mid-December. Sandwiched between the daily drenching of the monsoons which subside in November and the oven-heat which parches the land from April onwards, this was the peak holiday season in Burma. Yet we were the only family there. Not that it was sinister. The breakfast staff were very attentive, the fresh guavas, watermelons, papayas, and stubby bananas were plentiful and the tranquillity as the sea breeze played with the tablecloths was very welcome after the maelstrom of Rangoon. The girls snorkelled among the coral and tanned themselves on the beach to the bemusement of locals, who did their best to keep out of the sun. But after a day or so of indulgence, we were yearning for something more real, to get behind the shop window of opulence. We didn't have far to go.

The hotel was the only one on this particular stretch of coast, but wandering a few metres across the main road we came to the hand-painted sign of Zaw's Restaurant. A small rustic building, it had three or four tables with plastic cloths invitingly nestled in the shady interior. Out the back was a kitchen and, I guess, sleeping quarters for the Zaw family. The ambiance may have been informal, but the food was to die for. Our first meal, a pungent prawn curry, danced in our mouths. From that moment we happily sacrificed the starched napkins and stretched noodles of the restaurant of the hotel we were staying in. Daw Zaw turned out to be the main cook, while her daughter taught in a local primary school:

'It's not worth my while teaching,' she said, 'the pay is poor and the schools are in an awful state. We are happy here, cooking for occasional visitors.'

There was a contented feel about the place.

'We have our own rice fields.' Daw Zaw said, 'although we do have to take it in turns to sleep out there because it will get stolen otherwise.'

Helped by the fact that April's rusty Burmese was returning, we quickly formed a bond with this family. 'What do you want to eat tomorrow?' she asked us. She wasn't being pushy, just treating us like family. 'Why not come to the market with me and we can choose the ingredients together'.

So it was, the next day, that we crammed into a truck-taxi and trundled into the local town. On the way, she pointed out to sea: 'See those fishing trawlers. They're factory ships, mainly Thai. They process the lobsters and fish on their way back to Thailand'. Similar to China's sequestering of opium and precious stones in the north and western natural gas companies off the coast, it summed up Burma's plight. Other nations siphoning off her natural assets.

In the centre of town, we were confronted by a rich and aromatic palette of local produce. In the open area, all kinds of vegetables and fruit, bicycled in from the field before dawn, was on display under tarpaulin shades, a riot of colour. The girls started wrinkling and holding their noses as we approached the covered central part of the market. Old women sat impassively flicking flies off the fresh and dried fish with bamboo fans. Blushing lobsters half a metre long hung on racks and small, yellowy chickens were laid out on another stall. We came across one particularly rotund lady sitting cross-legged, with a mound of muddy brown paste in front of her. We took a wide berth due to the pungent odour. 'Oh that's *nga-pi*,' our impromptu guide remarked, 'fish paste is the basic ingredient of most Burmese dishes.' As a family, we had indeed tasted this over many years of home-cooking, but not seen or smelt it in its raw state.

Having stocked up we headed back along the beach road. Ladies, straight-backed and swathed in checked longyis, walked home with bundles of market produce balanced on their heads. Bicycles and whining mopeds sped by with sometimes whole families clinging on. And, as if we needed to be reminded in this remote outpost, loudspeakers strung to telegraph poles blared pro-military propaganda and patriotic music. Nobody seemed to take much notice.

'I wonder,' said April, as we sat on the balcony that evening, 'how many tourists come this way? Given its vacation season, there aren't

Stall-holders at Ngapali market, 1995

many around. Although we are bringing much-needed custom to
the locals, I still feel slightly uncomfortable.'

'Why's that?' I said, but I knew what April meant. Were we just
the latest in a long line of opportunistic tourists, business speculators
and—going back a century and more—proprietorial colonialists,
who had descended on this country to plunder what they could?

Many have advocated economic sanctions against Myanmar
and disapproved of tourism. Others have argued that the so-called
liberal West should have exploited to the hilt the chance to invest
in Burma after 1988 when a democratic door began to creak open.
Not just for the sake of profit, but by way of setting better examples
of employment and business practice inside Burma. Similarly with

tourism. Once the invitation of 'Visit Myanmar Year' was made in 1996, some would say we should have gone there in our millions. If only by the process of social osmosis, Burma must surely have changed. In the event, limiting contact with the outside world plays into the junta's hands.

'Do write,' Daw Zaw said as we bade our fond farewells on the last morning of our time in Ngapali. When we returned to the UK, we did. And, unlike our parcel to Aung San Suu Kyi, which was intercepted or just failed to get through, we did hear back a year later. The spidery handwritten letter said simply: 'Is it possible to come again to Myanmar? If you come again, I and my family will welcome to you with happiness.' I often think of that family but we've yet to return.

We were back in Rangoon for Christmas. For the girls and me it was weird to be celebrating this festive occasion associated with turkey roast and snow-laden gardens, by consuming curry and rice in the dry heat of the city. Conversation turned to other places. April's father Austin had often spoken warmly about the town of Chauk on the Irrawaddy. Somewhat removed from the swirling unrest in the capital, it was a reasonably fun place to be in the 1940s and 50s. The nodding donkeys of oil derricks peppered the horizon and it was Austin's job to ensure the crude oil was transported safely by river to Syriam, outside Rangoon. Largely owned by Burmah Oil, in a paternal-style reminiscent of the Quakers' Bournville village in the UK, the town boasted a school, a hospital, employee homes, plenty of domestic staff, and a social club. It was here, April told us, that she spent her early years with her sisters and forged a strong bond with her nannie, a young local Burmese woman named Ma Mhay.

Given that it was her first visit back to Burma in thirty-two years, April asked after Ma Mhay's welfare when we were in Rangoon. News came that she lived in the same house and was still alive but frail. Thus started a mini-mission to get to Chauk as soon as possible. April's cousin Steven worked for the Myanmar TV station. We weren't sure how he managed his distaste for the military regime and the need to tow the party line. His job was to commission nationally produced documentaries and nationalistic soaps from Thailand and Korea. We didn't probe. Learning of our intention to travel up-country, within a couple of days he had procured a minibus and a driver.

As dusk fell on New Year's Day, we headed out of the city, Steven upfront with the driver, and us, a ramshackle bundle of excited travellers, in the back seats. The airport road soon gave way to rutted tracks and potholes as we left the city behind. The driver's technique was to drive at full speed to skip the holes and jump the ox-tracks. The bundle of travellers became even more ramshackle and a whole lot less excited as we lurched and bounded along. We gave up trying to stay seated and lay down in the back of the minibus. Only a couple of unscheduled stops served to break up the unremitting discomfort. The first was the call of nature. Around midnight we pulled into an unpromising shack-motel. The loos were out the back, rotting steps rising to two bamboo privies on stilts. In the pitch black, we stumbled around and then someone mentioned snakes. Quick as a shot, four female figures were squatting in the middle of the road as the shy moon looked on.

Two hours driving later we blinked from fitful sleep and peered through the minibus windows in disbelief. We were slowly weaving our way through a village where a night festival was in full swing.

'This must be some kind of *pwe*,' April said, 'See that main stage over there, that's where they are putting on their plays and reciting poems. Sometimes it's written down, sometimes folklore being passed down the generations. No doubt they'll be poking fun at the government.'

In the dead of night, the village was buzzing. People singing and dancing and sampling local delicacies from street stalls. We saw and smelt battered aubergines and courgettes, white-fleshed gourds, sticky rice in bamboo sticks, sesame brittle, coconut milk with a palm sugar called *jaggeri* . . . but there was no time to stop to join the festivities.

April and Ma Mhay are reunited after 30 years

The moment we arrived in Chauk will be etched in my mind forever. It was early morning when the minibus finally pulled into the village, axles and shock absorbers bruised but intact. A few children were playing in the street and the welcoming smell of woodsmoke hung in the air. They scooted off, seeming to know who we were. Our girls wandered down to watch the fisherman out on the Irrawaddy. Some minutes later, the small, slightly bent figure of Ma Mhay emerged from the doorway of a small house, her silver hair tied into a tight bun. Despite being frail, she shone in a simple white blouse, an *aingyi*, and mauve longyi. Her eyesight was all but gone, so as April approached, Ma Mhay gingerly held out her hands and gently stroked April's face. As she traced the contours with her bony fingers, a smile of recognition registered and soft tears began to fall from both of their eyes. Thirty years melting in a moment. A child she had loved and nursed two generations ago was now in front of her. Neither expecting to see each other again, April had returned to whisper 'I love you'.

Was it the psychologist Carl Jung who first used the word synchronicity to describe a meaningful coinciding of unrelated events? Sometimes intuition tells us we are in the right place at the right time. People talk about the planets lining up, fate smiling upon us, prayer being answered, the cookie crumbling in a favourable way. The point being, I suppose, that it is not something we control (wholly, if at all), as mind and matter, timing and place come together in a portentous manner. The backward-looking episodes we experienced on our family trip had a mix of both. Our unanticipated meeting with Aung San Suu Kyi and a chance sojourn with the Zaw family felt fortuitous. Synchronous you might say. Yet, for all the government overtures of 1996 Visit Myanmar Year, our stay at the beach hotel felt strangely odd. We were out of step with our novel surroundings and the timing seemed awry. Maybe, as tourists, our visit to Ngapali was a year—or a decade—too early. In the case of Ma Mhay at Chauk, we were almost too late.

Our children were profoundly affected by the five-week stay in Burma which spanned from Christmas 1995 and took us into 1996. Zoe took to wearing longyis, and raising funds for the refugees following Cyclone Nargis. Sundy Lin and Louisa were subsequently spurred to take extended trips across South East Asia, savouring an array of cultures and snapping some evocative pictures along the way. For Mala Su, our youngest, the full impact came later as she began to take a keen interest in Burmese politics and travelled back to Yangon a couple of times.

As for me, I was also rocked by a series of emotional depth-charges going off during the following months and years. My very limited, and in retrospect, naïve view of Burma had been thoroughly challenged. Downtown Rangoon had a ravaged feel. The wide, tree-lined boulevards and Victorian edifices of the old British buildings leading to the Sule Pagoda, looked uncared for. The grand facades overlooking the harbour had no doubt enjoyed their heyday in the early part of the last century when the port was bustling with freight and passengers. Top civil servants and military brass would have taken high tea in the salon of the Strand Hotel, among the palms and the sound of a tinkling piano. But now most of the buildings were shabby and unkempt, a ghostly reminder of colonial days which the current regime was happy to neglect. Mandalay was not much better. It failed to live up to the romance of Kipling's description, which, it has to be said, was based on his imagination rather than an actual visit. We found it to be a fairly characterless town, driven by Chinese immigrants, dominated by its pagoda on the hill. The old royal palace looked impressive, but less so when we discovered that the moat and regal walls had been restored by slave labour.

The people we met were invariably gentle, generous and placid, yet most were living in dilapidated housing, commuting to work on bicycles and overcrowded buses and simply eating, with very little energy left over for leisure or recreation. Outside the cities, the countryside was stunning in its beauty, but the roads were woeful and rutted by ox carts, the once efficient colonial infrastructure was neglected and an air of weary resignation hung over the bamboo villages we passed through. Some roads were being restored, but the labourer gangs were mainly women and it was shameful to see them patting down the tarmac with their bare hands. No petrol stations, no banks other than the national one where bribes were necessary even for simple transactions, no TV channels other than state-endorsed news and documentaries, regular Army checks and, in homes and tea shops, tight-lipped loyalty to the regime for fear of government spies.

Many years later, I asked our girls to note down what they made of the family visit to Burma, with the passage of time. 'How did it feel to be pulled out of school and piled onto a plane to connect with distant relatives on the other side of the world?'

'The heat and humidity. That's what hit you first and stayed with you for the duration,' said Louisa. 'The musty smell in Rangoon, the scent of cheroots that were being smoked on every corner by men and women, combined with petrol fumes and smell of spices.'

'Children seemed to be happy everywhere we went, always wearing a natural smile and not especially bothered about us "tourists" or Sundy snapping photos. They seemed to be happy with what little they had.'

'I remember the contrast between rich and poor being quite shocking. And between the traditional and the modern. Maybe this stood out more to us as we were not used to seeing temples and palaces of this grandeur, much like people from Asia are not familiar with English heritage, cathedrals or castles.'

'That trip,' said Zoe, 'gave me a greater sense of pride in having Burmese roots. A better understanding of mum, my aunts, and grandparents. We met the wider family who in the same way were kind, gentle but strong in spirit, humble, hospitable, generous, quick to smile or laugh.'

'The welcome we got from granddad's extended family,' said Mala. 'It was a type of hospitality we hadn't experienced before, almost like we were royalty. Surrounded by people watching us intently, while we sat around a long table covered with plates of rice and curry, being told to eat, and then eat some more . . . considering they lived modest lives, we all felt the warmth and appreciated the generosity of this family.'

Hearing April speak Burmese for the first time was a revelation for Sundy. 'Not full sentences but the odd few words as mum became reaccustomed with the language. By the end of the trip, I think she was picking up most things.'

'I had absolutely no knowledge,' continued Sundy, 'about the complex political history that now seems to attach itself to every news story from Burma. I can't get used to using "Myanmar".' Turning to April and me, Sundy wondered: 'Why didn't you share with us more about Burma when we were younger?'

'I'm not sure,' I said slightly taken aback. I didn't have an answer.

'It seemed there was a strong sense of community,' Zoe said, 'with the extended family living all together. This was a given. I understood why granddad could tolerate most things but not disrespect towards elders. He didn't like the way I spoke to you sometimes and would pick me up on it.'

Zoe also mentioned chatting to a cousin her age in Burma. 'She spoke of dreams to go to university in America. But that wasn't an option as she needed to look after her mother who wasn't well. There was a deep respect and obligation to put her family before her own hopes and wishes. I found this humbling. Especially coming from my last year at University with a higher education that I had taken for granted, and surrounded by students who were also self-seeking and without any real sense of responsibility.'

Hearing these recollections confirmed in my mind that taking that trip to Burma in 1995/96 was one of our best family decisions. For our children, it was a bit like rummaging through an attic and discovering faintly familiar memorabilia that filled in lots of gaps about themselves, their family, their forebears. The attic had always been there, of course. But now it had been explored, smelt, handled, held up to the light . . . the dust of an unreached past had been blown away, cultural connections made.

For April it was a bitter sweet experience. There was much that she recognized and this was comforting, but the lack of improvement in living conditions, in the buildings and the roads saddened her. If anything the country had slipped backwards since she left in 1964. It finally removed that vague hankering for 'home'. Britain was now where she belonged. Our return coincided with April embarking on her counselling training and practice.

'I became less reticent,' she told me a lot later when we talked about this period. 'I still struggle to express things. But I found that my own experience of pain, of reconciling my past insecurities was helpful in helping clients deal with *their* past hurts. It's no good trying to be strong, like I had done for so long.'

For me, the country remained an enigma. In my albeit selective experience of Burmese folk, I had found them to be warm, welcoming, and hospitable. How could such people, renowned for their geniality and steeped for centuries in benign Buddhism allow—and in some cases perpetrate—brutal reprisals against unarmed protestors in Rangoon and persecuted minorities in non-Bamar areas of the country? Where had things gone astray? At the time, there were few commentators who could help me and there was precious little interest from the outside world to prize open this clam-like conundrum. For a period, interviews by foreign correspondents with newly released Aung San Suu Kyi were reported in *Time*, *New International*, and a few Sunday supplements. Much hope was pinned on her capacity to bring democratic reform to the militarized regime but the newsfeeds soon dried up after 1996. She was put under house arrest again and all went quiet.

CHAPTER NINE

(1996–2008) CONVICTIONS

Over the years, and well before our five-week heritage trip to Burma, Austin and Margaret—who started out in rented accommodation in south London—moved several times in Sussex, Herts, and Northants. In each location, they attracted people around them. Much of this was down to their generous hospitality. Austin enjoyed nothing more than seeing family and friends eating delicious Burmese and Indian food, often cooked by himself. Often guests would be greeted by rows of chopped cauliflower and carrot drying on trays in the sun, ready to be pickled with chilli. The sound of pestle and mortar pounding fresh ginger and garlic and the pungent aromas of fish paste from the kitchen were familiar to their visitors.

I was slightly uneasy about possible prejudice when they announced their move to a quaint and conservative English village near Daventry. I need not have worried. It wasn't long before their beef curries were being enjoyed by neighbours and their famous curry puffs were taking the church fete by storm. As his three daughters got engaged and married Brits, their sons-in-law were quickly enfolded in this Burmese embrace and cooking tradition. If they were wishing for grandsons, it wasn't to be. Eight granddaughters arrived, including our four, in quick succession.

By the early nineties, short-term tourist visas for Burma were being issued. Somewhat to our surprise, April's parents immediately took the opportunity to return. In the interim since their departure nearly thirty years ago, many members of the family had passed away. Surviving brothers, sisters, cousins, who had stayed behind were, of course, delighted to see them and turned out in force to meet them at the airport. I wonder how the reunions affected Austin and Margaret, as they looked into the tired eyes of their family and close friends. A resignation of spirit, a loss of hope, decaying buildings, a broken country. They returned to the UK with many albums of photo opportunities. Endless groupings of relatives, bunches of shy faces in dim rooms lit up by a flash, seeming almost startled at this unexpected, familial brush with the West.

But it wasn't all one way. There was a fascinating gift on the other hand which turned out to be life-changing. Margaret's elder brother Walter was a pilot, who had flown a Spitfire for the British alliance in Burma during the Second World War. Following the War, he became a civil aviation pilot for Burma Airways. So trusted was he that whenever he took a flight, General Ne Win insisted that Walter be at the controls. Ironically, such favour was of no help, when in 1987 the superstitious Ne Win decreed that all banknotes with the denomination of ten be removed from circulation. At a stroke, thousands lost their savings, including Uncle Walter who was never able to finish building the family home.

One day Margaret, who must have been in her sixties, showed April and me a letter she had received from Walter, now retired in Rangoon.

'Walter is so excited,' she said. 'He and his wife are talking about being *born again*. What do you think he means?'

Margaret wondered what we made of all this and we did our best to explain that the Christian faith was more than rule-following and church attendance.

'It's more about knowing and following God in a personal way,' April said.

'God is not some far off disinterested being,' I added. 'He wants to be involved in our lives, day by day.'

We both were slightly hesitant. I guess for several reasons. First, we were talking to our parents, not an easy thing to do in matters of personal faith and values. After all, they had been the primary shapers of our life principles and moral code. I recall having a similar conversation with my mother when I was home from university one Christmas vacation. Dad had been very ill and it had shaken her to the core. What was life about, she wondered, anticipating that she could be on her own shortly. Very tentatively I sat down at the kitchen table and told her what Jesus meant to me.

I was almost as surprised as my mum to hear what I was saying. Back when I was living with them at home, I had listened to others, watched their lives, read the scripture passages they recommended. In some ways, I had imbibed a 'foreign' lifestyle, inherited a belief system, and entered something I would never have contemplated: a Christian subculture. For all my parents knew, it was indeed a cult. At university, I was initially slightly schizoid. One evening I'd be evangelizing in a hall of residence, the next I'd be boozing at a party. I wanted a foot in both camps. My non-believer friends tolerated my spiritual inclinations with bemused goodhumour and my Christian friends gave me the benefit of the doubt. As I was talking to my mother, I think she saw that my beliefs were real, I had not been brainwashed. They were coming from my heart. The first century Jewish rabbi who claimed to be the Messiah was indeed real and someone I was getting to know better as each day passed.

Another reason for our hesitation was that both April and I had experienced enough to know that living as a Christian believer was no easy option. Incredulity, and occasionally outright ridicule from those around us, was not uncommon. Also, the churches we had frequented were full of amazing people but far from perfect, and not always a good advertisement for the compassionate and loving God we talked about. I was, and still am, disappointed about this but have come to see that, like all organizations, churches— despite their heavenly aspirations—are earthbound. They are human constructions with the capacity to hurt and heal in equal measure.

Added to all this, we were aware that both Austin's and Margaret's mothers were Buddhist. April's parents wore such beliefs lightly and were content to tick the Christian box, but we didn't want to disrespect their existing beliefs. As it was, they were both intrigued by news from loved ones in Burma and the way it resonated with our faltering attempts to explain God's impact on *our* lives. From that time on, it was exciting to see them read the Bible with fresh hunger and to find a deep joy in their relationship with God. All in all, these conversations helped me see the value of convictions. Personally held beliefs, hammered out through life experiences, refined through the fire of setbacks and found to be sufficient whatever the circumstances. Not limited to a specific culture, to special people, or to a given time.

April's parents may have escaped much of the mindlessness and brutalities of the military junta in Myanmar, but their country always retained a special place in their hearts. This was revitalized by their first visit back home in 1992, to be followed by further trips in subsequent years.

As a grandfather, Austin would beckon one of his grandchildren from his favourite armchair. As they came close, he would gently pinch the back of their hand, asking them to do the same on top of his, then repeat so that there were four pinching hands on top of each other. Then he would recite an ancient Burmese rhyme, followed by their squeals of excitement as the little 'tower' of hands dramatically came apart on the last '*che*'!

'What does it mean . . . what does it mean, Pa Pa Gyi?' they wanted to know.

He would chuckle and say something like: 'The prawns are clinging to each other. Then, when the little boy comes in and slams the door, all the prawns scatter!'

No great significance but it was the opportunity to play a funny game with granddad that was the attraction. Austin's large hands were a cartographer's dream. His bony knuckles a mini-mountain range with raised veins like dark rivers flowing down across the parchment plains of his stretched skin blotched with mauve moles. It was impossible to feel uncomfortable in the presence of April's father. Perhaps it was because he reflected the warmth and happiness of his own family.

Once, when we were driving past some orchards in Kent, Austin told me that as a teenager he had spent long, carefree summers playing with his cousins in the country and that he often dreamed of living out his days in just such a quiet, rural place in Burma. He spoke of owning a rice plantation, tending his fruit trees, and enjoying Burmese and oriental foods surrounded by relatives and friends. I got the impression that left to his own devices, he would have stayed and seen out his days in Burma. Although the political circumstances would likely have thwarted his dream.

In his early eighties, Austin's health was beginning to fail, and as is often the case, Margaret as the main carer was the first to pay the price. Although a shock, perhaps it was fitting that this dynamo of a lady should not be stricken by a lingering illness but by a single blow, a massive heart attack in 2004. April, like her sisters, was hit hard by this loss and there were many private tears. It was like a main guy-rope had been severed and the family tent sagged for a while.

Austin's mind was lucid and his wit remained, but his body gradually deteriorated with Parkinson's disease. He lived with April and me for a couple of years. Some moments were difficult like getting him back into bed after falling out in the night. Some were humorous like when he came down in the morning with his cardigan back to front. 'Which way are you going, Austin?' I'd say. Sometimes funny and sad at the same time: watching him gingerly step from one room to another, a concentrated confusion of balance. For all these frustrations, he was a star at the local lunch club, which was his one major outing each week. The blue-rinse ladies would vie to sit next to him to catch his low-key, infectious charisma. He would often return triumphant with a prize from the raffle, even if it was the same pack of biscuits that he had taken.

His youngest daughter Gay and her husband Graham took him for what they all knew would be his final visit to Yangon in 2006. If he'd had his way he would have stayed, surrounded by adoring nephews and nieces. However, now wheel-chair-bound for much of the time, seeing out his days in that way would not have been practical or fair on his Burmese relatives. When he could no longer eat his favourite foods and enjoy his evening tipple, we sensed he would not last long. He passed away in 2008. As with Margaret, the family gathered for the funeral.

It was a crisp day at the end of March. Family and friends walked behind the coffin to the graveside in the small Buckinghamshire village of Mursley. Although scarves were needed to combat the chill we were warmed inside by fond memories. Daffodils nodded in honour as the cortege passed in dignified slow motion. He was buried alongside the indomitable Margaret, whom he had married in 1947. The word that came up often in conversation that day was 'gentleman'. He was also remembered with much irreverent fondness by his granddaughters who spoke at the funeral service:

'One of granddad's greatest sources of amusement,' Sally said, 'was to tease us and if we couldn't take the tormenting from him, he would say: "if people tease you it means they like you".'

'He teased me about my Burmese nose, telling that if I pinched it every morning and evening then it would turn into a nice pointed English nose.' Thida said. 'I realized this wasn't strictly true after he claimed he had done this to mum when she was little!'

Zoe said, 'When I was young I remember granddad gently shaking my head, making the sound of water swilling around . . . being gullible, I think I actually believed him. Granddad was very hospitable, always ensuring we had another helping of his delicious curry or insisting we have another drink whether we were driving or not. I think his favourite phrase was "Have, have! Eat, eat! . . . don't be shy." We looked forward to family gatherings for weeks. I can still hear grandma and granddad's laughter now.'

I think it was Jess who said, 'He taught us the invaluable skill of being able to flare our Burmese nostrils. His laugh was infectious and sounded like it came from deep within, almost like a wheeze, that made his eyes disappear behind his cheeks. The joy he took in his family . . . a bunch of eight granddaughters who all look the same but different.' To this Amy added, 'We'd like to thank papa for his constant encouragement in all our academic endeavours and for his reassurance that it was just puppy fat and that we were, in fact, solid.'

Austin Horace Francis; his father's favourite, so beloved of his mother and revered by his siblings as the eldest son. Little did he know that at a formative age he would be leading reconnaissance patrols in the Arakan, running an oil depot on the Irrawaddy and perhaps, most difficult of all, severing ties with his wider family and country in the prime of his life. Well, retirement with fruit trees and a rice plantation in rural Burma remained an unfulfilled dream. But along with the ever dynamic Margaret, they did create a succession of welcoming homes and lovely gardens in England. What happened to the grey leather handbag and the fifty-rupee scarf I do not know. But perhaps as important as that early exchange of love gifts in Calcutta, Margaret and Austin showed their extended family, now well over twenty in number, how to create a place of understated warmth, of ready acceptance.

As we visited their graves a few weeks later to bring fresh flowers, it seemed like the closing of an era. The cherry blossom was dropping extravagantly from nearby trees, and April's gloved hand was in mine. I looked across to the fields, recalling my 'first love', my first encounter with the Francis family. As a naive teenager, my eyes were opened to another world, my taste buds were teased by strange cuisine, and my imagination stirred by anecdotes of old. April's parents had effortlessly but powerfully demonstrated that all were welcome in their family home. Perhaps instrumental in this was the decisive move they made in 1964. They had chosen to leave their early lives behind and—having tasted exile from Burma—they knew the value of inclusion.

SECTION 2

REALITY CHECK

'Mandalay is one of the few place names in Burma that has not been changed by the Burmese military government . . . The generals were rewriting history. When a place is renamed, the old name disappears from maps, and eventually, from human memory. By renaming cities, towns, and streets, the regime seized control of the very space within which people lived.'

Emma Larkin (2004:11) *Secret Histories*, London, John Murray

CHAPTER TEN

(2010) CHILD BY CHILD

Our family visit to Burma—now rebranded Myanmar—in 1995–96 left an enduring impression on us all. Yet, for all the fireworks that initial encounter had set off in our heads and hearts, it took another fifteen years before April and I returned to her homeland. I guess the emotional roller-coaster of guiding the girls through their teens, their tentative steps towards courtship (which we as parents were usually the last to hear about), and then arranging three weddings as Sundy, Zoe, and then Louisa were married to their lovely husbands, all took its toll. This, together with the fairly relentless pressures of work, counselling for April and lecturing for me, conspired to keep thoughts of Myanmar at bay. The country and its people were deep in our hearts, but our thoughts were elsewhere.

In the event, this all was changed by an unexpected invitation in 2010. An invitation that led to successive visits, seven over the next eight years.

Lincoln directs a small Bible college north of Yangon. He has just a few staff, most of whom are part-time. He struggles to pay them from month to month. The name Lincoln may conjure images of gas-guzzling classic automobiles in the USA but he is a far cry from this. He is a mild-mannered visionary, five foot four, and unofficial leader of the Zanniat churches, part of the Chin people group. The youngest son from one of the poorer groups of Christians among one of the least privileged minority groups in

Myanmar. Good credentials to be used by God if one thinks of David, the teenage shepherd, youngest of the smallest Jewish tribe who was later crowned king of Israel. While Lincoln dreams, his wife and fellow Chin, Leah, organizes and makes things happen. Not by giving orders but by showing love.

We were given the names of Lincoln and Leah from two unconnected sources. One was April's younger sister Gay, who had met them on a visit to Yangon. The other was a friend of our daughter Zoe, who had gone to the delta region of Myanmar to help in an orphanage following Cyclone Nargis in 2007. Both spoke highly of Lincoln and Leah's compassion for deprived young people and children. Having exchanged a few emails Lincoln trusted us enough to come and teach alongside him at the college for a few weeks each year.

He wanted April to train the students in listening skills and for me to run a module on biblically-based leadership.

Lincoln was convinced that his college should prepare their students not just theologically but equip them with the leadership qualities to positively inspire their communities. His invitation rekindled the strong connection we had made with the country during our 1995–96 visit, the college's needs meshed well with what April and I could offer and the timing was good, now that our daughters were all independent. We didn't want to revisit Myanmar just to sightsee, but to contribute in whatever way we could. Most of the students were non-Bamar, mainly Chin, and came from remote villages, in some cases a journey of two or three days. In a way, it also closed a circle for us family-wise: it was in the Chin Hills that April's grandfather had practised as a civil surgeon in the 1940s.

We knew Lincoln and Leah and their four children lived in the Karen quarter in north-west Yangon. In another telling connection, this was also where April's mother's family resided. As a family we had enjoyed many a meal with her uncles, aunt and cousins back in 1995–96. What came as a total surprise was that, of all the strands of

Lydia, John, Leah, Mary and Lincoln (Ruth away at college), 2011

spaghetti that make up the city of Yangon and its outer townships, Lincoln and Leah had ended up living a few doors down from April's family. They were neighbours.

I wander to the top end of their road. Without any signs or fanfare, the street gradually evolves into an open market. Soon after dawn, stalls open up with fresh produce for the local community. Some are little more than a piece of plastic sheeting on poles, others are the shady front rooms of their homes that open up straight onto the street. Amidst the low hum of conversation and the gentle jostle of brightly clad customers and frail old ladies in cardigans, the important business of the day is taking place. I stoop down to see different types of rice being poured out onto weighing scales by children. Housewives bustle past me with bundles of sorrel, pak choi, and bamboo shoots wrapped in the *New Light of Myanmar* newspaper. Some who could afford it have a piece of pork or some chicken drumsticks. Then there is the lady with the mound of *ngapi*, which no Burmese market would be without. Not even the fragrant aromas of turmeric, saffron, and other spices can compete with the pungent smell of fermented seafood. The fish stall is at the far end, probably because this is where the flies gather.

Things go quiet in the afternoon as households nap. Later, around sunset, space is cleared. A bunch of local lads hitch up their longyis and form a rough circle. Keeping a bamboo ball in the air with feet, knees, shoulders, heads, everything except their hands, they display their skills at *chinlone*. By mid-evening, the dimly lit shops finally pull down their blinds. As I hop through side allies, I see through the cracks of timber shacks, families gathered inside, the TV flickering on their faces.

Lincoln and Leah's home brought new meaning to the term open house. I lost count of the number of people dropping by and the waifs and strays they have 'adopted'. One was Tin Oo who had lost her husband and was destitute. She was befriended by Leah who taught her patchwork quilting from oddments of material. After a year or so she was able to set up a small business with a small sewing machine we took out for her from the UK. Then there were the young girls from poor families in Myanmar who often disappear into the sex trade on the Thai border as a means of income. Lincoln and Leah's extended family provided a safe alternative for many until they were able to find jobs locally.

We found the college to be a fairly run-down tenement, a two-up, two-down rented building in an adjacent district. A collection of grinning flip flops greeted us at the foot of the open tread stairs, which rose to the main and only classroom. Thirty-plus students, crowded into old-style wooden desks, beamed at us as we did our *mingala bas*. The extent of my Burmese at the time was this greeting accompanied by a slight bow of respect. Teaching technology comprised one whiteboard nailed to the wall. The upper rooms doubled as dormitories for the men; the women had separate accommodation down the street. The kitchen and loos were out in the back in a makeshift bamboo privy. I soon learned only to visit in emergencies. At that time, to have permission for Christians to congregate in this way, Lincoln had to twist the arm of the local township head, although restrictions have eased a little since then.

The students sang songs from an ancient hymnal with gusto, had well-thumbed Bibles and scribbled earnestly in their notebooks. Their thirst for learning and desire to make up for lost time, given their deprived backgrounds, electrified the classroom. Being asked questions, working in small groups, role-playing were unfamiliar experiences, but they grew taller before our eyes. For the weeks that we participated during that first visit, I was out of my comfort zone on so many levels, yet I have rarely found teaching more uplifting and satisfying.

'Come on,' said Lincoln, half-way through that first visit. 'I want to show you something.'

Little did we know that he was taking us on a forty-minute drive out of Yangon to Taukkyan. We trundled north in his van with two friends and Leah. Leaving behind the airport turnoff, we passed the Army barracks with soldier activity at each entrance, and on into the countryside. It was the road we, as a family, had taken to Chauk all those years ago. Lincoln said that since then it had been spruced up for Hillary Clinton's visit. Then, just I was dozing off, we took a sharp right down an unpromising tarmac track. We slowed for cyclists and pedestrians heading for the main road. They were oblivious to stacks of plastic rubbish which spilled from the ditches. A field with the huge trunks of teak lumber, freshly cut, labelled and waiting to be transported, was visible through the trees. Ragged collections of bamboo huts came and went, some with a tethered cow, a pig or two, and chickens pecking at the bare earth. Young children were assembling at their rudimentary school gate, the sound of their chatter overlaid by Buddhist chants from a nearby monastery.

'So this is it,' Lincoln said, pulling up at what seemed to be the end of the road.

'What are we meant to be looking at?'

Having not explained the destination, he was enjoying the slow reveal. 'We bought this two acre site a while ago when it was going for a song.'

Our faces must have registered bemusement.

'The lease has expired on our college rental in Yangon. In a way it's good. It has forced us to do something with this land.'

Like intrepid explorers, Lincoln and Leah swished their way through the undergrowth and a jungle of trees to point out the perimeters of the plot, a crumbling brick wall on one boundary but otherwise fairly indistinct borders with neighbours' homesteads and wilderness in the other direction. The one landmark was a well and water tower rising in a small clearing and it was here that we gathered.

'By 2020,' Lincoln said, smiling but with no hint of arrogance, 'I want to have a college here, providing Christian education for young children through to students.'

'Including a pre-school,' added Leah, beaming.

We couldn't quite grasp it. 'We'll back you in whatever way we can,' we said, not knowing quite what that meant. Little did we know that we were standing on the threshold of a miracle, and destined to participate in it.

As we sat on the bed, our notes spread out in front of us the evening before one of our first teaching sessions, April looked pensive:

'You know, it's all very well teaching them active listening skills, but you wonder who is going to listen to *them*?'

The following morning, the students were attentive and leaned forward, notebooks at the ready. But, the fresh faces deceive. The students, ranging from late teens to early thirties, struggled to understand. As we got to know the students individually, we heard some awful stories. Many had experienced shameful levels of humiliation, persecution, and bullying. Sometimes on account of their poverty, occasionally due to their Christian faith in a predominantly Buddhist country and often simply because they were not from the dominant Bamar people. Of the many minority groups in Myanmar, the Chin are typically regarded as the lowest in the pecking order, excluding the Rohingya who are not regarded as legitimate citizens. For all their social and educational disadvantage, the hope is that these students will return to their villages better equipped and motivated to take up leadership roles.

As I gazed along the row of faces in the room, I found myself thinking about the connection between language and love. On succeeding visits to Myanmar, April found she could pick up more Burmese and was able to speak to locals with some confidence. Indeed, it came as a revelation to me to hear her converse in her mother tongue. When I first witnessed this, I saw and heard a new April. It was like a door being opened to a forgotten room and the dust being beaten from elegant antique furniture. Each trip was a discovery for me too, a voyage into the uncharted territory of Myanmar's conflicted history and cultural traditions. Even at a visual level, I was bemused by the appearance of the writing. To my untrained eye, the Burmese alphabet was an indecipherable series of joined up 'o' shapes, and the spoken word, unlike the European languages, was tonal.

I had a go at pronouncing some Burmese words. From April's frown, I needed a lot more practice. 'When it comes to the verb *to do*,' April mused, 'Burmese people tend to say *we'll do it*, even if they cannot or do not even intend to. This is because saying *no* is difficult culturally.'

'Mmm, I think I've already come across that.'

'Actually, I'm not sure how you say *no* in the language,' April was talking to herself more than me, 'although it's a common word in English.'

A few days before, a friend and fellow traveller had shown us a photo he'd taken of a sign in a local Yangon park. In English, it listed the following park rules: *Fishing in the lake is not allowed. Swimming is not allowed. No football play. No sex. No music. No selling.*

'Basically, few pleasurable activities left then, apart from walking!'

'I guess so,' he chuckled. 'It reminds me of a notice at the swimming baths back in Kirkstall: *No diving. No spitting. No canoodling.*'

When spending time in Myanmar, it was a case of constantly recalibrating. My comfortable English ways and words were robbed of impact in this new sphere, an experience which was at the same time intoxicating and inchoate. My spontaneous jokes, once they had reached the other end of lengthy translation, fell flat. Yet laughter erupted at innocent things I did or said. As I began to inhabit the world of April's past, chatting with her cousins and their children and engaging with the students at the college, I experienced a degree of disorientation, an intangible feeling of being confronted by *the other*, the *not me*. I'd encountered this before, of course—concerning gender, age, and class. But here the issue was ethnicity. A different way of viewing the world that challenged my assumptions of what was acceptable: little things like eating rice and curry with your fingers, making a 'kissing' noise to get the attention of waiters in a restaurant, burping loudly as a sign of appreciation after a fine meal, dropping down on a straw mat in the middle of the floor when sleepy, smiling politely even when you don't agree.

April's father had been a master of this with Margaret. Better a minor sacrifice in untroubled waters than the risk of drowning in a flowing torrent. As for April herself, I am still learning to 'read' her when the book is firmly closed. To pay attention to her first time because that is the time that counts. To show kindness rather than talking about it. To lay aside my fuzzy intuitions in the face of what she sees as 'patently obvious'. To avoid hugging her in public (not just in the park!) because such touchy-feely stuff is definitely private for the Burmese. Compromising here, adapting there, the concentrated effort to be self-forgetful does not come easily. But love, love for April, for these hungry-to-learn students, and for the unfathomable, endearing ways of her country and its perplexing language, this is what binds us together. Keeps us coming back year after year.

Although formal accreditation of their studies was not yet possible due to poor English language, the college graduation was taken seriously with a formal ceremony complete with gowns, mortarboards, lengthy speeches, and attendance certificates. Lincoln opportunistically found me a gown to preside over the occasion. As ever, the 'passing out' celebration concluded with a meal cooked by the students. Sitting at long tables and benches, mounds of fluffy rice, a wonderfully tangy green bean salad with tamarind paste, and chicken curry are loaded onto our plates. As I helped myself to more *balachaung*, a kind of sambal made of fried shrimp, garlic, onion, and tamarind, I was interested to know from Lincoln how he squared his sincere but tiny endeavour with the complex and deep-seated ills of his nation.

'I am a dreamer,' he said. 'I dream of a day when we can provide education for pre-schoolers through to mature students on the same site.'

It's an impressive vision. He hasn't wavered from the 'impossible' dream since he first told us about it in 2010.

Having supervised the cooking, Leah slides onto the bench beside us. 'I also have a dream,' she announces. 'In Myanmar, infants are farmed out to the wider family and largely left to their own devices

Pre-school children at Blossom

during the working day. That's why I have set up a pre-school. It's called Blossom.'

It was little more than a bamboo hut, with 'open-air' windows and an outside play area with some sand covered by a tin roof. From 9 a.m. the little scamps arrived and deposited their slippers at the entrance. As each trotted into the cool of the interior they took themselves to one of several play areas. Some went to soft toys and puzzles, some to cutting out, and others to drawing and painting, each corner supervised by one of the helpers. Being enveloped by love is the only way I can describe it and I found my eyes moistening as we watched each child welcomed and made to feel at home. The initial awkwardness of little newcomers quickly melted. Meanwhile, lunch was being prepared, Leah pooling and sharing out the helpings of rice and vegetables that most had brought in their little tiffin carriers, so that each child had something to eat.

After a while, a circle formed, helpers and children, singing and dancing in a glee-filled procession. The children were invited to start a new song and several did. Then it was 'story time' and anyone who wanted to, could come to the centre of the ring and relate a little incident or sing a song. Some shyly wriggled as they did this, others were uninhibited and revelled in their moment of glory. One girl explained her highlight of the weekend with much aplomb. 'I had a haircut,' she announced, flicking her curls. The next lad was less forthcoming but wanted to say something, so repeated the haircut story. Even though it was a straight copy, everyone gave him a hearty clap. It was almost as though their self-confidence was growing before our eyes, nurtured by affirmation. What we witnessed is probably commonplace in the developed countries, but there was something about the atmosphere of unconditional acceptance, so contrary to much else that is happening in this country, that warmed our hearts. Sadly, this kind of pre-school is unusual in Myanmar. During our visit the following year, we gathered that UNESCO has recognized the groundbreaking nature of this example of child-centred learning. Leah now trains staff throughout the country.

Schools for older children are poorly funded and firmly set in a traditional mould: highly prescriptive, learning by rote, and heavy on memorization. Primary and secondary education is hit-and-miss. So Lincoln and Leah's desire to provide more child and student-centred schooling in an environment where they feel safe and loved, is refreshing. The three-to-five year olds at Blossom are just a few in number—around twenty-five when we visited—but getting an enviable start in life. And at the other end of their education, the Bible college students are gaining the much-needed skills and confidence. Already several hundred alumni, who have graduated from the college over the past eighteen years, are bringing compassion-based leadership to churches, hospitals, schools, and communities across Myanmar, especially in the more deprived rural areas.

Lincoln and his family and small staff team face an uphill struggle with finances. They encounter suspicion and occasional antagonism from the local Buddhist township which borders their Christian college. And for sure, their effort seems tiny amidst the huge needs of this nation. Yet despite local harassment, a lack of resources, intermittent Wi-Fi, no administrative support and a library full of books consumed more by termites than by students, April and I couldn't but admire their quiet tenacity. Child by child, student by student, cohort by cohort, their dream is being realized.

CHAPTER ELEVEN

(2011) SOME BURN UP

An early and lasting impression of the streets in Yangon was that of incessant toil. Working people straining every sinew to make a living and keep their family above the poverty line. April's uncle Abu was one of these working people, but he was thinner than most. It was as if life had pared him down, sloughed off any excesses, extinguished any illusions. Tall, wiry, more soul than body. We had met him on our family visit in 1996; he was our first port of call after arriving, on our way from the airport to our guesthouse. His wife had just died and as is the tradition, neighbours, family, and friends were dropping by to pay their respects throughout the day. Hospitality and food, however simple, is central to any such occasion. The monks were the first to arrive soon after dawn. They ate in dignified silence, then hitched up their robes and filed off down the street, shielding their shaven heads from the sun with lacquered parasols. Abu looked on, a little distracted but not distraught. He was doing what any good Buddhist family would do: 'adopting' monks and gaining merit by donating rice and food. For their part, those parents who initiate their sons into novicehood, believe they avoid hell in the next life. Despite the sadness of Abu's loss, a certain reciprocity is in play and everyone seemed content. But beneath the benign exterior of golden pagodas and saffron-robed monks, is all as serene as it seems?

A few days later Abu had invited us as a family to dinner at his home. At the 'wake', the six of us had sat down to mohinga, with our

April's uncle Abu with his family

hosts looking on attentively. This time it was more informal, sitting cross-legged on the floor with a low table of rice, soup, curries, and pickles laid out before us. Our girls tucked in with enthusiasm as various younger family members of Abu's clan came and went to refill dishes and bring drinks. Perhaps because they were shy about their poor English, they did not tarry. Being a member of the older generation, Abu was fluent. As smoke from his cheroot formed an eerie halo, he had been only too happy to fill us in on the Buddhist rites of passage.

'At the birth of a son, the local presiding Sayadaw delivers Mingala sermons and blesses the newborn for his future well-being.'

'. . . a Sayadaw?'

'It's the monk. He deliberates on the planetary dispositions to forecast the destiny of the child. The village astrologer sketches a horoscope with a steel stylus on a palm leaf . . . a chart to be consulted in his entire lifespan.'

Abu poured himself another scotch and continued in a mellow tone. 'As a boy, Buddhist parents entrust their offspring to the care and guardianship of the local monastery. He will be trained by the senior monks in Buddhist teachings. This includes moral behaviour and becoming a good citizen.'

Serious stuff, I thought. Nothing less than laying the foundations for a civilized society.

'They participate in dances and songs on festival days,' Abu said, 'and they perform daily chores, clearing the compound, hauling water from the wells and accompanying the monks on almsgiving.'

'One of the precepts instructs abstention from a solid meal from noon till dawn the next day. People give food and other gifts generously.'

Many times we had seen a line of monks in their coloured robes, shaking their silver alms bowls, sometimes with novitiate boys in tow. There was no doubt the customs Abu described were fundamental to Burmese life. 'I wonder whether it could lead to an unreflective set of rituals!' I said, 'The danger, I suppose, of any religion or faith system.'

'It's woven into the spiritual soul of the Burmese,' Abu replied. 'Parents are overwhelmed with joy to see their son become a disciple of Buddha. When Buddhists pray they believe they'll gain merit as at that moment, they are pure and untainted with evil and sins'.

I'd often pondered our chat with Abu since that evening. In the years following, I was surprised to discover the somewhat embattled situation that Lincoln and his team found themselves in. His college on the outskirts of Yangon has experienced persistent petty interference from Bamar Buddhist neighbours. Then there was the small church we visited outside the city. It comprised around a dozen Christians meeting in the home and courtyard of a couple in the village which was majority Buddhist. It was exciting to meet with Charity and her husband and their small congregation, including a bunch of adorable kids. Only later did Lincoln tell us that they had stoically put up with rubbish being routinely tipped into their tiny front garden, and having a back fence repeatedly torn down by resentful neighbours. As it happened, when Charity started an after-school club to care for all the unattended children in the village, with pencils and colouring pens provided, attitudes slowly softened.

It is now 2011 and April and I are on our second visit to Rangoon. As I draw closer to Burma's heartbeat, I find myself both attracted, and on occasions, concerned by the country's love affair with Gautama Buddha, who lived 2,500 years ago. Prospect Burma in the UK provides scholarships for Burmese students and they put us in touch with Aung Zaw Moe. One evening we meet up with Aung Zaw, a man who, I'd guess, is in his early thirties. We gather his grandparents are Shan on his mother's side and Burmese on his father's. His early memories of growing up in Burma are vivid:

'As a child, I helped my father on the farm, about fifteen acres. He grew paddy rice in the monsoon and peanut or green beans in summer. This was in Kamarnut, near Bago, north-east of Yangon.'

'My mother managed the home. She also had a family business making cheroots. When I was eight I had to help my mum in the kitchen, learning how to cook, wash, and clean. But it was watching my grandfather . . . that's what shaped my thinking. He was at the centre of things when it came to community affairs. He inspired me . . . his leadership, his motivation, and commitment to help others. I am his clone. The way I think, the way I behave is completely like him. Being with him for eight years changed my life into a mature one.'

For all his youthful looks, there is indeed a maturity etched into Aung Zaw's face. He speaks earnestly, yet in an almost dispassionate tone. Not for the first time, I find a Burmese person distancing themselves emotionally from the setbacks and sacrifices they have endured.

'The event that changed my life is Cyclone Nargis in 2008. I was working in HIV projects in Yangon and I volunteered in cyclone-affected delta area for two months. That completely shocked me and arose me to do something to build community resilience. I worked in the delta area for two years before studying in Bangladesh.'

Now, Aung Zaw tells us, he has a Master's in Public Health from a university in Dhaka. He refers to himself as a community-development consultant, working for four weeks in the field and then four weeks off. He knows very well the challenges of living and working in Myanmar. Poverty and privilege, militarism and pacifism, belief and secularism rubbing alongside each other uneasily.

Intrigued to know what motivates this young man, I ask about his beliefs, where he gets his energy.

'I am lucky to study Buddhist way of life from my grandparents as well as from my community. I stand out from comfort zone and seek for the truth of Buddhism. I try to practise meditation.'

'Say more.'

'What I mean is I am not so-called Buddhist—traditional one—but I am practising novel way of Buddhism, practical one. Since 2003, I am practising meditation and learned deeply about Vipassana meditation. That guided me to be a true Buddhist to keep in line with the teaching of Buddha.'

He speaks fast and in a dutiful tone, as if there was no other way to conduct your life. I can't help admiring his zeal.

'I grew up under supervision of my grandfather. Since I was eight, I used to help him. To gather donation money, to assist his accounting, to visit to monasteries, to take part in community meetings, and so on. He is my idol.'

'Not many Western children would refer to their grandfather as an idol.'

'These experiences teach me to be a community leader,' he continues. 'I also do reading and most of my books are about Buddhism, all teach to serve for others who are in need. For Buddhist, our ultimate goal is Nirvana, similar to "Heaven" in Christianity. If you are planning to go to Nirvana you need to practise love, compassion, giving to others . . . and meditation.'

There is something sublimely simple yet profound about his worldview. Almost like catching a train to a desired destination. It is all about helping others with a pure mind.

As our conversation with Aung Zaw draws to a close, I ask the question I like to ask all the young people we meet: 'What do you hope to be doing in a decade from now?'

'I have a couple of dreams,' he says readily. 'To be a monk or a teacher in a university to train young people on various development subjects like Public Health, Business Management, Social Science, etc. Since 2012, I wanted to do a long-term meditation as a monk; however, I had less chance to do so. Maybe, I will be a monk in coming ten years.'

I feel I've learnt a lot about Buddhism from Aung Zaw. It's as if there is a golden thread, a seamless connection between what he does now in community development, his village upbringing, and his Buddhist beliefs. It comes across as an enticing mix. I don't think many people have questioned him about his beliefs before. It was as if he was articulating something and, in so doing, a clarity emerged. Was it T.S. Eliot who said: 'We only have the words for what we no longer need to say?'

On the way home from meeting Aung Zaw that night, my mind is travelling far faster than the taxi as we bump along the dimly lit streets. I feel I have been plumbing the hidden depths of Myanmar and need to know more. Not for the first time, Thant Myint-U's book *River of Lost Footsteps* comes to the rescue.

'In the tenth and eleventh centuries,' he writes 'Burma was part of a far-flung and dynamic conversation, a component of the Buddhist world that linked Afghanistan and the dusty oasis towns of the Silk Road with Cambodia, Java, and Sumatra, with scholar-officials in every Chinese province, and with students and teachers in India.' But by the twelfth century: ' . . . the conversation was shrinking. Burma's Buddhism would become even more impassioned. Not part of Christendom, the Islamic world, or the cultural worlds of Hindu India and Confucian China, Burma, proud and resolutely Theravada, would be left largely to talk to itself. This is not to say that Burma was ever sealed off,' he remarks, 'only that a constant effort was required to connect and overcome a natural tendency to look inward'.

April reminds me that Myanmar today remains a predominantly and devoutly Buddhist country, at around 90 per cent. 'The Bamar,' she says, 'are the dominant people group in the Irrawaddy valley and they hold most of the top jobs in government.'

The intricately carved gold and vermilion entrances to the Buddhist temples are in all the cities and towns. Even in more remote areas, white pagodas and stupas punctuate the skyline. Buddhist chanting is the background muzak across many streets, and Burmese households have a small room with an altar, consecrated by a monk. This consists of a simple shelf on which statues of the Buddha and offerings are placed. It seems plausible that this veneration, embedded deeply into the country's psyche, has contributed to its self-contained stance. Maybe it's the military that has then taken it a step further, from introversion to isolation.

The night air is still warm and the low hubbub of conversations from neighbouring homes keeps me from sleeping. I recall the way Margaret, April's mother, sometimes sat and reminisced wistfully about her childhood. Often she mentioned the Festival of Lights. She described how in Shan State, there were hot air balloon competitions to celebrate this event on the Buddhist calendar. The night air filling perilously with fire-powered paper lanterns, each seeking to outdo the other in their ingenuity of colours and patterns. The balloons are hoisted to the sky in homage to the Culamani Pagoda of Devas. The successful ones rise high above the clouds beyond. Some are unable to leave the ground. Others burn up midway.

These customs and names, so unfamiliar to me at the time, conjured an enchanting picture. As I doze, that phrase 'some burn up midway' comes back to mind. It seems an apt metaphor concerning the fate of the many pagodas and monasteries from past generations. On our travels so far, we had seen so many Buddhist works of art meticulously created by enterprising and farsighted devotees. Some were alive with activity and reverence, but others now lay in ruins due to lack of proper care and maintenance. As the elderly writer, U Ba Than wistfully notes: 'Our Myanmar mentality is equated with

Tumbledown temple in up-country Myanmar

straw and fire and mineral water, where zest and fervour only last a fleeting moment.'

In the eleventh and twelfth centuries, Bagan was the centre of a vast Buddhist kingdom stretching from Tibet, through much of present-day Burma down to the straits of Malacca. The people of Bagan were fervent practitioners of Buddhism and increasingly Theravada Buddhism. With the rise of Confucianism in China, Hinduism in Ceylon and Sumatra, and the advance of Islam from the West, they saw themselves more and more as defenders of a threatened faith and an island of a conservative tradition in a hostile and changing world.

'The royal residences have long since crumbled away,' April tells me, 'but Bagan is still a breathtaking view, especially at sunset. Thousands of pagodas rising from the mist like other-worldly silhouettes. Sadly many local villages were demolished to make way for the photo-snapping foreigners.'

'Is it near Chauk?'

'Just a few miles upriver. We often used to visit as a family, taking a picnic and staying for the day. In those days I was too young to realize the history and significance of the place. I didn't ask my parents and they didn't say. To me, it was like a child's playground to climb and clamber up.'

Far surpassing Bagan and other holy sites in Myanmar in terms of both spiritual significance and visitor numbers is the Shwedagon Pagoda in Yangon. This holiest of shrines with its principal gold-leaf dome along with sixty-four lesser pagodas rises majestically above the steaming skyline of present-day Yangon. On top of Theinguttara hill, its distinctive gold dome is visible from air and sea. Tradition has it that two Burmese merchants from Rangoon met the Buddha by chance, soon after his enlightenment, when travelling in North India. They offered him rice cakes and honey and as a token of their visit the Buddha gave them eight hairs from his head. These are said to lie enshrined within the Shwedagon and ensure its iconic status. It was one of the first places we visited as a family in 1995. Having deposited our flip-flops at the downstairs booth, we made sure we were respectfully covered and padded up the steps to a vast marble platform. As U Ba Than reverently notes: 'We slip off our shoes when we enter pagodas and monasteries or places of worship. In the same manner, we slip off words when we enter the sacred space of silence.' We squinted as the mid-morning sun dazzled, catching the shimmering surfaces of gold. Devotees sat cross-legged at their shrines, each one dedicated to the day of the week that the worshippers were born. Bare headed monks were shrouded by the heady scent of joss sticks and incense.

April and I decide to return to the shrine again. This time the sun is setting. The distant skyline is a smear of flame orange, then blood crimson as it sinks below the horizon, punctually at 6 p.m. The atmosphere is quite different to our first visit, quite lively. The worshippers are there, of course, wrapped in their holy silence with hands cupped in the lotus bud form of deep obeisance, seemingly unperturbed by visitors as they file by to light candles and take photographs. Indeed the whole atmosphere has the feel of a vibrant marketplace, complete with flashing neon lights in some of the shrines, chattering guides, and the rhythmic chanting of worshippers. It is sincere for sure, but also very accessible. What a refreshing contrast to some privatized expressions of religion I have come across.

It causes me to ponder our Western non-conformist tradition which is sometimes so eager to avoid distraction and idolatry. In the process, I wonder whether we have robbed our church services of richness, such that they become 'thin'. Spoken and sung words with a brief homily from the pulpit. This is not the worship experience I read of in scripture. To take Psalm 45 for instance, which heralds the coming of a King. This refers both to David, king of Judah, but also looks forward to the return of Jesus at the end of time, as a majestic King and awesome bridegroom. The imagery is 'thick' and evokes our five senses and more. This is my paraphrase:

How can I contain my tongue
with what I see and have to share?
My heart is bursting with a song,
my senses ravished and laid bare.

To receive His kiss is to taste grace
and everlasting favour,
so feast your eyes on the face
of your majestic saviour.

By truth he has cancelled out
every demon of deceit;
all evil has been found out
and placed beneath his feet.

Be stirred by his righteous rule,
feel the release of all toil,
as he embraces you with joy
and anoints your head with oil.

Smell the fragrance of his robes,
rich palatial spices confer
and infuse his royal clothes
with aloes, cassia and myrrh.

Listen well when he calls,
it's incredible but true,
He sees us as beautiful,
and the King, he comes for you.

'I love the reference to the rich fragrance of the King's robes,' says
April. Then proceeds to give me a mini-lesson in herbs and spices.
'Did you know all the spices mentioned have medicinal properties?
Aloe vera, you must have heard of that? It's an African succulent and
fights bacteria. It heals burns and improves skin tone.'

'Cassia comes from the bark of evergreen trees, which are native
to China and here in Burma. It produces a warm, spicy aroma and
drinking it's tea, it's supposed to boost your immune system.'

'And myrrh . . . ?'

'That's a natural resin extracted from small, thorny trees in
Egypt. It's a spice used for perfumes, but also a natural antibiotic
with no side effects!'

I'm impressed with April's knowledge and so thankful
to our God who wants to engulf us in the full measure of his
creative and healing presence. Both this side of heaven and—
more completely—beyond. That's the kind of sensory overload
I can cope with! Perhaps for too long, I have been pursuing the
spiritual *or* the sensual, when in God we have a full measure of
both. It is strange that, at a time when my Christian pilgrimage
had become somewhat arid, it takes an encounter with Buddhism
at the Shwedagon to reawaken my appetite for God's presence. To
plunge afresh into his grace.

'What do you make of it all? Myanmar's Buddhist heritage?'
April asks as we slowly descend the steps from the Shwedagon to

retrieve our sandals. I'm not sure I have an answer, but a few days later, I've had time to process my thoughts.

We are at breakfast and enjoying our favourite dish: refried beans, or pe pyote kyaw, with crispy fried onions and wafer-thin nan bread.

'There are many endearing aspects. I love the joyous festivals that involve food and envelope whole communities. The self-discipline engendered at an early age, I'm jealous of that! It seems a high premium is placed on education founded on moral precepts. The respect paid to the Buddha, to monks, to elders, to teachers and parents . . . '

'Yes, and in that order. Maybe we should have instilled this in our children,' says April with a half-smile.

' . . . there's also something admirable about the class-less, non-combative stance. I don't see an insistence on "right" theology. The holy teachings and heart-attitude of Buddhists seem to thread through all that they do.' Later, other attributes come to mind. There are no compartments. There's no pressing need for aggrandisement and there is plenty of compassion to go around. All this is refreshingly different from a world where celebrity leaders rely on image-management, hashtag followers, and the pretence that they are in control. The fiction that they are central.

'Can you see why I'm often telling you not to be in such a rush?' says April, bringing me back to the present.

She is right. I remember once when the children were young, I said to Zoe, 'Sorry, I can't do that now, daddy's in a hurry'. To which her little voice piped up, 'I can hurry with you'. How sad to be passing on these facets of Western paranoia! Sometimes it seems that reaching my goals, winning my arguments, proving my point, have become all important. Life in the fast lane easily becomes unreflective. Too readily, I rely on head knowledge and disconnect myself from meaningful relationships with others as well as with my surroundings. My day too easily descends into a series of calculations and transactions.

April's ability to stay in the moment is a wonderful antidote to all this. Perhaps centuries of Buddhist meditation have seeped into her soul. Other spiritual traditions, including Islam, Judaism, Taoism, and Hinduism advocate and practise their own forms of meditation. As for the Christian faith, this is a timely reminder for me to re-embrace the contemplative tradition. It was integral to, and beloved by, the so-called desert fathers and mothers. These were the monks and nuns from around the third century BCE who blazed a sacred trail for both Eastern and Western Christian traditions. I am reminded of a statement made by Archbishop Rowan Williams:

> 'To put it boldly, contemplation is the only ultimate answer to the unreal and insane world that our financial systems and our advertising culture and our chaotic and unexamined emotions encourage us to inhabit. To learn contemplative practice is to learn what we need so as to live truthfully and honestly and lovingly. It is a deeply revolutionary matter.'

As we approach the end of this visit to Yangon, my mind turns again to Uncle Abu. By an uncanny coincidence, Austin and his two younger brothers Abu and Eric, all died within a space of a few months in 2008. Although my understanding is still only skin deep, I'm grateful for the time Abu took to explain things on our first visit. Brother to Austin and middle child of six siblings he seemed poised and at one with life. Back then in 1995, his wife's death had hit him hard, but he was getting on with things in an unruffled manner. Much as Austin did when April's mother passed away. No drama, no emoting, almost a fatalism that things cannot be changed.

For all the atrocities and injustices perpetrated by their government, I find it difficult to visualize men like Abu and U Ba Than as revolutionaries, taking on the authorities, leading a public revolt. They do not wear their beliefs belligerently. Aung Zaw is a different matter. His convictions run deep and I can see him at the barricades.

Contemplation and revolution may appear to be strange bed-fellows but perhaps the British ex-Archbishop has a point. Buddhists are not alone in emphasizing meditation and wholeness, but this attitude of mindfulness towards body, mind, and spirit does appear to be very evident within homes and communities. It shapes the dreams of the Burmese we have met. For the most part this remains passive. But there comes a point at which the strong chords of patient benevolence and tolerance start to fray. In 1988, Buddhist monks were part of the student rallies of resistance in Rangoon, and again in 2007, they were at the forefront of the so-called Saffron Revolution, leading marches in protest against the military government. Junta troops began firing on the demonstrating monks and civilians leaving thousands injured and hundreds dead. There was national and international outrage at a situation that was dumbfounding on at least two counts. First the extremity of the situation that pushed habitually peace-loving monks to revolt in the first place. Then, incredulity at witnessing Bamar troops fire on their holy brothers, who have been venerated for centuries.

Given that the vast majority of Bamars—the dominant people group—are devout Buddhists, this raises puzzling, if not worrying, contradictions. The elitist military machine which, over the decades, has ground down opposition by fair means and foul: this does not feel like justice; the patently unequal distribution of power and wealth that leaves millions on the breadline—this does not demonstrate compassion. The persistent intolerance and sometimes vicious treatment of other ethnic people within their borders; this does not speak of kindness. As far back as 1962, Ne Win and his generals oversaw the destruction of mosques, the confiscation of belongings and the redistribution of Rohingya land among Arakan's Buddhist population.

Such political and social crimes are not confined to Myanmar, but they are certainly not to be expected from a people professing Buddhist beliefs. To be sure, there is a right and proper place for Buddhism within the Burmese government. Given the historically close connection between the state and the clergy, any positive future vision for Burma must surely heal the divorce between politics of nationalism on the one hand and moral and spiritual values on the other. If reaching Nirvana, for Uncle Abu and all his fellow Buddhist believers in Myanmar, is based on merit and compassion in this life, then there is some soul-searching to do. Like the paper lanterns hoisted into the night sky in homage to Buddha at the Festival of Lights, we can but hope that these aberrations 'burn up midway'.

CHAPTER TWELVE

(2012) LETTING GO

Our annual visit to Yangon is becoming a regular winter jaunt; this is our third. While we don't relish the long-haul flight, it all seems worthwhile once at our destination. Initially, I was impressed. We'd got our visas from the Myanmar embassy in London with comparative ease, although having to report our eye-colour on the application form was a little sinister.

The queue for the 'foreigners' passport control at Yangon International Airport was not as long and tedious as usual and we'd managed to secure a decent exchange rate for currency at an airport kiosk. In past years, we'd had to fuss with foreign exchange certificates (FECs). Not this time; dollars were acceptable tender. There was even a new X-ray machine to detect suspicious items. After a very slow start through the nineties and noughties, Myanmar is catching up fast as a traveller destination, I thought. Then it all went wrong. April and I loaded five items of luggage into the X-ray detector tent. Five items in, a bit of confusion as a fellow passenger bundled past us . . . then four items out. Our initial bafflement turned to mild panic. The missing case just happened to have pretty much all that was essential for our trip. We could have done without some clothes and gifts, but we had come to do some training at Lincoln's college. So to find ourselves without iPad, notes, reference books, and for April to be detached from her diabetes medicines, was worrying.

At first, I started to fantasize in a light-hearted way. Is there some shadowy force sabotaging our attempts to work alongside our Chin friends? Two years back I had drowsily arrived in Yangon with a heavy cold, which unusually for me, had decided to infect my larynx. The next year I left my spectacles at the transit check-in at our stopover at Dubai airport. Now this year I was without my notes. On the first occasion I was voiceless, on the next trip I couldn't read. And now I could speak and see but, robbed of my notes, I didn't know what to say. As the dark humour of the situation subsided, a more rational mindset kicks in. Having exhausted enquiries at the airport, we determined to call security each day for updates. Surely someone took it by mistake. The more I dwelt on this scenario the more it seemed like wishful thinking. Then I had a light-bulb moment. Surely Apple has a way of detecting the location of their iPads. Feeling clever in a *Spooks* sort of way, we caught a taxi downtown on our second day to find an Apple store to log in my serial number. No joy, they were just a sales outlet with no detection facilities. Half a day wasted but on reflection I am relieved. The thought of arriving at a stranger's doorstep down some shady alley to confront burglars in the Queen's English was starting to alarm me.

We were staying at a modest hotel near the airport. They charge top-dollar rate for foreign visitors but the ambiance remains quaintly old-fashioned. On each floor a youth was sleeping at the end of the corridor, scrambling to attention as we approached to show us to our room. This is well intentioned but hardly necessary. When his hotel telephone rang, echoing down the landing day and night, it did tend not to make for a restful stay. Staff are plentiful. Porters, cooks, and cleaners bustled about, cheerily calling to each other. It seemed as though a whole village had been transported onto the premises and we as guests were bystanders. Above the lift in the lobby a big yellow smiley-face notice had the following instruction: *Focus to the task. Not to the person.* I presumed this was aimed at staff, but it seemed odd on several levels. Why display it in a guest area? Why issue internal instructions in this rather megaphone manner? And, important though the task is, are people not important in a hotel? It seemed to sum up the confusion and ambiguity of how to handle the international clientele they sincerely want to serve. As part of re-branding itself as 'Myanmar' in the mid-1990s, the Burmese government made a push for tourism, hoping to attract a flood of overseas visitors and inward investment to follow. But more than twenty years later, there is a long way to go. Indeed, many of the plush new hotels in downtown Yangon are under-used and the generals who invested their ill-gotten gains so heavily are losing out badly.

As if managing to misplace a precious suitcase on arrival was not enough, more self-abasement was to come. I was living up to the label of an absentminded professor rather too well. Two days later, I discovered that the spare mobile phone that our host Lincoln had lent me to ease day-to-day communication during our visit had also been 'spirited away' to a place unknown. He brushed off my apology and endeavouring to retrieve the lost mobile, he dialled its number. Repeatedly each day. No one answered.

'I've noticed locals all have mobiles,' I said to Lincoln.

'Yup, telecoms literacy is high here. Most adults connect via Facebook and Viber.'

' . . . yet will happily ride hanging off the back of a clapped out bus,' I added, 'or take a taxi with its internals stripped down like it's a stock car.'

'It's part of the paradox of modern Myanmar. Here's another one. The country is rich in natural resources, but the majority don't benefit. Or take our trade in precious gems. Most of the revenue is siphoned through the bank accounts of government ministers.'

As Lincoln kept to the middle lane, cars and trucks overtook and undertook at will. The seemingly endless outskirts of Yangon rattled by. The majority of city dwellers lived from hand to mouth in makeshift shacks or dilapidated tenements.

'Once we were the so-called rice bowl of Asia. Now we're a net importer. We have plenty of hydro electric capacity, but we are having to buy electricity from Laos. How crazy is that?'

The more time April and I spend here, the more we find the seemingly placid public face of Myanmar is misleading. It masks deep injustices, incipient corruption and nepotism by senior officials and their cronies. While most of its South East Asian neighbours have excelled in trade and commerce, Myanmar is a country frozen in time since the 1960s, sliding from relative prosperity to economic obscurity sixty years later.

During our first family visit to Rangoon in 1995–96, I was caught up in the first flush of enthusiasm. I recall we wandered around the stalls of lacquerware dishes and antique boxes wrapped in newspaper, of woven baskets smelling of saffron, of jade necklaces and carved elephants, of embroidered scarves and exquisite paintings. The six of us sat on high stools, sampling street vendor delicacies in Scott Market. We observed monks and locals pay homage to Buddha at their shrines, the sun seeming to set alight the gold-leafed dome of the Shwedagon. We wandered down from the Sule Pagoda towards the harbour, the wide streets flanked by the ornate facades of colonial

Old colonial buildings in Yangon pockmarked with mildew

buildings. The old embassies with ample frontages, the imposing Post Office, the Port Building were all still there.

Although much of the past grandeur had long since faded, I see now that I was in danger of romanticizing these sights, allowing nostalgic images to cast a pleasing veneer over the boulevards that once proudly administered this outpost of the Empire.

As we unpeel the history, of course, we find the reality to be more complex, each age a giddy cycle of hope, brutality, and decadence. There was the self-consumed and out-of-touch monarch, Thibaw, last king of Burma in his glass palace at Mandalay. Overthrown without a shot being fired in 1886. Then, the early decades of the twentieth century ushered in an era of increasing prosperity and improved infrastructure. But was this simply to serve the needs of the British and a way of subjugating the nation to a distant imperial government? The Second World War saw lower Burma overrun by Japanese forces with stories of shameful cruelty in POW camps before repulsion by the Allies. The early days of Independence were full of optimism but cut short by assassinations and coups. And since the early 1960s, a military regime has resided, as grim as the once-splendid Rangoon buildings now decaying with mildew, their windows like the hollowed eyes of neglected children. That is pretty much how most of the population now feels.

'No era is without its share of shame and pride,' says Lincoln. We are in his favourite tea shop. He gestures for a refill of our flask. 'Country names and street names can be changed, political parties can be rebranded, but the conversation in places like this is the day-to-day reality check.'

'For the most part,' I say, 'the mood I pick up is one of weary resignation.'

Lincoln nods solemnly and pours more tea. Outside the surreal presence of Wayne Rooney does little to lift spirits. A life-size poster gently rocks on its stand, arms folded across his puffed-out chest. There's something incongruous about a boy from Everton, in his Manchester United kit, marketing Mandalay Beer on the streets of

Yangon. Customers must know he earns more in a day than they will in a lifetime.

Lincoln leads us through the uneven side streets of downtown Yangon, dodging between market stalls, knife grinders, and children squeezing sugar cane through mangles for juice. I think again of April's family, the ones who remained. Austin, the oldest sibling, left behind two brothers and three sisters. His wife, Margaret, part of a close-knit family living in the Karen district, said goodbye to two brothers. Apart from a sister, Jessie who emigrated to Denmark, neither Austin nor Margaret would see those they left behind and their families for another thirty years. What nobody could have foreseen, even in the turmoil of South Asian politics of the time— with North Korea, Pakistan, and Thailand all subjected to fledgling dictators—was that the 1962 coup in Burma would kick-start a military regime which remains intact to the present day. The ruling generals have always shown an uncanny knack of handing the baton to a new generation of military men.

In some ways, the original intention was uncomplicated, perhaps even noble. At the outset, it was generals and their foot soldiers who took control. Their mindset was to rebuild national pride and promote a new identity for Burma. To get back to the morally pure and culturally esteemed foundations of Buddhism. For Ne Win and his colonels, the notion of democracy was as alien to them as a dictator is to most Europeans.

In their defence, the country has survived. The economy, having slumped on more than one occasion, is now just about ticking over. Myanmar lies seventh out of ten South East Asian countries, with just Cambodia, Laos and Brunei lower in terms of GDP per capita, according to the International Monetary Fund. Myanmar is a member of the economic club called the Association of South East Asian Nations. The National League for Democracy (NLD) has seats in parliament, though still not a majority due to the percentage of seats guaranteed to the Military. And increasing numbers of international non-government organizations(NGO) now have access to bring in humanitarian aid and know-how. But the unflinching rule of the junta has come at a huge cost. For sixty years successive cadres of generals have demonstrated an almost myopic obsession with self-preservation, never mind the needs of the wider population and their basic human rights. It's like the notice in the hotel lobby writ large: *Focus to the Job, Not the Person.*

When Austin and Margaret returned on a couple of occasions to visit relatives, to sit with those who had been bereaved, to share family stories with nieces and nephews, they were witnessing the streets and homes they might still be inhabiting. Never ones to be sentimental, they did not dwell on this. And the Rangoon families seemed content to stay. For all that, the silent gulf, in material well-being, in political freedom, in expectations for their children's future, was huge.

It is now 2012 and the country's attempt to woo and embrace tourists is still stuttering. New Korean cars are flooding in at the ports but little has been done to the highways since Independence. We are back in Lincoln's van. A journey of a dozen miles takes two hours on clogged roads in the rush hour. Aspiration is written all over the sprawling shopfronts as we weave through traffic from the landmark junctions of Tenth and Seventh Mile. Makeshift enterprises with gaudy signs advertise: *Sweety—Home Mattresses*, *Marvellous Wedding Planning*, *Ben Hur Trading Company*, *Ever Right Engineering*, *Perfect Building Supplies*. A small green-painted tea shop simply calls itself *Splendid* and another, less fortunately, calls itself *Taste Wind*. I suppose if a better life is a long way off, neon superlatives help to bridge the gap.

Now and then a procession of children comes into view, barefoot and swathed in their Buddhist robes, boys in saffron and girls in peach pink. Some have matching parasols to shield their shaved heads from the stifling sun and they rattle their silver bowls for alms. It makes me wonder what an equivalent six-month stint of religious observance and austerity might look like for youngsters in Leeds or Lyon. Would it yield a more spiritually aware generation, weaned

Girl with her child on a bike on the outskirts of Yangon

off their plugged in, secular diet? Here they comprise a pretty tourist picture, but it is salutary to recall that one reason that 'The Lady'—a staunch Buddhist herself—is politically gagged could well be down to a small group of Buddhist extremists in her government. They are anti-Muslim and have been ruthless in the ethnic cleansing of insurgents from minority tribes, whether Rohingya in the Rakhine district, Shans in the northeast, or Karens on the Thai border.

I am also struck by what you *don't* see in Yangon. Rarely do we witness anyone run, except perhaps to skip across a three-lane highway, dodging between hooting taxis and overcrowded buses. Begging and graffiti are conspicuously absent, no doubt due to zero tolerance from the authorities. Nor do we see many arguments or even raised voices. Perhaps this is because time is elastic and arguments require energy, and for most, the passion has long since ebbed away to leave a kind of blanket acquiescence. What is there to hurry for, what is worth arguing about? It's been observed that the

Burmese don't 'do' emotion. If they do not agree with you they just stop talking and don't let you know what their feelings are. Another noticeable absence is immodest dress. No bare midriffs or thigh-hugging lycra here. Not yet anyway. Despite the pressing heat and ever-present dust, young people in their crisp white shirts and bright school uniforms and women in their colourful-patterned longyis speak of winsome dignity.

Much more brazen and unabashed are the condominiums, hotels, and apartment blocks, thrusting into the skyline as we approach the business district. They elbow their way onto the edge of Kandawgyi Lake, towering over palm trees and dwarfing nearby pagodas. Funded by foreign investors from opportunist neighbour countries, these urbane buildings—all gleaming glass and marble atriums —point to the wealth of an elite. It's an open secret that it's the military and their business partners who constitute this top echelon. No trickle-down in sight. Indeed no middle class to speak of. As Lincoln tells us: 'We used to live to eat, now we eat to live'. Given that talking about and enjoying a good meal is central to the worldview of the Burmese, this is indeed a low point in national well-being. I'm reminded of another adage: 'Every day that you do not eat, you are eaten.'

Will tourism ever take off in this country? Will the service sector start focusing on the person and not just the task? In some ways, one hopes not. So long as simple things take perspiration and effort, so long as the government remains obstructive, so long as internal transport remains arduous and hotels prohibitively expensive, Myanmar will resist or repel the clamour of package tours. However, by the same token, the ills and injustices of the land will also remain veiled and overlooked by the West. Out of sight, out of mind.

One week into our stay, we took a few minutes pool-side at our airport hotel. An attendant explained swimming was not possible today due to cleaning chemicals in the water. Sure enough, we found a hand-printed sign strung across the ladder into the pool. It said simply: '*Under progressing*'. April and I smiled at each other. As a way of describing this wonderfully impossible country, that kind of says it all.

But does it? Lincoln gave another try to locate the whereabouts of his mislaid phone. The likelihood of retrieving it appears remote but his expression registers excitement. The person who answers is none other than a taxi driver who had just discovered the phone beneath the back seat of his hackney'd carriage. It must have slipped from my pocket as I clung on to a fraying strap for safety, weeks before. Fifteen minutes later we are at a rendezvous point and I am taking a selfie of the three of us using the returned phone: me looking mightily relieved, Lincoln looking mildly surprised and the taxi driver appearing bemused at all the fuss. He wants no money and only reluctantly takes the bundle of *kyats* pressed into his hand.

There is a happy ending to the saga of the lost suitcase too. Again it involves lots of phone calls and return visits to the airport. On the day before departing for the UK, we decide to make a last-gasp attempt to locate our errant luggage. In the meantime we had borrowed books, I had rewritten my notes and we'd bought replacement medicines at a tiny shop in the Karen district, which was selling everything from paracetamol to antibiotics over the counter. Airport security guards brusquely point us to the permit office. A long conversation ensues with the officer. Entry beyond the public area requires identification papers and stamped documents. I get the distinct impression that my guide and interpreter, Lincoln, is being given a hard time, no doubt because he is Chin. He takes it all in good humour. Once armed with entry permits we return to the security guards who, still with no hint of a smile, now direct us to lost property office within the terminal. The lady at the desk looks uninterested as Lincoln translates my story of woe and lists the inventory of lost goods. At the word 'Bible', there is a shift in her attitude. I am not sure why, but she becomes more animated and helpful, making rapid-fire phone calls. Cupping the receiver she asks me to describe the lost luggage, Lincoln translates and she proceeds with the call.

'It is possible that Qatar Airways have a bag of that description,' she reports as she puts the phone down and gives us directions.

A further ten minutes and having gone to an adjacent building, passed through more security and climbed a back stairway, we are outside the Qatar Airways office. As we are invited in by the purple-suited staff there, looking somewhat like a naughty teddy bear who'd done a runner and then regretted it, was the familiar sight of my long-lost case. Everything seems intact and I want to hug it.

It was great to be reunited, but I was left wondering about the subliminal purpose behind being detached on arrival and then reattached with our precious belongings just before departure. It is a bit like the year before when I managed to retrieve my spectacles on the way *home* at the Dubai International lost-property office. Was it an object lesson in abandoning my 'developed world' props, letting go of my security blanket, and learning to sit with a different pace, a rhythm uncluttered by accoutrements? Maybe my assumptive slide-rule of what constitutes progress in this country is misplaced, after all. For every instance of poker-faced officialdom and miscued customer service, and for all the rigours of simply travelling from A to B in shabby taxis alongside gutters of raw detritus, here was a country yet to be mugged by cynical crime. A city yet to spawn homeless beggars in shop doorways and ragged orphans clutching at us for handouts. Here were working people deprived for decades of human rights and basic respect by the authorities and cowed by a cheerless military regime, yet men and women who found in themselves a willingness to serve guests with gracious dignity in hotels and restaurants. Taxi drivers honest enough to return lost goods. Airport staff helpful enough to assist a disoriented tourist get reunited with his luggage.

CHAPTER THIRTEEN

(2013) SCHOOLMASTER TO STATESMAN

Each time we land in Yangon, usually in the early hours, family and friends turn up to greet us. Margaret's family lived in the Karen quarter and Austin's were in a district closer to the centre of town. They didn't have a lot materially but without fuss, they shared generously from the little they had. For me, it brought a whole new meaning to the word 'grace'. One family member stands out: Austin's nephew, Monty. Born the first son of nine children in the year the Second World War ended, he may have been named after the Allies' General Montgomery. Monty is not tall, perhaps five foot two, but stands erect as befits a naval man. His short black hair is slicked down and his fresh shirt is tucked into a checked longyi. Unfailingly, he manages to look dapper, despite the vicissitudes of crossing town on public transport. He always seems a little stern. But I soon gather his reluctance to smile is not due to a lack of humour, but absence of teeth. When he does chuckle he manages to do it without opening his mouth. Now retired, he has time on his hands and he tells us he is only too glad to have foreign relations to look after. Following his hour-long 'constitutional' in the cool of the early morning, it gives him a mission, a welcome structure for the day.

The Summit Park View Hotel, with its cool interiors and a floodlit pool, is within walking distance of the Shwedagon Pagoda. Although now surpassed by the gleaming tower blocks in central Yangon next to the Scott Market, it remains one the flashiest. It was here—a couple of years later—that we as foreign guests were advised to gather inside by the British Council during the Myanmar 2015 elections, just in case there was any trouble on the streets. We shortened our stay at another less salubrious hotel. Bumping into teenage girls in the lift, on the arms of wrinkled old white men, was too much to stomach.

Whatever our chosen accommodation, we have come to count on one thing: April's cousin Monty takes it upon himself to keep us fed while we are in town. It's as if he doesn't trust the hotel to sustain us. Taking two or more bus rides from his home, he arrives hot-foot in the foyer with plastic bags full of provisions. Fresh produce bought in the market at dawn and prepared by his family that morning. We smuggle him up to our room at which point he unloads his booty. Tiffin carriers with curry, rice, soup, stir-fried vegetables—different ingredients every day—are spread out on the dressing table as we phone down for some plates and cutlery.   .

He doesn't eat with us and is already planning the next meal: 'What do you want to eat tomorrow? How about chicken and coconut rice? And I can bring some *achin-hin*, a nice sour soup with sorrel? Or would you prefer *hin-gyo*, a peppery soup with courgettes and marrow? I can bring *bhagis* too?'

He picks up the delight from our faces. For April especially, this is home-cooked food which evokes the tangy tastes and spicy aromas of childhood.

'What are you doing today? Is there anywhere you want to go?'

Again, it's not that he doesn't think we are capable of getting about, he just enjoys overseeing our trips. Being white and tall, I am an obvious non-local and he thinks taxi drivers may overcharge me. So we have a little routine. I stay out of sight while he hails a passing cab and bargains with the driver. Currency is swiftly exchanged, then I emerge from the bushes and we all jump in. Not all drivers will impose a tourist surcharge, but it keeps Monty happy that we have saved some *kyats*.

On this occasion, taking a break from our teaching at the Bible college, Monty took us to the docks. We were admiring one of the

April with her cousin Monty, our unofficial tour guide, in downtown Yangon

river steamers being kitted out for tourist cruises up the Irrawaddy to Bagan and Mandalay. Burnished brass-fittings glinted in the sun and the timbered cabins smelt of sandalwood and shone with polish. Stairways with roped handrails led up to an open deck. Beneath a wide awning, there was a sturdy dining table to host guests wealthy enough to afford the luxury trip.

Just as we were visualizing ourselves at impossibly expensive, candlelit dinners served by white-jacketed waiters on the *Irrawaddy Princess* . . . out popped one of the crew members working on the refit. He and Monty greeted each other undemonstratively but warmly. It turned out he had worked for Warrant Officer Monty in the old days. We weren't surprised to hear his high regard for his naval boss.

'Monty would always treat us with a hearty meal at the end of a successful exercise,' he told us. So this is where Monty honed his love of delighting others with good food. Old habits die hard.

For a while, I had been in the process of rapidly scaling down my enchantment with Myanmar. Things were not nearly as simple as I had imagined. It seemed the country was deeply divided and I was keen to find out where the fissures began. On one of our trips downtown with Monty, I was quizzing him about the history of his country, particularly the period since Independence, and the conversation turned to Burma's forgotten hero, U Thant.

'Not long ago, U Thant's family house in Yangon was restored. It's open to the public. You should go.'

April and I arrange to visit the following day. I had already gathered enough to know that U Thant was a rare thing in Burmese affairs: a conviction-led politician. I was interested to hear how things panned out for this unusual man.

Windermere Park is a residential area in Yangon, once favoured by colonial administrators and still home to many city and regional officials. April and I make our way down a leafy drive, where we come upon a 1920s detached house. Although the white painted walls with long, shuttered windows and first-floor balconies are modest, the place is in its own gardens and well-secluded from the main road. It's another bright, dry day with a slight breeze stirring the trees. This is the family home where U Thant spent much of his life.

As we enter, a young man pads towards us. He has faintly Chinese features. He introduces himself as Noe Ley, a volunteer guide at U Thant House. He tells us he is from the north of Myanmar and is currently a student in Yangon.

'You know,' Noe Ley says, 'after all the excitement of his student days, U Thant returned to his hometown for a career in education. He started out as a school teacher and later became a headmaster. He loved to write and he published a book about the League of Nations.'

Noe Ley falls into his practised patter with ease, but enthusiasm shines through.

'He felt strongly in the right of nations to govern themselves and the need to accommodate minority peoples. He was also very wary of a nationalism fuelled by martial spirit. He didn't have time for harking back to Burma's past glory days of all-conquering warrior kings. Whereas many in Rangoon and beyond held an intense distrust of the outsider.'

I was struck by a photograph of U Thant as a student. It depicted a young man with soft features, in a formal and somewhat studious pose, wearing a shiny silk jacket over a white, cotton collarless shirt. A pile of books at his side. I was now seeing beyond that donnish portrait as someone who was not afraid to form his own mind.

'Wasn't he a contemporary of Aung San?'

'Yes at the start of the Second World War, Aung San was one of the Thirty Comrades, trained by the Japanese. The so-called 'Thirty' have been written into our folklore,' says Noe Ley. 'They later became disillusioned with their soldier-trainers. In 1943 they switched sides to combat the Japanese invasion of Burma through underground resistance. After the war and much soul-searching, General Aung San exchanged his military credentials for civil leadership. His goal was to make Burma independent.'

'Anyway in 1947,' says Noe Ley, sipping his water. 'U Thant received a call from Aung San. He wanted U Thant to become press officer for the Anti-Fascist People's Freedom League. U Thant always had ambitions to be a journalist or become a top civil servant, so no persuasion was required. Even better, he was reunited with his old friend from Rangoon days, U Nu. In 1948 U Nu became Burma's prime minister.'

'I guess the post of Press Officer suited U Thant's skills?'

'It did, but U Nu also saw talent in his old student-friend for diplomacy. He had no time for the superior attitude of the Bamar people. Their disregard for Burma's many minorities was blatant and sometimes brutal. This bothered U Thant and was to become a burning issue later in his career.'

Noe Ley beckons us to another room. The photographs that adorn the walls illustrate the next episode of U Thant's life.

'He rose swiftly through the ranks of administration. Although when he was appointed as secretary for Information and Broadcasting in 1950, that raised a few eyebrows.'

We stand beneath a photocall of U Thant surrounded by Indian dignitaries on his first overseas trip to Delhi in 1951. 'Typically such posts were the preserve of the Indian or Burma Civil Service, members of an Oxbridge-educated elite. Remember U Thant only had a modest degree from a Burmese university.'

I wonder about Noe Ley's education, but don't ask. He seems very clued-in.

'Despite the mutterings, the friendship with U Nu prospered. U Nu was the frontman. Meanwhile behind the scenes, U Thant, as secretary to the Prime Minister, wrote his speeches, managed international visits, hosted foreign guests. Most importantly, he was U Nu's closest advisor and confidante. He proved himself to be loyal, tactful, incorruptible. One of the few people willing to argue with the PM.'

Here then, I think to myself, is one of the ironies of U Thant's life when contrasted with the national destiny of Burma. Someone who has the courage of their convictions, who isn't afraid to question the status quo. How badly the generals who run Burma have needed that kind of internal critique over the years. It seems, from what I have heard, that the military junta quickly disappeared into a bubble of power, driven more by self-preservation than any manifesto that would benefit the country.

We arrive at a wood-panelled wall festooned with black and white photographs. It's like a Who's Who of the 1960s. In each frame is the benign—now bespectacled—figure of U Thant, shaking hands, addressing conferences, awarding certificates.

Noe Ley sees us smiling. 'Yes, you can see how busy U Nu and U Thant were at this time, spreading their message of neutrality and friendship. They travelled the world meeting with state officials . . . Premier Kruschev in Moscow, Mao Tse-tung in the Forbidden City, Ho Chi Min in Hanoi.'

I'm struck by the visual incongruity in the photos. The two Burmese statesmen in their characteristic white *gaung baung* or traditional headdress. Even with this formal piece of Myanmar head attire reserved for special occasions, the photos typically show them dwarfed by their smiling hosts.

'But . . . ' Noe Ley's voice becomes a little softer, as if not wishing to be overheard, 'as U Nu and U Thant were winning friends and influencing people on their international trips, things were shifting on the home front. The Anti-Fascist League was running out of steam. By the late 1950s, the government was disintegrating and there was uncertainty as to what would happen next.'

'Ne Win?' I asked.

'Yes, of course. Ne Win was also one of the Thirty. Now a General, he and a revolutionary council of his loyal lieutenants had been biding their time. Choosing their moment, they sacked the entire top layer of bureaucrats. All those who were trained and capable.'

'Wow, what took their place?'

' . . . Army officers. They were drafted in to run local councils and the judicial courts. But there was no clear ideology. It's not unusual to have an Army regime, but this was different. It was soldiers—not civilians—who held all of the key posts. Can you imagine, untrained military men, running the government!'

This was a further irony brought into stark relief by U Thant. At a time when he and his Prime Minister were wooing the world, the government at home was turning in on itself, losing touch with its own people and gaining few allies abroad.

Noe Ley is a handsome young man with a shock of black hair. Undeterred by a pronounced lisp, he seems to enjoy sharing what he knows about Burma's forgotten hero.

'For all the troubles at home, U Thant's star continued to rise. In 1957 he moved from his home here in Windermere Park to New York to work for the United Nations.'

Noe Ley points to a photo of the family on the steps of his official residence, a stately red-brick house, surrounded by lawns on the banks of the Hudson river.

'He was earning a reputation as an impartial and capable leader but also a statesman with strong compassion. Look at this . . . '

Noe Ley directs us to a statement made by U Thant at the time:

'Burma's imagination has been fired by the high idealism and lofty purpose of the [UN] Charter . . . a world in which discrimination based on race and colour would be eradicated, and a world in which the traditional under-dog, the masses of Asia and Africa and Latin America would at long last begin to enjoy a fairer share of the good things of the world.'

'Around the same time that U Thant was being sworn in as head of the United Nations in 1961 . . . back in Rangoon, Ne Win was rounding up all senior members of parliament—including U Nu as part of his coup.'

We enter the hallway, from which the stairs wind upwards. It was this wooden stairway that U Thant's grandson encountered as a termite nest four feet high when he first discovered his grandfather's home in 2012. At that time, the grounds were overgrown and the roof of the two-story house was nearly collapsed. Originally built in 1921, it had been U Thant's family home for many years, but in recent years, had fallen into disrepair. With the help of many donors and permission from President Thein Sein, the house has now been restored as a telling testimony to U Thant's life and work, a tranquil oasis in the heart of Yangon.

We pause at a family portrait of U Thant with his wife, Daw Thein Tin, and their two children. Another son, Maung Bo had died as an infant. This was taken just before they left for New York in 1957. Then, on to the living room where each wall recounts some of the Secretary General's achievements: shuttle diplomacy to help defuse the Cuban missile crisis; helping to end the war in the Congo;

U Thant, Secretary-General of the United Nations until 1971

lobbying hard against apartheid in South Africa and the US military intervention in Vietnam. The visual displays speak of a person driven by a strong belief that many of the world's conflicts were linked to scarcity and need. A sentence from U Thant's memoirs underscores the breadth and cornerstone of this vision:

> *'If we can . . . free ourselves from the shackles of hatred, fear and prejudice, as well as from want and disease, we may hope for a new great resurgence of creative activity—a vast spiritual and intellectual reawakening of mankind.'*

'When U Thant headed up the UN he launched the World Food Programme and the UN Development Programme. He connected issues of public health, education, job training, and food security.'

Less publicized was his role in launching the International Convention on the Elimination of All Forms of Racial Discrimination (ICERD). Not the snappiest of titles but a significant international stand against apartheid and colonialism. For the time, this initiative was as ambitious as it was prescient.

Noe Ley returns and checks his watch. He's had a long day as a volunteer at the Centre. Most visitors have gone and a gentle breeze stirs. Early fallen leaves, toasted and frail, are caught in endless eddies as they scuttle along the veranda outside, rustling like the incoming tide. He has his own lectures to attend but I am intrigued by U Thant's work to combat racial discrimination.

'Do you know where your country stands on the ICERD?' I ask.

'In the early days, it was considered important to the people groups of Burma. There are around 135 in all. As Secretary-General of the UN, U Thant introduced the global Convention which was designed to give autonomy to ethnic groups.'

'So, what about now?'

Noe Ley has done his homework and looks a little sheepish: 'Today, there are just fourteen states across the world that have yet to sign or ratify the ICERD. Eight are island nations. This leaves five other nations: Brunei, Malaysia, North Korea, South Sudan, and . . . '

'Don't tell me . . . Myanmar.'

'I'm afraid so.' At these telling words, Noe Ley gives a little bow and takes his leave. As a member of the Lisu people group, he is one of the minorities yet to be recognized and protected in Myanmar. In a way that sums up the ultimate irony. U Thant's principled and influential life as an individual throws into stark relief the tragedy of Burma as a nation over the last century. Incredible promise, only partially fulfilled. Unrivalled power in South East Asia diminished to shadow-boxing. The resilience of the masses persistently compromised by a lawless elite.

Later, back in the UK, I discover the difficulties of ICERD ratification. Once again making progress in Myanmar is by no means straightforward. The first step is to establish the legitimate 'national races' of Myanmar. These designations are hotly contested, not least because race membership is linked to citizen's rights. For example, the Rohingya people, the subject of recent international and UN concern, are not recognized as a 'national race' at all. But other people groups are also excluded from Myanmar's somewhat arbitrary taxonomy. These matters are further hampered by decades of authoritarian rule that has compromised the independence of its legal system. After the protests of 1988, the University of Yangon including its law school was shut down. Even after it reopened, no lawyers were trained there until 2014. Nevertheless, it would seem to a neutral observer that Myanmar is pre-eminently a country where the rights of minorities and indigenous people groups urgently need protection. Signing up to ICERD was a declaration initiated by Myanmar's only global statesman of the twentieth century. Yet Myanmar remains one of a handful of countries yet to sign up to this accord.

It is likely that the nature of this and other ironies are entirely lost on the military regime. When U Thant died of lung cancer in 1974, after a gruelling second term as Secretary-General leading up to 1971, the world mourned. Tens of thousands lined the streets of Rangoon to pay their last respects when his body was flown home. True to form, General Ne Win, always suspecting him of connivance with U Nu, refused to accord him any special honours. He was denied the dignity of a state funeral and there was a tense stand-off with furious students. The soldiers finally wrested his coffin from the protesters, killing an unknown number in the process. Aung San Suu Kyi, who was daughter of Aung San, U Thant's friend from university days, was one of a very few Burmese compatriots to recognize U Thant's contribution on the world stage, as UN Secretary-General. 'It is,' she said, 'a matter of pride not only for Myanmar citizens but for all Asians.'

For decades the name of U Thant was absent from school textbooks and passed over in historical literature. Thanks partly to the restoration of his family home in Windermere Drive, Yangon, there is now something of a revival of interest in him and his unique place in the annals of Burmese history. For the dedicated schoolmaster and lover of literature from Pantanaw, this would be pleasing to know. Yet when I bring to mind U Thant and his restored reputation my mind also goes to folks like Monty, Noe Ley, and a host of April's relatives who remained in their homeland. Ordinary Burmese people like him who have a keen sense of justice, who are independent-minded and warm in their hospitality. People who, over the generations, have remained stoical, all too aware of the ironies and unbowed by the inequalities around them.

CHAPTER FOURTEEN

(2015) THE ELEPHANT

It's the end of another teaching day at the Bible college and we are unwinding with Lincoln in his front room. He and his wife Leah continue to have an 'open house'. Children flit to and fro with little swirls of *thanaka*, a natural sun lotion made from ground up tree bark, on their cheeks. There's the rattle of pans from the kitchen and occasional visitors wander in through the front door which stays ajar. Tea from a waiting flask and snacks are always offered. Twilight mosquitoes gather around our ankles and the old colonial-style fan sluggishly shifts the air above us. I am wondering whether, after half a century of military rule, there is a softening stance as the government edges towards greater democracy. Lincoln becomes nostalgic as he often does:

'You know when older folk gather they often reflect on the golden era of Burma under the British. In those days, "Made in Burma" meant something, Rangoon Airport was a transport and commercial hub.' His tone is more philosophical than bitter. 'The university was famous and many Westerners came here to study.'

' . . . and now?'

'Now university education is in a poor state. For what it's worth you can buy a thesis from Rangoon University.'

We are sitting in chunky, old-style chairs. Cabinets, with books and papers spilling out, divide us from the dining table. The gaps in the springy floorboards that I noticed last year, eaten away by termites, are still there.

On the wall is the striking image of Lincoln's father William, looking earnest with a crew cut of white hair, swathed in traditional Chin colours of emerald green, red, and black. Catching my gaze, Lincoln remarks, 'He was revered by Christians among the Falam group. You know he translated the New Testament and many songs into our language.'

Lincoln speaks with a deep affection for his father. But I also sense the responsibility of continuing his father's work weighing heavy on his shoulders. Carrying on the dynasty as it were. It was William who started the College eighteen years ago and now Lincoln, his youngest son leads it with a small team of various relatives.

'I was born in Falam,' Lincoln says.

'That was where my grandfather was stationed,' says April. 'He worked there for a while as a civil surgeon in the 1940s.'

Spurred by this surprising connection, Lincoln jumps up and rummages in a cupboard. He pulls out some photographs of the remote hill station, a collection of buildings set into a densely wooded and slightly misty hillside. 'That's the hospital. That's where your grandfather would have worked.'

Lincoln has a broad grin as he describes the cold, sometimes frosty, mornings, the cascades of pink cherry blossom and fruits like Asian pear, plum, and Japanese apricots hanging from the trees. The only time he gets back to the Chin Hills is each spring when he goes recruiting for his next intake of students. Given half a chance, I think he'd stay there.

'There are dozens of ethnic group among the Chin people,' Leah says, as she joins us, 'each with their language. They live in the mountains of north-west Myanmar bordering India. We'll have to take you there one day.'

It sounds like a place we'd love to visit. But like many things in Burma, the idyllic goes hand in hand with the arduous.

'Transport is a real problem.' Leah sighs, 'There are a few roads. To get to most villages requires a long hike through rough terrain. Especially during the monsoon rains, the tracks are all churned up.

We had mudslides again this year . . . roads and some villages washed away.'

I am reminded of how the journalist Peter Popham describes the region as having the feel of the Wild West. He reports from Hakha, the main town deep in the Chin hills, having made a fifteen-hour drive in a four wheeler from Mandalay. He follows the fate of Arthur and Laura Carson. They were American Baptist missionaries from the US Midwest, who decided to move their mission work from the Burmese lowlands to the Chin Hills in 1899. The Chin peoples were renowned for their headhunting, slave raids, and animal sacrifices, and had never encountered the Bible:

'Seven years later, in 1906, the Carsons made their first convert. Two years after that—shortly before expiring from appendicitis—Arthur Carson baptised number one hundred. This pioneering, inexhaustible couple had learnt the language, written it down in the Roman alphabet, taught their converts to read and write, and had translated several books of the Bible, including the Gospel according to Matthew and the Acts of the Apostles, into Chin and had them published.'

Influential young chiefs were won over and native fears about evil spirits and cursed fields were dispelled. The Chin began to see that this new faith could raise their status in the eyes of the British Raj and allow them to hold their heads high in the presence of the lowland Burmans who had always despised them. Today, because of the seeds planted a century ago by Arthur and Laura Carson, Chin State is overwhelmingly Christian.

Popham concludes that, 'The Chin have left their savage past long behind, and thanks to Christian missionaries, they are also literate. But in the process, they have been deposited in a kind of ethnic limbo: Christians in an overwhelmingly Buddhist land, Burmese citizens who feel neither Burmese nor anything else.'

I am not sure Lincoln would wholly agree. 'Ne Win expelled all the foreign missionaries in 1967,' he says, 'but since then a vibrant and indigenous Christian faith has flourished. It is a core part of Chin identity. One of the things which binds them together.'

'So, how big is the Christian minority in Burma?'

'Apart from the Chin? Well, there are also sizeable Christian communities among other non-Burman ethnic groups such as the Kachin, Karenni, Naga, and Karen people. Overall, I'd say possibly 10 per cent. But this would be a lot lower in Mandalay and Yangon.'

Lincoln does concede however that a lot of the dynamism of the Christian faith has been lost. He shakes his head in a despairing way: 'Today, in a place like Kalaymyo, there is a church on every street corner. Sadly though, it's become a competition of who has the biggest church building, who can raise the most funds. You know, there are even some pastors who wait at the airport to solicit wealthy-looking visitors as they arrive from the overseas.'

Leah places a tray of steaming Shan tea on the low table in front of us. We all agree that religion has a habit of bringing out the worst in people. 'You know,' Lincoln says, 'throughout Burma, Muslims— and not just the Rohingyas—have long been the targets of hate speech and violence. Christians also face restrictions, discrimination, and abuse. Even Buddhists themselves who try to counter extremist Buddhist nationalism are taking a huge risk.'

'How do the Chin people fare?' April asks.

'Since the 1990s, there has been a campaign to destroy churches. Crosses built on hilltops and by roadsides have been removed. This comes from the State. Church services get disrupted. Church leaders have been assaulted and pastors conscripted for forced labour. Can you imagine, sometimes they are pressed into building Buddhist pagodas and monuments.'

Lincoln goes on to tell us that the treatment of Christians has improved slightly since Burma's transition towards democracy in 2011 but they continue to be subject to human rights violations and institutional discrimination.

April with Bible college students. The one on the right was stoned and chased out of her Buddhist village when she became a Christian

'It's because there is a close tie between religion and ethnic identity. Violations of freedom of religion or belief have always been part of the story of Burmese Christians.'

Sometimes I think that there is an intolerance towards Christians in the West, all the more perplexing given the Christian foundations to our society. But hearing this gives me another perspective.

Lincoln and his wife Leah have been our litmus test for the mood on the streets in this beleaguered city over the years. The NLD had just been able to take up their seats in government, which were won in previous elections but had never been recognized by the military junta. According to Lincoln, the cautious optimism that accompanied the change in government is fading fast:

'The NLD has precious little experience in political leadership. People on the streets are growing impatient with the lack of tangible change since the elections.'

'The benefits are just not reaching the poor,' Leah adds. 'Prices of basic food like rice and eggs or renting a property are rising far faster than wages. In the public sector corruption is rife.'

'Why?'

'Because their pay is so low.'

I hadn't realized things had got so bad. It's not easy to read the true emotions on the inscrutable public face of Yangon. I look down at a newspaper on the low table in front of us. The domestic press coverage of Aung San Suu Kyi is plentiful nowadays, no doubt an attempt by the regime to win favour.

'You know, she's losing credibility internally as well as outside,' Lincoln says, who stays abreast of international news. 'They're giving her a hard time for her apparent inaction over the Rohingya exodus.'

'Why is she so unwilling to denounce the atrocities in the Rakhine district? Or at least publicly distance herself?' This is the number one question for people we know.

'Aung San Suu Kyi cannot speak out.' For Lincoln the quandary that bothers so many is simple. 'If she does, this will lead to political reprisals from the government, and this will weaken her influence even further. On the other hand if she doesn't, she will be blamed internationally for not helping to resolve the Rohingya crisis. This is exactly what the military is hoping for. They are gambling on that because she will lose face in the West as the "poster girl" of Burma. This will enable her to be removed from power.'

He tells us that there is a strong nationalist Buddhist faction in the government. A small number of extremist monks in Yangon who are influential in carrying through anti-Islamist policies:

'She is swimming with her arms and feet tied,' says Lincoln. 'The old guards are retreating but who will take their place? The intelligentsia is leaving the country, the few educated people like doctors and university professors are going to Thailand, Philippines, Japan for better incomes . . . young people are asking questions but it seems there is no one capable of stepping into this vacuum.'

Lincoln's verdict is delivered without obvious emotion and tallies with other snippets we have picked up. The inevitability of it all brings, if anything, a sense of weariness and resignation. Although the members of the NLD are now in government, they do not hold a majority vote and still need the support of other minority parties to influence policy. A quarter of seats are block-reserved for the military. Also, for all their passion and sacrifice, they have precious little experience of government, even in opposition. What is more, hundreds of NLD sympathisers are still imprisoned and subject to torture.

As for Aung San Suu Kyi, her role as state counsellor gives her little say over internal matters like the Rohingya crisis. The heavyweight ministerial posts of Home Affairs—which include the control of the Police, Border Control, and Defence—are all held by Army officers. Based on her past writings, her staunchly pacifist Buddhist beliefs, and her singular dedication since being parachuted into the cauldron of student protest in 1988, locals are prepared to give her the benefit of the doubt. But for how long?

Aung San Suu Kyi has always been passionate about education. Whether she can receive some credit for it or not, an effective school system is beginning to be reassembled. This is badly needed. Fewer than one in ten adults have graduate-level education, although this is changing fast. Interestingly, women comprise a higher proportion of the highly educated in all regions, except among the Chin, the people group which Lincoln and his team primarily serve.

It comes as some relief from the gloom of our conversation when Leah calls us to the dining table. We tuck into a bowl of delicious *khao-swe*, a traditional noodles meal, combining chicken, coconut milk, fish sauce, fried onions, boiled egg, and lemon juice. This signature Burmese dish always puts me in mind of family occasions back in the UK, with Austin and Margaret cooking and presiding. They derived great pleasure from seeing their children and grandchildren enjoying their gorgeous food. We discuss the ingredients. April is intrigued by the Chin custom of adding a touch of fresh mint. Lincoln also has a personal penchant for a side-dish of fresh chilli which he dips in salt. He knows it's not good for his health, but Leah has given up trying to hide the dish.

Having chatted about different food ingredients and recipes for a while, which the Burmese love to do, I inadvertently plunge us back into more solemn matters.

'What baffles me, is the way the Rohingya crisis has been seized upon by the international media when many other minority groups have been systematically persecuted for decades'.

'In fact,' says Lincoln sneezing into his arm as he overdoses on raw chilli, 'ethnic cleansing started back in the late sixties with the expulsion of Indian and Chinese nationals. It wasn't reported because Burma was closed to the West and surrounding nations.'

Lincoln goes on to relate some sinister incidents, smaller in scale but as black as the night that has so swiftly descended outside. A policeman with three bars, presumed to be a sergeant, who refused to take bribes from drug lords was forced to quit his job. He and his family were later found knifed to death.

'It is so funny . . . ' Lincoln allows himself a half-smile, 'the authorities reported that he did this himself! There is a Burmese saying, "there is nothing, not even a tree, the elephant is walking for all to see".'

'I'm guessing that roughly translates as the emperor has no clothes'.

'There was this other incident,' Lincoln nods, 'concerning a prominent Muslim lawyer, U Ko Ni. His career was going well and he helped draft the constitution for the new government. His downfall was finding a flaw, a loophole in the constitution that permitted Aung San Suu Kyi to take office which the administration had to grudgingly allow.'

April and I wait as Lincoln allows the tension to build.

'After returning from a trip to Indonesia, he was gunned down in broad daylight at Mingaladon Airport. The rumour was that the CCTV cameras were conveniently turned the other way. The case remains unresolved. Of course,' Lincoln adds, 'such events go largely unnoticed in the press, but they do serve to intimidate anyone who is tempted to step out of line'.

Once again, we were having the curtain lifted on some of the less seemly aspects of this supposedly peace-loving land: deep rifts between the Bamar—the dominant Burmese people group—and other minority peoples, with brutal reprisals going back decades. An eye-watering gap between those with wealth and influence and those with no access to power. Those who have benefited from the sixty-year rule of the military junta comprise a thin top layer of generals and their families and business networks. The rest live in shabby squalor. On Friday afternoons we hear the rhythmic thud of helicopters overhead, transporting ministers back from the capital and government HQ in Naypyidaw for weekend golf in Yangon.

They live in plush homes, having negotiated advantageous deals with their business partners, and remain immune from everyday hardships suffered by their compatriots. Gated communities are springing up all over Yangon, hosting huge villas with ramshackle huts clustered against the exterior walls. The winners and the losers living cheek by jowl. Whichever index is used, it is clear that for the majority of people, whatever their ethnic background, life has been grim over the past couple of generations. The homeland April and her family left behind is beset with low wages, poor working conditions, a corrupt government, no political voice, a censured media, and is largely cut off from the rest of the world.

Now, as if the distribution of power were not already tilted enough, we are learning of further levels of injustice. According to Lincoln, it seems this Bamar-dominated Buddhist nation is struggling to become a society in which the diversity of different ethnicities and religions is respected and celebrated. Hate speech, persecution, and institutional discrimination are alive and well.

But there are chinks of light. Anna Sui Hluan is the wife of Myanmar Vice President Henry Van Thio. Born Chin and growing up in Yangon, she is a linguist, researcher, Christian preacher, and social activist, writing extensively about language, human rights, and female emancipation. In an interview, she notes that in the eighteenth and nineteenth centuries, European and American missionaries were astounded by the liberty afforded to women in Myanmar culture. During the dark days of the twentieth century, this equality was eroded and diminished through authoritarian methods, political and religious. But now a new wave of global gender activism is starting to wash over contemporary Burma, buoyed up by social media. In her doctoral dissertation, she argues that women's empowerment is supported by Christian scripture. 'It's the people that use the religion that are the problem. Religion itself teaches many good things.'

This year is the first time we have been able to teach in the new college building. It's quite a drive out of Yangon, but tremendous for the faculty and students to have their own space. The main octagonal classrooms are built on two floors, with more buildings to come. In a way, the unfinished teaching block seems to typify the ambivalence of the country. It feels like Myanmar is teetering on the brink; an enterprising project underway but the promise yet to materialize, many doorways are leading nowhere. Yes, Aung Sang Suu Kyi is in government but her hands are tied. The NLD is represented in government but still largely powerless. Working people go about their lives increasingly unhindered, but those who step out of line are summarily eliminated in broad daylight. Meanwhile, the country's most prominent Buddhist monk, Sitagu Sayadaw, is telling the military—in a sermon broadcast live on TV to over a quarter of a million people—that it is not a sin for Buddhists to kill non-Buddhists.

As electricity stutters to a halt, it seems a good time to bid Lincoln and Leah good night. April and I make our way down the road, thankful for a full moon. For the first time, we, as foreigners, are staying with a relative rather than at a hotel, without endangering our host. A sign perhaps of a slight slackening of suspicion, although April's cousin is still obliged to register us as guests with the township boss.

We say little to each other as we turn in for the night. April tends to ruminate on things internally and I have learnt not to chatter in these moments of reflection. There is a lot to process.

I wake early to a cockerel crowing, echoed by another several blocks away. In the half-light I gaze dreamily through the mosquito net at the teak paneled ceiling above us. Buddhist mantras start to chant hypnotically across sleepy streets.

A cockerel crows a third time and I wonder who has betrayed whom in Burma's murky past. Familiar household sounds begin to stir, suggesting normality. But, at a country level, I sense denial is in the air. Somewhere, a clock strikes, dogs yap, and a family argues across the road in muffled sing-song Burmese. The shadows in the yard below are still deep and secretive. For all the heady history of this land, the coming and going of colonial power, the fortunes and follies of political leaders, the ebb and flow of religious fervour, domestic life goes on. The man next door raucously clears his throat. I hear the swish of mothers bathing at outdoor stone tanks, the call of hawkers shouting their wares as they push their carts down the dusty road outside.

By 9 a.m. the children's staccato chanting of their times tables escapes through the slatted windows of a nearby school. What kind of country will they inherit, I wonder? Lincoln's college and Leah's pre-school give hope that the tide can and will turn. They are just one indigenous couple among many other dedicated civil activists, local charities, and NGOs. Orphans are being cared for, nutritional support is being given, medical education is being offered and grassroots community leadership is being developed. Perpetrators of crimes against humanity and preachers of hate have yet to be brought to justice, but it's good to know that many are working strenuously to defend freedom of beliefs and promoting interreligious harmony. Hopefully, creatures, more impressive than the blinkered elephants and far more dignified than the naked emperors, will soon be walking for all to see.

CHAPTER FIFTEEN

(2016) MUSEUMS AND MAUSOLEUMS

On this our fifth trip, we have arranged to take some time out of Yangon when the Bible school teaching is finished. For April and her sisters, Reservoir Road in Taunggyi has a special place in their collective memory. A rented bungalow up in the hills is where her parents, Austin and Margaret, escaped the desert heat of Chauk for their family vacations. For Elizabeth and April, away at boarding school in Darjeeling for much of the year, the family gathering together with their mum, dad, and younger sister Gay, each January and February was an oasis. That was in the 1950s. Now, several grandchildren later, April is curious to see what had become of her childhood haunt.

Privately, I think the chances of finding the place are low and even if we do, it will only lead to disappointment. But I keep these doubts to myself. I'm uncertain where this downbeat feeling is coming from, but it chimes with my misgivings concerning Myanmar as a whole. For all the excitement of teaching at the college in Yangon and catching Lincoln's vision for transformed rural communities, I am becoming somewhat disillusioned about the plight of its peoples. So much around us; the long history of internal conflict, the vice-like grip of the generals, the passive fatalism of most citizens, and the indifference from the international community, all this seems to stack the odds against lifting spirits and improving conditions. And while retracing steps

and chasing childhood dreams can be rewarding, I ask myself
what is the use of these backward glances to bygone days when the
present is so bleak? If anything, it simply underscores the pathos
of a once-proud nation.

Dawn breaks and we are bumping along winding roads cut
into the rust-coloured earth and valleys dense with semi-tropical
vegetation. At each town, the tea shops are busy with customers
stopping off for breakfast on their way to work. They sit on low
stools, hunched over steaming *mohinga* and flasks of tea. It is still
misty and the dark interiors of these tea shops have a secretive feel.

After a sing-song conversation in Burmese with the driver, I
am told we are heading for Inle lake today. Much photographed
for tourist brochures and magazine covers, it would be a pity not
to take in the atmosphere first-hand. The small town of Nyaung
Shwe is only an hour's flight from the choking chaos of Yangon and
a shortish taxi ride from Heho Airport. But it may as well be half a
century away. Situated in the south-west corner of the massive Shan
State which borders China, Laos, and Thailand, the majestic lake
is 900 metres above sea level and twenty-two kilometres long. It is
cooler here and the vegetation lusher. Like other ethnic groups, the
Shan people are fiercely independent, and back in the early part of
the last century, the region was relatively autonomous. Local areas
had their appointed leaders called sawbwas, who were held in almost
regal esteem. Thant Myint-U sums up this era well:

'By the 1950s the sawbwas were all men who had grown up under
British rule. Nearly all had studied at a school in Taunggyi, set on
a hilltop amidst pleasant grassy fields and run in the manner of an
English boarding school, complete with imported headmaster and
a rigorous schedule of games. Some had also gone on to university
in England and America . . . Many were seen by the British as
gentlemen who combined the best of Eastern and Western
manners, and for a few decades the Shan States seemed to enjoy
an almost idyllic peace and prosperity'.

I was intrigued to know what had become of this privileged generation, but for now, our little group had its mind on other things. After a brief barter for a 'skipper', we are sweeping up the inlet toward the main lake in a narrow skiff, seated one behind the other using umbrellas to shield ourselves from the spray and sunshine. Soon a wonderful scene unfolds before us, everything becomes more still. A wide expanse of water with a ribbon of wooden houses and Buddhist stupas just visible on the far shore. Surrounding all this, the distant Shan Hills, fading greeny-mauve into the skyline.

We pass fishermen balancing their boats with their single-leg paddles as they cast and gather their conical fishnets with nonchalant ease. Out in the middle of the lake, we navigate between acres of tomato plants, a kind of suspended aquatic garden. Then we come upon the stilted villages, simple bamboo huts with verandas and shaded interiors. Access is by water only. Narrowboats chug past, ferrying people or goods down the side waterways under makeshift bridges. We stop by one of many weaving houses. Two bamboo floors of artisans are sat cross-legged at their stations. Some women sort the lotus leaf strands and with the ingenious use of bicycle wheels, others load the threads onto looms. As bobbins spin and shuttles rifle from side to side, pedals dictate the intricate patterns and woven longyi cloths emerge almost effortlessly. It is like watching an old newsreel of a Lancashire mill, except the dyes, dazzling turquoise, deep greens, and honey-yellows, are more vibrant.

Getting up close to this colourful cottage industry is a real tonic; pulsing with enterprise, suspended above the shimmering Inle Lake, surrounded by the wild beauty of the Shan State. For a while at least, my sullen mood is lifted.

The following day we resume our search for the bungalow in Taunggyi which was buried deep in the childhood memories of Elizabeth and April. As a young distribution manager for Burmah Oil in his thirties, their father Austin travelled widely

Women weaving cloth from lotus leaf on Lake Inle

in the Shan State, leaving his young wife and children at home on Reservoir Road. On the opposite side of the road was another marooned wife, Pat, a princess married to Saw Sai, a Shan prince or *sawbwa*. He had all the trappings that went with such nobility, part of which was an English education. We had met them years before when they were staying with Austin and Margaret on a rare visit to England. I recall Saw Sai was a small, wiry figure, with large owl-like spectacles, full of fun and mischief. Sadly he had passed away in the interim and Pat now lives in Yangon most of the year with her daughter who works at the American Embassy. Sitting in Austin and Margaret's garden, Pat had been happy to tell their story:

'After the War, Aung San knew he had a mammoth task ahead of him when he returned to Rangoon. The country was economically crippled. On top of that, the various people groups within the borders of Burma were agitating for autonomy.'

I felt privileged to be hearing about such events from a different perspective. No less than a princess! Although she made no capital from her royal connections, she spoke with authority and grace.

'It is to Aung San's credit that he was able to bring three of the largest ethnic groups to the table. That was in 1947 at the village of Panglong, to the far north of the Shan States. A historic agreement between the Bamar, the Shans, the Kachin, and the Chins. The Karen were not represented.'

'It all looked so hopeful at that time for the Shan people.' Pat spoke with quiet affection about this golden era. 'Sao Kya Seng represented the Hsipaw constituency. He served as a member of the Chamber of Nationalities and was secretary for the Association of Shan Sawbwas from 1954 to 1962.'

Pat's tone became more sombre at that point and we sensed a change of fortunes.

'The Shan people saw him as one of their national leaders. The sawbwas all knew each other and had a real expectation of federal power sharing in post-Independence Burma. After the military coup Sao Kya Seng was arrested. He was last seen being taken into custody at an army checkpoint near Taunggyi.'

I later read that it was in this same town that Aung San Suu Kyi arrived in 1989. Before her house arrest, she was making trips along with a band of other democracy activists to various parts of the country. Sometimes harassed by the authorities, but enthusiastically feted by the locals, she was cementing her connection to the downtrodden people she so loved. The visit was a heartfelt and symbolic gesture in recognition of her father's legacy. On 12 February , exactly forty-two years after the Panglong Agreement, the NLD central committee renewed their declaration for democracy and Suu Kyi made a short speech to around 2,000 at the local prayer hall. Thirty years on, the people of Burma are still waiting for full democracy to come.

'For a while, the regional *sabwas* continued to rule in local Shan states,' Pat continued. 'But Ne Win saw such fiefdoms as a threat to the new government. It was the same for many other minority groups. Government soldiers systematically smashed their rule and customs. It was brutal.'

April knew about some of this history but was nevertheless shocked at what Pat was telling us. I too was appalled, but equally struck by the even-handed way in which Pat related such events. Events which brought a catastrophic halt to the benign rule of the Shan princes and, more personally, to their own lives and futures. She hadn't quite finished:

'One night in March 1962 the military came to arrest President Sao Shwe—who was Shan—at his house in Rangoon. His sixteen-year-old son, Sao Mee Mee Thaike, ran out into the compound brandishing a sword to confront the intruders. Tragically he was shot dead.'

It was with such half-remembered stories resurfacing in my head that we came to Taunggyi. An important hub in the southern Shan region, this used to be a classy town with a string of notable eateries and stores on the main street. Leafy avenues led off this main thoroughfare to desirable residential areas. In the time of the Raj and post colonial days, it offered cool and comfortable living for those who could afford it. Maybe it was recalling Pat's chilling story which recast the town in a more negative light. It felt rather soulless to me as we ambled along. However, we hadn't come for the shops and restaurants. After drawing a blank on several roads leading up the hill from the high street, April started to recognize some landmarks. Following her hunch, we finally came upon the original bungalow where the family had stayed a lifetime ago. Excitement rose as we walked up to the property. Disappointingly it now had a high perimeter wall and looked rather unlived in. My pessimism at the start of our trip appeared to be justified. It reinforced my sadness about a country which in so many ways was a shadow of its resplendent past.

As the rain began to fall, our attention turned to Pat's house on the opposite side of the road. Through the iron gates, we could see the imposing porch of a fairly substantial bungalow, set in a small compound. It looked weathered but well cared for. Inside I imagined the panelled reception rooms would once have witnessed the coming and going of friends from neighbouring states. The shrieks and squeals of young children as they played in the dappled shade of the fruit trees. While family and friends took tea on the veranda, visiting from the heat of Rangoon, the muffled chatter of drivers, servants, and cooks would have come from the kitchen as they gathered to gossip about food and local events. Now, it is empty of people but redolent with memories.

Arriving unannounced, our small party peers through the gates, dripping with raindrops. A middle-aged man approaches. It turns out to be Aye Kyaw, the housekeeper, and after a little explanation, he invites us under the porch, and then into the house. Maybe it is just relieving his boredom, but he gradually warms to this unexpected visit, especially after hearing of the close friendship between Margaret and Pat as neighbours when their children were young. Much of the original furniture is under wraps and there is a slightly musty smell to the unused rooms with their creaking teak floors. Forlorn cabinets display Shan silverware and glass-fronted bookshelves offer Penguin classics in faded orange.

From the walls, sepia photos look down at us from a forgotten era. 'Here is one of their wedding day,' Aye Kaw says, pointing to an impressive picture of a smiling Pat with Saw Sai and several princes in their grand costumes and distinctive pillbox hats with a large bow on the side.

'And here's one of Saw Sai in his younger days.' It's a fading photograph of Pat's husband. We recognize Saw Sai as a member of the field hockey team at Cambridge University. He must have been the smallest player on the pitch but what he lacked in height he apparently made up for in charm and heritage. He was the son of the first president of Burma after independence from the British in 1947 when U Nu was prime minister. Each portrait conveys an age of ease and self-assurance borne of post-Independence optimism. For a decade or so it looked as though a federal solution might hold sway.

There is no hurry and as we pause and chat I am reminded of early conversations with April's parents. Part of the Burmese middle classes themselves, they frequently reminisced about the 1950s.

'In many ways, it was a golden age,' Margaret had told us. 'There was newfound freedom, a sense of progress, and some sense of hope for the future. With the exit of Europeans, the top civil service posts were up for grabs. The pukka houses of Rangoon's Golden Valley and Windermere Park became available. We moved into Inya Myaing Road. Austin was given more responsibility at Burmah Oil. Everywhere there were ample opportunities to take on business ventures, sometimes on the coat-tails of the Indian and Chinese.'

U Nu's government sent hundreds of young men and women to universities abroad as state scholars. But, as U Myint-U notes, few of these young professionals ever had a chance to use their privileged schooling to assist their country's development. Within a decade, from being one of the most prosperous trading hubs in South East Asia, with an efficient infrastructure and an uncensored media, Burma had begun to slide into social isolation and economic decline.

So our expedition to recapture childhood memories was partially successful after all. We had found Austin and Margaret's holiday bungalow, although as Aye Kyaw informed us, it was now owned by a Chinese man who rarely made an appearance. This hardly lived up to the nostalgia. More exciting by far was our spontaneous and brief visit to the house opposite. For me, it was a moving glimpse into a past age when days were relaxed and hearts were full of hope. Pat, long since referred to as Auntie and now in her eighties, still returns alone to open up the house for two months each monsoon season. As she wanders through the rooms and hallway there must surely be a wistful sigh as she 'converses' with these ghosts from the past.

But our trip is not quite over. We cross town to visit The Republic of the Union of Myanmar Ministry of Religious Affairs and Culture, Department of Archaeology, and National Museum. Long on title, short on exhibits. The hand-printed brochure explains that 'this is a celebration of the Shan state . . . the largest state existed in the east of Myanmar and divided into three parts such as east, south, and north'. The past tense of this otherwise hardly informative statement is poignantly accurate as the building appears to consign much of the rich heritage of these peoples to history. The first exhibition room comprises glass boxed mannequins dressed in the traditional costume of the thirty or so Shan tribes. It is like an artless shop window in a closing down sale. In another room much is made of the signing of the Panglong Agreement in 1947. A picture shows General Aung San and an assortment of Shan sawbwas in full regalia along with dignitaries from the Chin and Kachin in ethnic costume. The caption declares that their states would be part of the new republic and 'reveal the desire of all Myanmar nationalities to get the independence altogether from the British'. Do I detect a sense of relief and purging in this wording? Less evident is any sense of what was to come. Yes, the colonial rulers were overthrown, but what of the promise of a unified nation state? I pick up a brochure. It boasts of 800 Shan artefacts being displayed but these rather random and shoddily presented items make me wonder where the rest of the cultural riches of these proud people groups ended up. 'A museum that should be in a museum,' as Dylan Thomas once said of the one in Swansea.

This got me thinking about the difference between museums and mausoleums. According to dictionaries, a mausoleum is an external free-standing building constructed as a monument enclosing the internment space or burial chamber of a deceased person or people. A museum, on the other hand, is an institution that cares for and conserves a collection of artefacts and other objects of permanent value whether artistic, cultural, historical, or scientific. It occurred to me that the house on Reservoir Road, which has stood for a century, bears a poignant testimony to a past age, hosting treasured belongings with enduring value. Perhaps Pat's home is unintentionally deserving of the term 'museum'. Paradoxically, I can't help feeling that the threadbare national museum, which consigns the Shan peoples to an internment space, is more of a mausoleum.

CHAPTER SIXTEEN

(2016) HISTORY IN THE MAKING

Fed by the Himalayan glaciers high up in the mountains of northern Myanmar the N'mai and Mali rivers join forces to form the Irrawaddy. Here the currents are strong and the rivers barely navigable, cascading over rocks and narrow jungle gorges. It then gathers tributary rivers like the Chindwin, which winds through Sagain Division bordering India, and the Salween and Zawgyi rivers, with their source springs to the east. The Irrawaddy then drops south through lower Burma before fanning out into a silted delta beyond Yangon into the Bay of Bengal and the Andaman Sea. On the way, it provides a means of transport and travel, a place to swim, irrigation, alluvial soil, and an opportunity to wash and worship. There are echoes here of my relationship with April. We came together from very different hinterlands, our marriage carving its course, flowing deep and purposefully. The early days were a succession of emotive eddies and roaring rapids, especially when our four daughters reached their teenage years. We argued, we taxied, we swam. We sowed, we prayed, we sang. Passing like restless clouds, the children went their separate ways and we found ourselves meandering as relative 'strangers' to each other on an unfamiliar plain.

As it happens, our youngest daughter, Mala Su is with us on this trip with a friend Kelly. This is Mala's first return visit since 1996 when she was fourteen; she is now thirty-four. We arrange to join Elizabeth and John—April's sister and brother-in-law—on an excursion up country. It is Sunday morning at Myanmar's International Mingadalon Airport, November 2016, and we await our domestic flight to Heho, the hub for the Shan states and beyond. The take-off time for flight 7Y-151 with Mann Yadanarporn Airlines comes and goes with no sign of our plane. The departure area ebbs and flows with backpackers, travel groups with their bright badges, a few smarter-looking business people, and families with cute toddlers. The display screens blink impressively with flight information except the most important column conveying 'status', which remains resolutely blank. It is only when an attendant walks between the rows of seats with a handwritten notice board that we know our plane is finally ready.

Boarding is like stepping back in time. A fifty-seater twin propeller ATR-72 with smiling hostesses and background jazz.

'This puts me in mind of the old-style movies,' I say.

'How so?' says April with a slight frown.

'You know, Humphrey Bogart in a creased white linen suit sitting alongside a cool and collected Ingrid Bergman.'

'Well you're in jeans and I'm dark, not blond like Bergman,' April says.

Sometimes I wish she didn't have to be so literal.

As I gaze at the slumbering eiderdown of clouds below with occasional glimpses of tiny dirt roads and glinting rivers, I reflect on what has happened to this nation since the hasty departure of April's family in 1964. How has such a beautiful country become so beguiling? How come so little is known about its internal machinations? It occurs to me, as the unending forests of pine, magnolia, and oak stretch out below towards the Shan Hills, that perhaps part of the explanation is geographical. The Irrawaddy basin is surrounded by a great horseshoe of highlands, with steep-sided chasms and soaring snow-capped mountains that prevent any easy access to the outside world. Perhaps, this natural topography deters outsiders and encourages the country to be self-contained?

My speculative thoughts are interrupted by the tilt of the plane banking into the small aerodrome of Heho. We are an hour and a half late, and I chuckle to myself: 'We are well behind time, but hey ho, we are here!' The taxi ride to Kalaw takes us on roads that caress the hillsides. We overtake ancient trucks minus their bonnets and overfull buses belching out a miasma of fumes. Still coming to terms with the currency I try to pay the driver Ks450,000. One too many noughts. The driver is almost shy in his non-acceptance of my unintended generosity. We had booked our stay at Thitaw Lay House ahead of time with the owner, Marc. It's not long before he tells us his story.

'I used to manage a psychiatric hospital in Belgium before a midlife crisis and divorce. It took me to Africa and now to Myanmar.'

Good preparation for running a guesthouse for disoriented adventure seekers up in the hills, I thought. His Burmese wife works as a doctor in Yangon and he is helped by a lanky local man, Mo.

'Mo will take your orders for dinners and collect what you want from a restaurant in town. For breakfast, there's home-made banana bread, cooked in the clay oven outside.' We already find ourselves de-stressing after the human bagatelle of Yangon city.

The next day we dawdle down the hill into Kalaw. We cross the railway line and the deserted platforms of an unkempt station, that wouldn't be out of place in sleepy Sussex. Walking across the grassy railway tracks, it isn't clear whether the station is operational. Although we later discover a few trains a day pull in for a twenty-minute breather on their jog up into the hills from Nyaung Shwe. It is market day, so we head for the stalls, some little more-than-a-piece of tarpaulin on the kerbside. Dried fish, fresh papaya, huge avocados, chillies of varying strength, and bunches of bright flowers are all on offer.

Following our noses, we come across street vendors frying tasty samosas, lentil bhajis, and a shop with a man making nans and parathas in front of us. April immediately feels right at home. They

Flower stall at Kalaw market

eagerly rustle up some kyats to stock up on their favourite snack foods like plantain banana crisps, salted butter beans, small green oranges, and some pickled bamboo shoots to accompany curried pork. Elizabeth and John, who have spent much of their adult lives teaching in Mexico, are equally at ease in this market environment. For Mala, Kelly and me, everywhere we look and all the aromas we walk into are novel and intoxicating.

I am almost light-headed with joy and I can't put my finger on why. Yes, the prospect of a tasty meal later. Perhaps the laid-back feel of the market. But it's more than that. Then it dawns on me that I don't sense any pressure and hassle as I do in so many other places. Prices are honest with no need to haggle. Kalaw seems to absorb a steady trickle of tourists without seeking to exploit on the one hand or ignore on the other. Smiling is reciprocated. Gleaming white smiles on brown faces streaked with *thanaka*. Everything displayed on rudimentary open shop fronts. It's like local folk are saying: 'Take us as we are'. If any sharp practice or conceit is lurking in this pleasant town, I am missing it entirely.

The warm, wet climate is well-suited to the growing of vegetables and fruit, which the locals bring into the market. Mopeds whizz by, laden with great bundles of farm produce and small motorbikes ferry whole families, toddlers on the handlebars and girls riding side-saddle at the back. A pillion passenger speeds along on a motorbike holding a pane of glass two metres square. Needs must.

We stumble upon a small compound with a western-style coffee shop and submit to a half hour of more familiar fare. A teenage lad arrives on a moped with a spurt of dust to impress the girls. To our astonishment, April runs up to him and accosts him with her best Burmese. The next minute it is smiles and photos all round. 'What was that all about?' we ask April when she returns to our table. 'Didn't you see? His eyes, his features were just like Seth's. If Seth was dark, it could have been him!' Thinking about that later it made me ponder that perhaps April, who was referring to one of our grandsons, was still in a kind of no man's land. Maybe this visit was stirring some residual ambivalence about her cultural identity.

On our second day, we receive some stunning news from the other side of the world. My lightness of spirit is rudely intruded upon.

'You won't believe it,' says Marc, as he checks in with us at breakfast. 'Donald Trump has been elected the President of the USA.'

The UK Brexit vote a few months earlier caught a lot of Europeans by surprise but, in this distant rural outpost, people are walking around in shock that Hillary Clinton has been pipped at the post in Washington. It feels like history in the making and over supper that evening we find ourselves discussing the sorry state of world politics.

'How can Americans possibly bring themselves to elect someone like that?' Marc is not just dismayed, he is angry. He is spitting feathers about all the bigotry of right wing, God-fearing fundamentalism that Trump seems to represent.

'It is incredible,' I say, 'I was convinced that Hillary would get in . . . and I think she was too. Maybe she took her foot off the gas . . . thought it was a done deal.'

'That's democracy for you,' Marc snorts.

'Yes, it just shows how arrogant politicians can become.'

'The hubris of the White House and your lot in Downing Street. The same goes for totalitarian rule here. It's not much of a choice, is it?' Marc says, waving an arm at the countryside beyond the lodge.

I don't think he expects an answer. He's right, we are quick to condemn dictators and despots in the developing world, yet sometimes *our* governments have little to commend them.

But it is the particular political context of Myanmar that continues to puzzle me. How can a nation of such benign and hospitable people, suffused with centuries of Buddhist pacifism, become a rogue state bristling with militia? One of Burma's most revered kings is Bayinnaung, who ruled nearly five hundred years ago. He is still hailed as a cult hero because he was a ruthless general who was able to weld together a nation that was naturally inclined to fracture.

'You have to remember,' says Marc, 'The highlands of Burma are one of the most linguistically diverse places in the world. Hundreds of languages, unintelligible dialects and highly independent cultures, each nestled in its own mountainside niche.'

It's taken me a while, but I am realizing that Myanmar is, in fact, several 'countries' or people groups, each with their customs, their rich lineage of local royalty, and independently minded rulers. Like many colonially dominated regions of the world, country borders were often drawn with arbitrary disregard for such local, ethnic interests. As if the right colour on the world map took care of any administrative untidiness. Burma was no exception.

'By the eighteenth century,' says Marc, happy to induct his guests, 'the kings of Burma ruled from the royal court of Ava. It needed a strong rule to keep Imperial China at bay to the north and to subjugate a landmass that today would encompass Burma, Thailand

and Laos. But, as with other subcontinents, Burma became a target
of European ambition. Then, in 1826, came the most expensive war
in British–Indian history, both in terms of lives lost and financial
cost. That was when the seeds of Burmese nationalism first began.'

Marc pauses. I wonder if he, as a Belgian, is thinking of his
own country's record in the Congo. 'At first, many benefited from
the peace and prosperity in the late nineteenth and early twentieth
century. Roads were built, trade was encouraged, an education
system was put in place. But there was never any doubt who was
benefitting the most.'

Marc swats away a mosquito. 'The Burmese civil war started in
the 1950s. It's the longest-running armed conflict in the world up to
the present day.'

Here in the relative tranquillity of Kalaw, these realities seem
remote. It is easy to forget that the Shan State, where we are staying, is
home to several armed ethnic armies. While the military government
has signed fragile ceasefire agreements with most groups, vast areas
of the state, especially those east of the Salween River towards the
Thai border, remain outside the central government's control. In
recent times this territory has come under heavy ethnic Han Chinese
economic and political influence. Other areas are under the control of
military groups such as the Shan State Army. This story is repeated
among several other people groups, including the Karen and the
Kachin bordering China and the Rohingya bordering Bangladesh.
It is perhaps not surprising that a major preoccupation of the junta
has been to subdue these rebellious factions. What is less defensible
is the heavy-handed way they have gone about this task.

The next morning the sun casts serrated shadows across the
compound as it streams through the lush fronds of semi-tropical
palms, bamboo, and banana trees that surround us. Trekkers from
France and cyclists from Holland wave as they set off for the day.
They are stopping by for a night or two, using the lodge as a base to
explore the local countryside. Many have come before. They know
Marc's place well and value the unspoiled away-from-it-all location.

Rural clinic in the Shan State

'A lot of thought went into the wooden construction of this main house and the adjoining bungalows . . . but I have to say it was frustrating,' Marc says.

'Why?'

'My designs were constantly compromised by local workmen. They were unwilling to adapt to new ways of doing things. You've no doubt found that the bedrooms have a slightly damp feel? That's because the timber floors and ceilings went in without the desired drying times. That was one of many short cuts I had to put up with.'

At a more mundane level, this seems to be an example of obstinacy leading to unsatisfactory outcomes, much like the affairs of state. Perhaps this is one national trait that is questionable. The downside of determination is an unwillingness to do things differently, a preoccupation with the present that fails to consider longer-term consequences.

Dusk descends and we decide to sit outside one of the thatched bungalows. A huge spider has been spotted in the rafters, but the risk of its reappearance and the nuisance of mosquitoes is outweighed by the serenity of sitting on the bamboo veranda, eating Burmese curry, laced with pungent fish paste.

Marc drops by with a couple of lanterns for us and stays for a beer. Recent world events continue to spark discussion.

'It seems that everywhere you look, countries are in a state of flux or out of control,' I say, with my mouth too full.

'Well we shouldn't be that surprised,' responds Marc.

'Why so?'

'Well isn't it what Karl Marx said? All societies will be dogged by a cycle of struggle, resistance, and finally, revolution. This is the natural order of things'.

I have a momentary flashback to my days studying sociology at university. A department staffed by left-wing faculty from Eastern Europe, led by the flamboyant Professor Stanislav Andreski. At that time socialism did seem an attractive option. And students believed they could change the world.

'So where do things go wrong?' I ask.

Between us, we have no trouble agreeing that nations are in turmoil. Sometimes this is triggered by irresponsible rulers, sometimes by dynamics beyond their control. Less clear to us is where all the idealism has gone.

It sounds like the fire is still burning bright for Marc. Following a mental breakdown and a failed marriage he seems to have found his niche in the Shan State, his guest house offering a place of solace and tranquillity for those weary of chasing the next deal. He and his new wife, Aye Ma, are well-embedded into the local community. He believes that little by little, things can change for the better. Less revolution perhaps, more evolution.

'Well, it's certainly taking a long time here in Myanmar. I admire your optimism in the power of community to improve conditions.' I'm surprised at how pushy that sounded, but Marc appears unoffended.

'What else is there?

'What about the possibility of a voice from the outside, some way of accessing the love and wisdom of the divine?'

'Or a voice from the inside, which is more likely given that this is a Buddhist country,' Marc counters with a flicker of a smile.

'OK, but what I'm referring to is a belief in a spiritual world, beyond our immediate senses, that inspires the human soul.' I am wishing others would join the conversation but they seem content to observe me digging a hole.

'Yes, but don't forget the material world embraces the awareness of things like beauty, joy, and love. These can be glimpsed through the arts, the sciences, and creation like this around us . . . recognizing that life is not about "me" but rather about me in some energizing relationship with something bigger.'

I acknowledge this and given the oasis he has created here in Kalaw, I can see he is living his dream. Although I wasn't expecting a philosophical discussion, I am keen to pursue my point just to see where it goes:

'How about an alternative viewpoint which invokes supernatural agencies? Okay, most of us are oblivious to this, but maybe the rise and fall of civilizations, empires, nation states are not just the result of human agency. Perhaps, alongside the messy day-to-day decisions there is an eternal plan unfolding.'

'But that explains nothing. It's fanciful. It doesn't tell us why this country has been in the grip of the military for so long.' Marc's tone is polite but sceptical.

'Maybe so. But this way of viewing history at least allows for a divine hand behind the scenes. Nations are not just spinning out of control in a moral vacuum. Maybe we are not totally at the mercy of those individuals and elites who manage to wrest control.'

'Really?'

'I know it looks that way.' I search for an analogy. 'Isn't it a bit like a horse and its rider? The horse is human agency. Sometimes graceful, often forceful, occasionally headstrong and wild. But just suppose there is a rider. A sovereign creator-God giving men and women the freedom to act yet calling them to account for how they have used their finite wisdom and brute strength'.

'Not much consolation for the political prisoners and those denied their basic human rights. Some probably not very far from here.'

'Not much, but some.'

We pause and let the cicadas fill the silence. Our discussion is good-natured but it is clear that, in terms of understanding or explaining what's going on in Yangon, in Mosul, in Washington, we are poles apart. The candles in the lanterns flutter and darkness closes in so we retire to our beds. Are those barking dogs in my head or real?

The next day Mala and I set out on a short trek to the nearby village of Myint Mathi. It's great to clear my mind of the world's imponderables. We climb gently through the forest behind Thitaw Lay House, following an indistinct path that is occasionally overgrown with bamboo shoots. I go first. Mala later tells me she was afraid of snakes. I guess she thinks I will frighten them off or get bitten first. Having walked in silence for a while, we start to talk. Since our first family visit in 1995–96, she has been untangling the threads of her family history in Burma. Meeting and spending time with her cousins of a similar age, Sweetie and Matida, on that visit made a big impression in terms of their parallel lives and life chances as contemporaries in Myanmar and the UK. We chat about fragments of memories shared by her grandparents and surviving relatives here, together with bits of political and social history she has picked up.

'You know, a lot has changed since the first time we came twenty years ago.'

'Like what?' I say.

'Things are a lot more westernized now. It's good to see less military presence on streets now and there does seem to be more freedom.'

We had spent some time in Yangon and noticed teenagers in the parks, playing music, and gathering in spontaneous groups without hindrance.

'I have mixed feelings about all this,' Mala says. 'Of course, it's great that there is greater freedom now. But there's something about young people wearing jeans rather than their traditional dress and watching Netflix. I wonder . . . I hope, they are not sliding away from what is distinctive and special about their culture.'

I see what she means and I have to agree. It's easy to assume that greater exposure to the West is a bonus for a 'developing' country when there is much we can learn from the Burmese people. The high premium placed on family and taking care of one's elderly relatives puts many of us to shame. The need to make do with what they have stimulates ingenuity and sustainability in comparison with our throwaway, environmentally reckless mindset. And, sinking deep into the parliamentary quagmire of Brexit, I'm not sure our version of democracy is particularly commendable either.

The path drops away into a valley and crosses a little brook. I'm looking up at the sun, but Mala is looking downwards for direction: her phone is showing north, north-west so we are heading in the right direction. We start to emerge from the forest into the earthy warmth of a fertile valley. Bamboo hats are bobbing at the far side of a field and we wave. Two or three women wave back, they are picking tomatoes. The next field is heavily laden with chilli plants . . . I imagine a hardy caterpillar munching its way through that. The small path gives way to an ox track, the red mud churned by the cartwheels. In the rainy season this must be impassable by foot, but today in mid-November, we are just about able to jump the puddles to small islands of dry ground. We push on to what must be the main street of the village of Myint Mathi. It is little more than a dirt track but the bamboo houses, interspersed with occasional brick-built homes, are well ordered. As one or two mopeds sweep past we arrive at a small tea shop sitting at the corner with the main road. Up a couple of steps, we are glad for the cool shade and a simple bowl of Shan noodles and Burmese tea. These automatically await customers at all the tables. Through the open door, a couple of curious boys shyly peer in. We watch locals come and go. Seemingly

Two Shan boys in Myint Mathi

unperturbed, they are going about their business, conserving their energy with efficient unrushed steps.

'Let's hitch a ride back to Kalaw,' says Mala.

In our shared fantasy, we imagine speeding along on a couple of motorbike taxis with our hair blowing in the warm wind to the soundtrack of Dire Straits. As it turns out we hitch a ride in a huge truck laden with aggregate. It snorts and splutters along at a snail's pace, barely coming out of second gear, but there is no deadline and this enforced speed limit seems a good way of winding through this verdant valley. Although it's not the Harley we hoped for, the words of 'Brothers in Arms' still have resonance: *'So many different worlds, so many different suns, we have just one world, but we live in different ones'.*

On our return to the lodge we hear more shocking news, this time much more local. We gather from Marc that the authorities have apprehended his helper Mo and he is now in jail accused of gambling. Six months 'inside' seems harsh for being found at the wrong house at the wrong time. Once again the hard edge of the military presence of Myanmar, the so-called *Tatmadaw*, encroaches. They took over a country in the early 1960s which was still finding its identity after its independence. They purged what they saw as unhelpful influences. This included ex-pats, Indian moneylenders, and Chinese merchants. They dropped English from the curriculum of all schools for a generation, with devastating effects. They nationalized prosperous industries, replacing foreigners with indigenous but untrained Burmese. They decided that the only way to quell the competing interests of the many minority people-groups was via military suppression. Perhaps Ne Win and his generals began with good intent, but it seems they soon became intoxicated with power and nepotism. Two generations later, the majority of citizens are impoverished, the leadership is discredited and the government is corrupt.

Marc has worked hard to create a haven in the hills of the Shan State and appears confident that things can change for the better in his adopted country. Sadly Marc did not live to see any such improvements. A few months later when we were back in the UK, we received news from his wife Aye Ma. He died of a heart attack while doing something he loved. Cycling. We sent her our condolences and this chapter of my book. In an understated yet warm way, she wrote back:

> 'It's all the more tragic in that he kept himself healthy and fit. Thank you for your kind words and giving strength, I really need those for going through this difficult time. I read your texts and those are fine. Please go ahead your process for this book . . . I can see him again through your writing, so thank you for this.'

A little while later, Aye Ma wrote again:

> 'Our night guard, Mo is back to our BnB after twelve months in prison. He is taking care the security, gardening and taking care for take away

for guests in evening. He including all staff are working very hard as
Marc was with them before and they wants to keep the quality and
comfort for guests as Marc run the BnB. By the way, Thitaw means
forest, Lay means little. Little Forest house is the name of our place.'

Leaving Kalaw behind, like a treasure trove of bitter-sweet memories, we are in the air again. This time taking a broad sweep down towards Yangon. For a while the Irrawaddy comes into view, uncoiling like a huge brown serpent. The wonder of geography and the menace of politics seem to fuse.

'*We are what we have been becoming.*' I mumble, half to myself.

'What's that?' says April, dozing with her eyes still closed.

'Oh it's an adage that psychologists are fond of using.'

'What does it mean?'

'I'm not sure. I suppose it's like saying that we don't just arrive fully intact at a certain point in our lives. Rather, the person I am today—the good, the bad, and the ugly—has been steadily accumulating from a long way back.'

'. . . and?'

'Well, yes I guess we are all the sum of our past parts—you, know, the highs and the hurts—but do we have to be locked into this path? Surely, the cycle can be broken, bad stuff can be unlearned.'

'Like the river, you mean . . . it can be redirected?'

'Exactly. Isn't that liberating? To think that things don't have to stay the way they currently are . . .'

'. . . I've always thought that,' April interrupts, slightly taking the wind out of my newly hoisted sails. 'I believe people can change. If I didn't I wouldn't do counselling. Some people stay passive and fatalistic. Victims if you like. Others dig deep to create a different future . . .'

April is now fully awake and gazes out across the vast tracts of forest. '. . . they may look for that energy from within. Some will call out to their Maker.'

'Well,' I pause, ' . . . if human beings can change, it's got to be true for a collection of human beings, like a whole nation. As you say, people differ on how this takes place, but surely wrongs can be righted. Despots can be confronted. The unhelpful stuff we have been steadily accumulating over time, from way back.'

'Up-river, so to speak.'

'Exactly. That doesn't *have* to determine the future. We all have a part to play in changing things for the better. No matter how small. Each of us is making history.'

The steward collects our plastic cups and hands out boiled sweets. April and I fall silent, cocooned in our respective hopes, doubts, confusion. For me especially, but also for April in many respects, the last few visits to Myanmar have successively dented the romantic veneer of Burma past. Indeed a reality check. As the plane prepares to descend, we can make out little knots of people in the scattered towns and villages below us, going about their daily chores.

SECTION 3

HOPE

'It is not power that corrupts but fear. Fear of losing power corrupts those who wield it and fear of the scourge of power corrupts those who are subject to it . . . [. . .] . . . The quintessential revolution is that of the spirit, born of an intellectual conviction of the need for change in those mental attitudes and values which shape the course of a nation's development'

Aung San Suu Kyi *Freedom from Fear* (1991:180, 183)

CHAPTER SEVENTEEN

(2017) BORDERLANDS

For me, the afterglow of meeting April's family and the wonder of first exchanges with Burma had long since been eclipsed. On recent journeys, April and I had come face to face with some of the ugly realities of this secretive country. No wonder she had been reluctant to return to the Burma of her childhood when we initially planned a family visit back in 1995. Better perhaps to have left that attic undisturbed, to have let the language lie dormant and to have left her memories unsullied by Myanmar's sad slide towards national obscurity. Yet, alongside the desperate poverty and the blatant injustices of a fractured land, we have also encountered glimmers of hope: cousin Monty and Noe Ley's account of that man of principle, U Thant, now being rehabilitated in the annals of twentieth-century Burmese history; Aunty Pat's stories and Taunggyi home, keeping alive the proud heritage of the Shan peoples; the strong Buddhist core of compassion and non-violence explained by Uncle Abu and U Ba Than among others; Lincoln and Leah with their shoe-string college aiming to give pre-schoolers and young people a start in life; Marc and his eco-friendly lodge in the hills of Kalaw. And, threaded through countless conversations during our visits to Myanmar: the genuine, uncorrupted kindness of so many ordinary people, who—despite all the privations of daily existence—continue to be helpful and hospitable.

In her book *Freedom from Fear*, Aung San Suu Kyi expresses a belief that the people of Burma would, one day, achieve democracy and make it work for the good of the nation. She adds that she found the great majority of students she had met to be brave and resourceful and predicted that they would play an inspiring role in this nationalist movement. Three decades on, Myanmar is still tottering unsteadily towards democracy, but if there is hope for the nation, much of it may well come from students. In particular, young people who, as graduates, left Myanmar for crucial parts of their education, before returning to give back something to the country that had treated them so shabbily.

Prospect Burma is a charity set up for this purpose. They began life in 1989, following the pro-democracy uprising in Myanmar the previous year. Over thirty years, they have worked to help create a peaceful, democratic future for Myanmar. Though the scope of what they do has grown over time, their commitment to helping talented and dedicated young people from Myanmar to access vital skills and education remains. When Prospect Burma first started, their work focussed on supporting refugees who had been forced to flee the country. For a while from around 2000, I attended their trustees' meetings and we have supported the charity consistently since that time.

They began raising funds for books and classes in refugee schools and awarded one annual scholarship to an exiled student from Myanmar to attend university. This then grew to supporting more Burmese students in their graduate and postgraduate studies abroad. Much of the funding came from the Nobel Peace prize which was awarded to Aung San Suu Kyi in 1991. From their early days when it was started by Evelyn Aris—Suu Kyi's mother-in-law—Prospect Burma has grown exponentially and is now operated by a few dedicated staff from offices near Victoria Station in London. For April and me, their focus on providing higher education to students from Myanmar is close to our hearts and a precious investment in the future of the country. To date, they have awarded over 1,700 scholarships.

One recipient April and I are keen to meet is Kamaylar. She was born in rural Kayah State in 1986, to farmer parents. Kayah State is historically known as Karenni State. The so-called Red Karen, who take their collective name from the red-coloured clothing, live in the smallest of the seven designated 'ethnic' states on Myanmar's current political map. The local people have been trying in recent years to rebuild their communities following six decades of civil war. Like other ethnic nationalities in Burma, they have faced political deadlock and their ancestral lands and natural resources have been grabbed by the government.

We are on our way to meet Kamaylar who lives in Loikaw, one of the bigger towns in Kayah State. The road cuts through deep valleys and skirts rivers, which sometimes flow rapidly with ice melt from the mountains and now, in the dry season, wind languidly between wide, muddy shores dotted with narrow boats. These waterways form natural borders and delineate important cross routes between the Karen, Shan, and Bamar states.

As twilight approaches, we pull off the dirt road to absorb the view opening up before us. Distant mountains are a watercolour wash of gentle mauves, receding range after range until they finally fuse with the violet hues of the evening sky. As we stretch our legs, our driver gestures to the rocks around us.

'Many precious metals here,' he says, kicking the ground with his flip flops as if the gold, tin and tungsten might just come to the surface. 'And the hillsides . . . in my father's day these were full of teak trees. The rivers, they are perfect for hydro-electric power.'

He goes on to explain that many of these resources have been depleted during decades of conflict. He paints a complicated picture of different armed groups appropriating shares of the natural spoils during the fighting. On top of that, Thai logging companies have cleared large areas of forests in areas adjacent to the border with Mae Hong Son province. As if to echo the loss, ten minutes of twilight vanishes and suddenly we are in darkness.

The following morning we catch up with Kamaylar for an early breakfast on a side street just off the main drag of Loikaw. The town is dominated by a Buddhist temple with intricate wooden carvings, multiple gilded domes, and a narrow spire that pierces the azure sky, a petit umbrella—known as a *hti*—at its tip. For all this impressive Buddhist superstructure, we gather from Kamaylar that the majority of Karenni are Christians, mainly Baptist and Catholic. As we wait for the bowl of steaming mohinga to cool a little, I mention to Kamaylar a study I had come across by Amnesty International. In 1997 they reported serious human rights abuses were taking place with counter-insurgency operations against ethnic armed organizations in the Karen, Kayah, and Shan States in eastern Myanmar.

'Apparently, civilians were subject to arbitrary killings, forced portering and labour. Their homes and property were being destroyed as the Tatmadaw moved through their villages on patrols. Is this still the case?' I ask.

'Things have improved,' she says. 'There have been positive steps, especially since the ceasefire in 2012. Long-divided communities travel more freely now and talk together. But still many thousands from Kayah State remain in refugee camps in Thailand. Few dare go back to their home villages. Years of conflict have led to desperate poverty.' She pauses and sighs, 'Trust takes a long time to rebuild.'

A posh-looking Toyota Land Cruiser clears its throat as it trundles by.

'That's another problem,' Kamaylar says, looking down the street at the plume of dust. 'The Karenni are losing out to outsiders.'

'Who are they?'

'The Chinese, Muslims, the Bamar. They are the richest people around here . . . these big houses and shops in Loikaw, they all belong to the Chinese. We don't have native people who are rich like this.'

As we tuck into the delicious soup, Kamaylar begins to relax and chat freely. She knows we are supporters of Prospect Burma in the UK, so she is more than happy to tell us her story.

'I completed my undergraduate degree in 2013,' Kamaylar says, 'and decided to continue my studies in education. I applied for and received a Prospect Burma scholarship to take a Master's degree in Educational Administration at Assumption University in Bangkok'.

Education in Myanmar is still heavily restricted, so she decided to undertake this particular area of study: 'I can set an example to the young villagers of how much they can achieve and succeed by completing their studies. I wanted my thesis to be used to serve teachers in Myanmar and those working here in my hometown of Loikaw. My research showed that even though commitment is very high, most teachers are not satisfied with their job.'

Kamaylar volunteered for a year alongside her studies, teaching English to Burmese migrant workers living on the Thai–Burma border areas as part of the Overseas Karen Refugees Social Organization.

'Now I've completed my studies, I bring my skills and experience back to my home town of Loikaw. Right now, I am working for the Mines Advisory Group, an NGO that works with people who have been affected by landmines. This saves lives.'

Kamaylar excuses herself for a few minutes to greet the restaurant owner. This is her local eatery. The sun is beginning to bake the street and we are glad for the deep shade of the awning. I start to muse on the voluntary work April and I have been involved in, mainly in the UK, through churches and in various communities over forty years. Sitting in front of us, we have often encountered those in darkness and despair: some in severe debt, some with mental illness, those whose marriages are disintegrating, some with disabling pain, and more. The 'border' has not been as visceral as that between Thailand and Burma, the territory rarely a matter of life and death. Nevertheless these people were on borders of their own. Many living on the edge . . . between being accepted and rejected, between keeping it all together and falling apart, between hope and an abyss.

'What are you thinking about?' April says. When I tell her, she frowns. I'm not sure she approves of the comparison I'm making.

'Kamaylar's providing mine-risk education to people living on
territory littered with unexploded ordnance . . .'

I have to agree that our situations back home incurred nothing like
the risks and danger faced by Kamaylar, yet the anxiety experienced
by those on the receiving end often shook them to the core.

Maybe I will fly that kite with April later. I turn my attention to
Kamaylar who has returned to the table. We each discuss our plans
for the day. Kamaylar has a class to teach and we have some exploring
to do. As we prepare to leave, her face lights up. 'Actually, I have a
bigger plan than that. I want to work in an organization to benefit
my people and my nation . . .' she says, her face a picture of resolute
determination, ' . . . to identify issues of educational significance to
the public . . . I am strong enough to struggle towards my ambition.'
As April and I jump into a tuk-tuk taxi, we *do* agree on one thing.
We have no doubts she will succeed.

Another Prospect Burma alumnus is Taing Saing San, now
known simply as Sasa. He was born in Lailenpi village in the Chin
State to parents who had received no formal education. Like many
local families they couldn't read or write, and to this day Sasa doesn't
know his birthdate. He attended the village school, a small bamboo
structure which the students shared with livestock.

'The first job in the morning,' he says' 'was to clear out the cow
poo. There was no uniform, we just had hand-me-down clothes
from older siblings. No books. We used large stones as notebooks
with smaller coloured stones as pens and pencils.'

The Chin Hills, rising to 3000 metres in some places, consist
of a mountainous range dividing Myanmar from Bangladesh and
India. Unlike most of Burma it is cooler here, with frost on winter
mornings, snow-melt feeding rivers which flow north to south
through jungle-clad hills. Frequently these hills are wreathed in a
smoky mist, giving them a secretive look. Traversing this terrain is
laborious and sometimes treacherous.

'It was five days to a supermarket,' Sasa recounts, 'so mum and
dad would take us to their fields. Rice, corn, pumpkin. If we were

lucky we'd climb a mango tree and eat the fruit. We'd pick avocados, apples, cherries and pears.'

He recalls that there was no local knowledge to treat even simple ailments and accidents, like help for a child who broke their arm falling from a tree. There was a time when his friend was sick with pneumonia. 'With no doctors or medical centres, we had no option but to take it in turns to carry him across the guarded border to India. A trek of six to seven days. Sadly as we were wading across one river, the friend was lost in the torrent.'

I gasp inwardly at the unfairness, the injustice of this loss.

'One year when I was still young, a friend of my mother's died in childbirth, and three of my friends contracted diarrhoea and tragically died on the same day.

'That must have been heartbreaking.' April responds with heartfelt empathy.

'It was a turning point for me,' Sasa says, 'no one, at this time in human history and in the development of healthcare, should die because they don't have access to simple medicine. I realized then that education is the only way to save our people.'

With no local high school Sasa had to travel further afield. He went to Yangon to study which was something of a culture shock. Coming from a small village in a very rural area he had to have his wits about him, like how to cross a busy road and how to take a bus. He returned home when he completed his high school education.

'That was it. I couldn't continue studying because the military government had closed all the colleges in 1997. What I noticed after arriving back home was that my friends were missing the basic medical information I had been learning. For the next two years I became their informal teacher, introducing them to simple hygiene like washing hands to prevent disease.'

'What were your plans at this time?'

'I was thinking more and more about how I could contribute and help rural communities by providing them with basic healthcare knowledge. This, I thought, would make a huge difference to their quality of life.'

Across the border in India a new college opened. Teaching himself Hindi and English, Sasa walked across the mountains to continue his studies. From there, he went to Armenia for further studies at university, which meant another new country and another new language. Back at home, his mother cried many tears and his father offered up many prayers during his seven-year absence. It was a huge sacrifice for all the family.

'I couldn't afford the university fees and I was asked to leave. When I was in Delhi, some friends told me about an organization that provided scholarships for Burmese students to study abroad. Thanks to Prospect Burma, I was able to go back to Armenia to continue studying medicine.'

'Sounds like a special moment?' April says.

'Yes,' he says with a smile in his dark eyes, 'life began to change in ways I couldn't have imagined. I was introduced to a key donor and contacts from the UK. I was invited to spend Christmas with Baroness Cox and stayed on for a month in London meeting many influential people including doctors and Members of Parliament. During my degree I spent my holidays in London on clinical placements. In 2008 I was introduced to HRH The Prince of Wales, who later became the patron of Prospect Burma.'

'It was such a surreal experience,' he says, 'to go from this tiny village in Burma to meeting a future king just a few years later.'

However all this was rudely interrupted by an unusual crisis back home. Every forty-eight years India and Burma experience the blossoming of bamboo. The bamboo flowers *en masse*, producing a protein-rich fruit. The problem is that this fruit is a favourite menu item for local rats. In 2005 the flowering started in north-east India, and as it travelled down across India and into the Chin State in Burma, the rat population grew and followed the bumper crop of bamboo. In 2008 there was a huge increase in rat population, decimating crops resulting in a famine.

Dr Sasa at his Health and Hope Training Centre, Chin State

'I was in England at the time and managed to secure vital medicine to take back. When I got there, I distributed medicine and met with local people to offer treatment. As the only trained medic in the area, I was overwhelmed with patients, and at the height of the famine, I was treating up to 500 people a day. I stayed for three months, trying to treat as many people as possible and contending with regular visits from the military.'

After he finished his studies and graduated as a doctor, Sasa tells us he decided that the best thing he could do to help was to enable a new generation of Burmese to become doctors. To bring the necessary skills into the community.

'I decided *multiply himself*,' Sasa announces, quickening his pace to match the events he is describing. 'I called a meeting for village leaders from surrounding areas to come and receive health training, and over 400 attended. They were trained in hygiene, better nutrition and water safety. Basic health interventions that could have a massive impact on people's health and well-being.'

'What happened?'

'Well, hundreds of villagers came together. I was the only qualified doctor in the whole Chin State.'

There is no trace of boast in Sasa's words. More a sense of collective achievement.

'They had donated everything from chickens to cows to fund my medical studies. Now they brought nails, timber, aluminium to help build a training centre. So it was we who launched the region's first primary healthcare service, called Health and Hope.'

We gather that hundreds of health workers from over 500 villages have graduated from the six-month training course. The organization also now runs an educational scholarship programme to support the next generation of leaders in Chin State. It has expanded its health work to support the training of Traditional Birth Attendants and continues to respond to the critical issues of food insecurity and malnutrition across the region.

'How does it work?'

'It's a participatory approach to healthcare. Villages from across Chin State and beyond each send one man and one woman to Health and Hope. After the training at the residential centre, they return to their villages. Here they introduce basic healthcare practices. Preventative health education as well as essential medicines, vitamins and relief for illnesses formerly left untreated and helping with prevention.'

'So your father's prayer really has been answered,' I say, 'and your mother's tears were not in vain.' That evening I look at a picture of my father with me on his knee, a photo taken about the time that the welfare state was being introduced in Britain. I think of the ready access to doctors, hospitals and schools that we and our family have enjoyed all our lives. The final words of Sasa stay with me:

'The one who is free should help those who are not free.'

April and I are disarmed by the courage of Kamaylar and Sasa, young people the same age as our daughters. Their particular projects target differing needs in very different rural areas of Myanmar: education and training, mine risk instruction, community health care. However, we are struck by some common features. Both refer to the importance of early experiences, in many cases harrowing, and the influence of family members in forging their values. Both had the opportunity to receive education outside their country, which proved a significant springboard in giving them expertise in their professional fields. And perhaps most poignantly, both have chosen to return to their homeland to pass on their experience and invest these skills for the next generation.

It would be tempting to dismiss these as isolated cases of self-sacrifice and dedication which have little purchase against the monolithic problems facing Myanmar. Indeed many are pessimistic about the fate of the ethnic peoples and believe much more work is required on the socio political front. This is the view of Martin Smith, a long-time Burma watcher and co-author of a searching report on the current situation facing Kamaylar's people, the Karenni in Kayah State. We met up with him in London at a Prospect Burma event.

'It is only when ethnic groups are able to participate in decision-making on local projects that affect their lives that trust can begin to be rebuilt. There needs to be a moratorium on mining, logging, hydropower, and other intrusive businesses until political reforms are agreed.'

'Surely, with the landslide victory of the National League for Democracy in the 2015 elections, there is cause for hope?' I said.

Martin was less sanguine. 'The NLD appear to believe they have won national legitimacy. They're not showing much inclination to negotiate with other parties, whether armed, electoral or civil society.' This is not the first time I had heard this. I recall Lincoln voicing similar reservations.

'Since the NLD leadership assumed office,' Martin added, 'their main concern appears to have been accommodation with the Tatmadaw's objectives, rather than seeking political reform. Some of the blame also lies with the ethnic nationality forces. As so often in the country's recent past, they are not united . . . they have yet to achieve a common platform or negotiating position that brings all parties together.'

Martin's report traces sweeping and systematic attempts by the Tatmadaw to prise the Karenni from their homelands. First a *Phyat Lay Phyat*, or Four Cuts, programme was initiated in the mid-1960s. This was a sustained military strategy designed to cut the four key links between civilians and armed groups: food, funds, intelligence, and recruits. Then, between 1988 and 2000, amidst widespread evidence of forced labour, arbitrary arrests, and extrajudicial executions, an estimated 30,000 civilians were forced to leave their homes. The current prognosis, two decades later, does not seem hopeful. Ceasefires and peace conferences come and go. The promise of political rights and reform all signal good intentions. But these overtures will mean little to any of the minority peoples until internally displaced persons are returned to their homes with safety and dignity. The message I got from Martin is that the humanitarian impasse in the 'borderlands' cannot be de-coupled from the continuing political crises within the country at large.

He is right, of course. But while there is an undoubted need for radical shifts of thinking at a state level, April and I are stirred by the power of individuals following their community dreams. This dedication cannot be overestimated. From our conversations, it is clear that these young graduates have a special bond with the people and places where they grew up. Sometimes the well-resourced interventions of international agencies misread what is needed in local situations of need. And sometimes, as Nigerian writer Chika Unigew notes, a 'white-saviour' narrative has the effect of undermining or invalidating the impact of locals working in their communities. Inadvertently this reinforces the stereotype that native residents have no agency and are unable to help themselves. But people like Kamaylar and Sasa are quietly breaking this myth. Their empathic understanding of both the local culture and the wider political landscape renders them well-suited to make a deep and lasting restorative impact.

Perhaps there is hope for the minority peoples of Burma, that they will one day receive recognition from the government. For a decade or so following Burma's independence in 1948, several presidents from different ethnic backgrounds led the new country. The first was Sao Shwe Thaike, from the Shan State. Then a Bamar, Dr Ba U followed by the Karen, Mehn Win Maung. The fourth president was a Kachin, Sama Duwa Sinwa Naung. In those heady days of an experimental statecraft, there seemed to be a chance of some kind of federal solution. But since the military coup of 1962, the ruling Bamar people have refused to recognize the ethnic populations within their borders. For all their proud history and distinct subcultures, they have been consistently excluded from political processes, forced to leave their lands and abandon their livelihoods. Despite living on the edge, being deleted from the map, these peoples have retained their intuitive ideal of home.

CHAPTER EIGHTEEN

(2017) MAGIC

We are on the way to Mae Ya waterfall. It's about two hours by car out of Chiang Mai, that meeting point for trekkers and melting pot of cultures, halfway between gridlocked Bangkok and the porous border with Burma. April and I are glad to be heading east rather than north to the grim anarchy of those borderlands. Mary is driving. She is a little unusual. As Lincoln and Leah's middle daughter she belongs to the Chin ethnic tribe, but she has been educated outside Myanmar and describes herself as a third-culture kid.

'This alters my view,' she says, 'on Chin people, Burmese people, and the wider world. I feel like I don't belong to any group, even though technically Myanmar is my passport country and Chin is my tribe.'

Resembling the intricate patterns of the ever-present longyi, embroidered within the cultural fabric of Burma are colourful threads of myth, morality, and magic. Meanwhile, education has been sorely neglected. It could be argued that the opposite is true of the West; the enlightenment of education has trumped spirituality, and the oaks of folklore have long been uprooted. But maybe as 'developed nations' we have our own brand of superstition and the esteemed education of our universities sometimes misses the mark.

Having made our sixth trip to Yangon to work alongside Lincoln and Leah, April and I decided to break the flight home by taking a three-day stay with Mary, her brother, and her sisters, on our way home from Myanmar. We have known Lincoln and Leah's children a while and we always feel so alive when we're in their youthful company: their impish sense of humour, their ability to mimic different Asian accents, their refreshing outlook on life. There is a gentle parental expectation that each of them will help out at the College in Yangon, but, as yet in their own way, each is successfully procrastinating.

So far, they've taken us to their favourite eateries, we've climbed the sacred temple mountain of Wat Phra but, thankfully, avoided the elephant rides. Today's a relaxing day, as we leave behind the fringes of the city, and paddy fields come into view.

'I'm just me,' Mary proclaims as we set off, 'and I don't quite fit in any of the people-groups. My views and cultures clash quite a bit. It's quite sad really.'

The new shoots of rice are a lush lime green and almost iridescent, stretching a kilometre back from the road to low slung huts of occasional villages wreathed with wood smoke.

'Nine out of ten people in Myanmar are Buddhists. You just have to look at some of the auspicious occasions in the Burma calendar. It's an intriguing fusion of astrology, animism, and Buddhist beliefs. Take *Tazaungmone*.'

'Take what?'

'Sorry, that's November, it's regarded as a special time of year: it is the month when the Kyat-ti-Kar planet dominates the sky and all the stars of the zodiac shine brightest . . . it's also the month of many heart-warming festivals for the venerable monks of the Order of Sanghas. Everyone gets involved, old and young. Lay disciples donate new saffron robes to the monks to replace those worn out by the rains. Of course, this brings special merit to the donor . . . '

'So it's win-win'.

I wasn't intending to be facetious, but Mary shoots me down with a quick sideways glance.

'It's also the month when it is believed that celestial spirits and guardian angels smile on earthlings and herbs are blessed with added potency.'

Buddhist temples grace most villages

Mary breathes in the fresh air from her open window, as if the scents of these herbs can be detected. 'Especially cassia buds. They have medicinal qualities. Because they're bitter, they are mixed with sesame, groundnuts, fried garlic and sesame oil.'

'Ahh, sounds so good,' chips in April from the back seat, recognizing the ingredients from our kitchen cupboard back home.

'If taken on the full moon,' Mary adds, in a semi-serious tone, 'their medicinal value is believed to be most potent.'

'Do you go along with all this?' I ask, but Mary is distracted by an annoying truck loaded with huge logs in front of us. Wilful deforestation is rife in northern Thailand.

Guarding the entrances to many pagodas and temples I've noticed *chinthes*, mythical lion-like beasts, which are a symbol of Burmese iconography and used on many revered objects. My mind drifts back to Yangon. Propped up against the entrance to many Buddhist pagodas, stalls tout clairvoyance, palm-reading, astrology, and fortune-telling. A strange mix of spirit worlds, dark occultism rubbing shoulders with the pure-mindedness of Buddhism. Maybe, in a state wracked by uncertainty and fear, it's a case of covering all options or feeding all insecurities. As well as being devotees of Buddha, most Burmese are also careful to keep the spirits happy. I am intrigued by the so-called *nats* which are believed to inhabit special places like trees and houses.

'Nats are taken quite seriously,' explains Mary. 'Annual festivals are held to keep them happy. Devotees make offerings to gain future favours. Maybe for the well-being of the family, for success in business, for luck in an examination, for a job interview.'

Is it strange to find educated Burmese holding such strong beliefs that date back to before the arrival of Buddha? Probably not. I recall Aung San Suu Kyi saying that Buddhism demands extreme self-reliance from the individual. In Buddhism, there are no gods to whom one can pray for favours or help. One's destiny is decided entirely by one's actions. While accepting the truth of this, she notes that most people find it difficult to resist the need to rely on supernatural powers, especially when times are hard.

'I recount to Mary what Hsar Doe Doh,' a Karen Christian had told us, 'the spirit is very much alive and well in Myanmar. Having befriended many Karen animists in the areas where I am working, I am learning many things about animism and its spiritual practices. These beliefs are central to the survival of our Karen identity. They extend to clothes, musical instruments, poetry, everyday practices. Even managing and preserving the environment.'

'Talking of clothes,' Mary says, 'I have a funny memory of when I was growing up. I got into really big trouble because I hung the *htamain*, a female sarong, in front of the house to dry in the sun. Apparently, we're not supposed to hang them in front of the house but can only do it in the backyard where it's not visible to the public. I still remember it to this day.'

She smiles and frowns at the same time. 'People don't mind hanging the male longyi in the front but it's a serious matter for the female *htamain*! Also, I remember as a kid, while I was playing around, I ran under it and I got quite a big scolding from an elder. Another thing I had to learn quickly . . . it's a disgrace to walk under female *htamain* that is hanging up. To me, it was just "clothes on the line". It's just a piece of clothing, nothing serious. But I guess that's not how it works in the culture.'

Mary sees April's expression in the rear-view mirror. 'I guess you think all these practices are just empty superstition?' After a long pause, and while April is wondering how to respond, she answers her own question: 'For sure, these kinds of beliefs and customs belong to what you might call a pre-modern world. I don't suppose they have much relevance or credibility today. In some ways, they may even be misleading and unhelpful.'

Mary seems to be processing her thoughts as she speaks and I don't want to interrupt. What's going through my mind is quite different. In my encounters with Burmese people, I have been struck by the measure of respect afforded to monks, to elders, to teachers, to parents. And, in many instances, a healthy attitude towards the environment, if only to appease the *nats* and avoid natural calamity. If this is the product of long-held beliefs and customs, then who am I to argue?

It may seem old-fashioned to give alms to monks or for Mary to address me as uncle but I am not going to object and I am impressed with the respect given to teachers. In one household in Yangon, the teenage daughter went to the entrance to receive a visitor in the little front room reserved for the Buddhist shrine. She was giving a small gift to her teacher as a mark of gratitude. It was more than an empty ritual. Given the classroom battle zone often experienced by teachers in Western schools, this act of humility seemed quite enlightened. It also occurs to me that home spun knowledge about the healing properties of different plants, herbs and spices demonstrates a very healthy appreciation of the natural world. A kinship and wisdom far removed from most of us 'first-world' hypochondriacs who pop pills and consume medicines at will. Most of us make little connection between their healing properties and their origin found in herbs and plants.

Mary is waiting for a response to her pronouncement on superstitious beliefs.

'Well,' April replies finally, 'you're right. We in the West have developed a high degree of cynicism towards this particular brand of spirit-world. When I was growing up in Burma I was looked after by nannies and servants with beliefs in the spirit-world. I just accepted and went along with it. There was no detriment.'

'But I detect some pushback,' I add. 'Some people in the West are now saying that rubbishing the supernatural leaves us poorer. Spiritually impoverished, if you like.'

Mary bridges two worlds. On one hand, the traditional, semi-mystical world of her childhood in the Chin Hills and being raised by Lincoln and Leah, Chin Christian parents. On the other, she has encountered the postmodern discourse of Western campuses. It's as if she is wearing cultural bifocals.

'I can see the place of animist beliefs and ancient folklore,' she says. 'Just look at the havoc disaster caused by the likes of Cyclone Nargis in 2007 and the monsoon rain causing mudslides in the Chin Hills last year. In times like this, you need something to buffer you against such devastation, some way of explaining what's going on. But I've also sat through my fair share of lectures that put such disasters down to climate change.'

'Maybe the two worlds are closer than we think. Take my work. I have designed and delivered a lot of training courses for managers. Sometimes I have paused to consider what I am doing.'

April, who has heard all this before yawns and Mary stifles a laugh. Undeterred, I continue:

'No seriously. It's not possible to draw a straight line between training and improved performance in the workplace. It's not that simple. Yet, this does not stop employers spending vast sums on training their leaders. In a way, I have based a career on this imagined and hoped-for link.'

'How can you live with yourself?' Mary asks rolling her eyes in mock indignation.

'Don't get me wrong, I believe in the value of well-thought out and well-delivered development programmes. But the bottom line impact is difficult to prove.

'Surely we have to make some assumptions or we'd never get anywhere?'

'Okay. Of course. It's just the way businesses trot out all sorts of clever reasons to justify their actions . . . '

' . . . and then feed all these variables into a computer model which predicts corporate success,' Mary says, mimicking the Australian accent of her university professor.

'You've got it. There's no doubt the levers are slightly more sophisticated but surely they still amount to best guesses. Superstition, if you like. They may be more elegant, but are they not still like your "clothes on the line"?'

Traffic has eased and we are now humming along on the open road. I look across at Mary. Her jet-black hair is long and wavy, blowing in the breeze of the open window. She has the nut-brown complexion characteristic of the Chin people and a wide vivacious smile. She is stunningly beautiful. She is also very alone. Neither in her parent's world nor fully in that of her peers. She has the benefit of not being captive to either, but where does she belong? I ask her about her feelings towards Myanmar.

'One thing that stands out to me. What I enjoy most about my home country is food. Because we're surrounded by countries like India, China, Thailand, we have so many types of food available to us in Myanmar. The different ethnic tribes also offer such a variety of food options which are super awesome and fascinating!'

I am no longer surprised when I hear Burmese nationals waxing lyrical about food and cooking. It's not unique to this country, I know, but hospitality based on delicious home-cooked meals is buried deep in the Burmese soul.

She pauses. 'You know, some things annoy me about my home country as well. Littering. Everywhere you look around town, there's always rubbish. It's either rubbish lying around or it's the red spit from the betel nut. It's disturbing and quite sad. That we weren't taught the importance of cleanliness or that we can't abide by the rules. It frustrates me so much!'

'And, ten years from now . . . what do you hope to be doing?' I ask.

'Ten years from now? Hmmm, there are quite a few things I'd like to achieve! I'd love to be in Yangon, helping out with admin at my parents' Bible college. No teaching at all, just admin work, and hopefully do some business along the side. I want to specialize in training young adults in either cooking, baking, card making, anything that would help them be independent in their future while also at the same time teaching the love of Jesus.'

She pauses, her face brightening at the prospect. 'Later I'd hopefully open up a café or a restaurant or some tourist attraction like a cooking school, so that all the youngsters who were at the project can have a job opportunity at these places.'

'Sort of bringing two worlds together,' I declare. I marvel at her positive energy but there's something still niggling me about our earlier conversation. 'You know what irks me about Western superstition. The dodgy belief that economic growth and free markets will guarantee a fairer, happier, more equal society.'

'There are lots of places where this *has* happened . . . '

'Maybe, but lots where it hasn't. To top it all, we then have the arrogance to export it! We offer this somewhat suspect form of capitalism as the proposed solution for struggling regimes like that of Myanmar. You know, in the US there's this political theorist called Francis Fukuyama . . . '

'I did an essay on him, didn't he write *The End of History* or something like that . . . ?'

'Yes, and others. He has created quite a stir. Well, he looks at Indonesia and Malaysia. He sees them as encouraging precedents, as kind of case examples to prove that this model works.'

'Do you go along with this?' Mary is genuinely curious.

'I'm dubious. There's a guy working for human rights and environmental justice in Burma, Jared Naimark.' I rummage in my

Some old buildings survive - a throwback to colonial days

rucksack for my iPad to check the exact quote I'm looking for. 'Ah yes, here it is. He says: "According to Fukuyama's analysis, foreign investment, specifically competition from American companies, will magically force the cronies to fold, leading to economic growth which will then lead to democracy".'

'Notice that word he uses,' I add, '. . . *magically*.'

'So, those in the educated West,' Mary chimes in a tone of irony, 'are dismissive of the mixed bag of mystic rituals, animism, and irrational beliefs so embedded in Burmese culture. But, then, on the other hand . . . '

I cannot wait to complete her sentence, '. . . we have the audacity to replace them with our own box of *magic* tricks'.

We seem to have both arrived at this 'Aha' moment together. I am sure we're not the first to have tumbled to the fallacy in this loose version of liberal economics. When applied to Myanmar, unrestrained capitalism is flawed on many counts. It does nothing to address the human rights abuses—many of which amount to war crimes—that have simmered for so long. It serves to prop up corrupt political elites and their business 'cronies', who will be first to benefit from international investment. It allows the siphoning of wealth to a privileged few and conveniently paves the way for foreign companies to take their share of the cake. Meanwhile, the rights of ethnic communities remain ignored, political activists remain incarcerated and natural resources continue to be plundered. This is to say nothing of the devastating environmental damage that follows and the dispossessing of indigenous peoples from their land and livelihoods.

I dig out another quote from Naimark:

'Let's imagine an American company comes to open a factory in Burma. Their executives might fly there on Air Bagan, originally owned by blacklisted crony Tay Za. They'll arrive at the new international terminal and purchase an office block at Hledan Center, both constructed and operated by Asia World, a crony company founded by one of Burma's most notorious drug kingpins Lo Hsing Han. They might buy land that was confiscated from villagers by KMA Group and use Max Burma cement to build their factory, profiting regime favorites Khin Maung Aye and Zaw Zaw. They might have no choice but to purchase electricity produced by a dam that flooded the homes of thousands of villagers without their consent, built by crony company IGE.'

'That's enough to put anyone off investing in Myanmar,' Mary exclaims, throwing both hands from the steering wheel momentarily.

'Yes, he does rather nail it, doesn't he? It's not that different from Aung San Suu Kyi's stance on all this. Economic reforms are meant to bring a strong and growing middle class and eventually a more democratic society. Her view is that this classic theory is flawed. Or at least it is in the case of Myanmar. This is because there is no middle class, rather a small sector at the top of society benefitting from inward investment. She says that the rich are getting richer and the poor are getting poorer . . . '

' . . . and as long as new money comes in, the military has less and less incentive to change,' Mary adds.

'Yes, and Suu Kyi also notes that the British and all the other foreign investors know this full well . . . their policy is not something to be proud of.'

Open fields blur by. A few farmers are in the fields, but no sign of machinery. We turn off the main road and head into the hills. April, who has been dozing in the back seat remarks on the freshness of the air as we go higher. As we near our destination and the thought of our picnic beside the tumbling waterfall beckons, I want to get some kind of closure on this unexpected conversation I'm having with Mary. She is well placed to confirm or contradict an idea that I have been brewing.

'Mary, what bothers me about Myanmar, is that the majority of the population are grinning and bearing an intolerable regime. Their daily lives are a chore and there's little hope of a way out.'

Mary describes herself as a third-culture kid

'I can't argue with that. It's one reason why I'm here in Chiang Mai at the moment. Although I plan to return to Myanmar soon,' agrees Mary.

'The ruling elite seems to be in a bubble. They either don't see or don't care about the wretched conditions of the masses. They certainly have no desire to change. Why should they? Their lives and those of their families are very comfortable.'

'True.'

'It's clear that Buddhism holds sway in most of the country. Among the beliefs that this devotion to Buddha engenders are loving kindness and a strong reliance on the accumulation of merit for the next life . . .'

' . . . and a belief in self-disciplined non-violence,' says Mary.

'Okay, and it strikes me that these deeply ingrained attitudes are not exactly the stuff of revolution. Centuries of this mindset are unlikely to forge the weapons of rebellion or incite the masses to bring down a despotic regime. So in the meantime, the generals are safe. The political status quo persists.'

'Yep. I guess Buddhism is conservative by nature.'

While the luxuriant scenery glides by, George Orwell's classic book *1984* comes to mind. Many people think that the 'big brother' authoritarianism he describes was partly based on his time spent in Burma.

'What about trade . . . ?' Mary suddenly asks, coming out of her own thought train. 'There's no shortage of commercial activity in places like Yangon and Mandalay?'

'Yep, as far as I can see, foreign businesses continue to invest and partner with the military. Openly in the case of countries like China and Korea, more indirectly in the case of the West.'

'They all turn a blind eye to appalling breaches of human rights,' Mary adds.

'And what happens? This bankrolls the military regime. It keeps the ruling generals and their families financially secure. What do they care about poverty on the streets.'

Having reached this somewhat gloomy conclusion, it's a relief when Mary tells us we have arrived at our picnic spot. After a short clamber up hill, we are all lying on the big rocks. Drowsily the three of us look up at the sky through the dappled sprays of eucalyptus and wild fig. The pungent perfume of fresh pine is in the air. We unpack and spread out our lunch. Grilled chicken and papaya salad. April starts on her favourite, glutinous sticky rice with sprouted yellow peas and fried onions.

'One more thing about where I want to be in ten years,' Mary says licking her fingers and looking into the waterfall, 'I'd have my own YouTube channel where all the content would be everything Myanmar-related! I can't wait to make all of these things come true!'

I want to bottle the moment. The bubbling of the stream. The purity of the air. The excitement of youthful dreams.

CHAPTER NINETEEN

(2018) THE PARROT

It's 6 p.m. on a drizzly Thursday evening and a diminutive figure stands at the front of a darkened lecture hall in north London. The Birkbeck amphitheatre is almost gladiatorial but she holds the attention of 250 undergraduates on a first-year management course. Perhaps not that remarkable, until we bring to mind the pitiful state of education in her home country. Swe Swe Than is Burmese, from a devoutly Buddhist family. Her father U Ba Than is a writer and was a civil servant until early retirement. Her mother died when she was young, but her father and her respected stepmother—like many parents of the forgotten generation when the cupboard of schooling in Burma was all but empty—were determined to see their daughter find the path to a good education. And so it was she found herself in the UK on a rare scholarship and arrived at Birkbeck, London University, where I was teaching at the time. She became my PhD student and walked the lonely path of deciding a research topic, collecting data from several countries, navigating complex statistics and completing the long-haul of writing up to achieve her doctorate. All in five years and all in a second language and despite an unremitting teaching load. But perhaps most admirable was her hope for the future. On one occasion when she was over for a meal with April and me, she shared her heart:

'Once I finish my studies, I want to return to my home country. I want to put something back into Myanmar,' she calmly insisted.

Swe Swe Than at her training centre in Yangon

True to her word, she completed her doctoral studies and, following three years lecturing at another UK university, Swe Swe is now back in Myanmar.

When conversing with Burmese nationals, it is not long before the issue of education arises. There is a chronic shortage of human capital as a result of the country's isolation. Literacy rates are improving among the Bamars and in urban areas, but ethnic groups are still playing catch-up with illiterate households running at over 10 per cent among the Chin, 17 per cent among the Kayin and nearly a quarter in Shan State. A similar pattern emerges for school attendance. There are many reasons for children not attending school; the main reason, identified by recent census data, is affordability. April and I have heard stories of pitiful resourcing at primary and secondary levels, with Buddhist and Christian tutors supplementing tuition. State teachers are often absent from their classes in order to boost their income from private tuition. Only a relatively small proportion—just over 7 per cent, or about two million—of the population aged twenty-five and abover have graduated from university or a higher level of education. This is skewed heavily to those in Yangon. Burma stopped teaching English for a whole generation in 1964 and closed Rangoon University for three years after the student protests in 1989. At the time, most universities were 'broken up' by the government, relocating whole departments, with the intent of minimising the possibility of concerted student protests.

Added to questions about the amount and quality of education is the pedagogic style. Teaching, such as it is, is typically by rote and memorization. Culture dictates that you revere your elders and teachers, a laudable value to instil. But unfortunately, it can lead to an unquestioning, passive approach to learning. My experience of lecturing students from South Asia in UK universities, and our experience of teaching those of Burman, Chin, Kachin, Shan and Rakhine origin in Yangon, is similar. The very idea of discussing ideas in class or a small group with fellow students is met with perplexity. Initially, at least, they deem it a waste of time since the professor is deemed the expert and it is his or her job to teach.

It might be thought that one good thing to come from British rule was improved education. Yet, while the British conquest is rightly framed as political subjugation, less publicized is that it also represented a moral shock to Burmese society. One significant consequence of colonialization which the British ignored, or at best, underestimated, was its impact on Buddhism. There were several seismic aspects to this imposed divorce between state administration and religion. The fall of the monarchy in Mandalay in 1885, ended a long line of royal Buddhist patronage dating back more than a thousand years. Pragmatically, the British withdrawal of traditional state support for monasteries disrupted village economies, with monks struggling to finance their daily activities. Collectively, this signalled a perceived decline of the teachings of the Buddha and a lowering of respect for monks. In educational terms, this led to an almost irreversible break from the monastic transfer of religious and cultural values, good manners and moral conduct.

When we were with Aung Zaw Moe, the millennial activist we met in Taunggyi a few years back, I asked him about the effects of poor education. His response was immediate and telling:

'Critical thinking,' he said. 'Most MPs are not grown up with a good education system. Second, we need to learn from others like Thailand, Indonesia, Vietnam . . . how they have transformed themselves in a decade or so. Thanks to Prospect Burma, I was trained in medical school and then outside Burma in Dakha, Geneva and Washington. I decided not to join the government service because it has no place to grow yourself as a continuous learner. You have no authority to give feedback to your boss. It's a dictatorship, you follow what your superior says. There is no motivation to learn. Third, the government is reluctant to change its position. All the Ministries have failed, they are just wasting public money, we don't encourage feedback or to criticize. This has happened since 1962 for two or three generations. It's difficult to replace this quickly.'

Aung Zaw is doing what he can. Part of his role is to work with local NGOs in Yangon and to train political leaders. He told us that four of his trainees, all women and NLD members, had been elected to parliament in the 2015 election and were now serving as MPs.

'As yet they have little influence. Partly because the old guard, predominantly male and much older, don't pay much attention to them. Also, they need time to learn the ropes. I am hopeful that with experience, their ability to influence policy will improve.'

On a couple of occasions when we have been in Yangon, we have taken the opportunity to catch up with Swe Swe. She and her sister Mi Mi, live downtown in the family home.

'When I first returned from the UK', she tells us, 'I wanted to take soundings for a couple of years before setting up shop. I had been away from my home country for a long time and I needed to test the market. I took some consultancy assignments with firms in Yangon'.

'What did you find?'

'Most organizations have little in the way of systematic processes for managing staff . . . it's all about hire and fire'.

Swe Swe is setting up a training and development company in the heart of Yangon and is eager to show us her new premises in Latha township. We pull into the car park of a ten-storey office block which is still being finished. Workmen are pulling cables through walls and builders are busy erecting internal partitions. Bamboo scaffolding, which looks impossibly perilous to me, is being dismantled from the exterior. The space for her centre on the ninth floor is almost complete. It comprises a reception area, classrooms of various sizes, break-out rooms and some offices for her small team, Mo and Sule. I always knew she was enterprising but we are curious to know how she had funded such impressive premises.

'My sponsor is the vice-chairman of a CB Investment Bank. He owns the building. I shared my vision of providing training in basic HR skills with him. I told him I wanted to support organizations in forming sound policies and structures for their staff. He saw the value of what I was doing and was willing to invest.'

'What's in it for him?'

'In return for the training rooms, he gets a proportion of my business profits.'

April and I got to know Swe Swe socially in the UK and she never ceases to surprise us. She is deeply loyal to her country, her family, her traditions, yet she has a resolute ambition to change things for the better. She is softly spoken and outwardly serene but this veils a deep determination to succeed. She has suffered setbacks with her health, the early loss of her mother, a workplace accident when she was younger that confined her to bed for six months, yet she resists any self-pity. She has no husband, and with her sister, takes care of their now elderly father. Her career passion has always been human resource management (HRM). It is a relatively immature profession in Myanmar. As yet, only the multinationals operating in Yangon have any semblance of HRM policies.

Students on their way to classes

'Western and Australian Universities are moving into Yangon fast,' Swe Swe says, 'they see an untapped market to offer diplomas and MBAs. Local businesses generally lack people management policies that have any consistency and fairness. So HRM is a popular subject.'

'Given the state of education in Myanmar,' she continues, 'accreditation is very attractive to Burmese students, especially at tertiary levels. But these courses are only affordable to the privileged and the wealthy. I want to do something about that.'

Swe Swe shows us the classrooms in her training centre, newly kitted out and awaiting her first students. She wants to introduce us to her benefactor who owns the building and decided to put his trust in her. We sit down while we wait and start discussing college education back in the UK. Having worked for a charity and then in industry for a decade or so, I landed up researching and teaching HRM and leadership development at four different business schools. These were fulfilling times for me, although I grew a little disenchanted as time went by.

'I do worry sometimes,' I say, 'that our business schools have lost their way. In their early days, they were set up to challenge the status quo. But I don't see much evidence of that today. Our universities are becoming ever more managerialist. It's all about rankings, performance metrics, student numbers. It feels like we are mimicking rather than challenging the morality of big business.'

'Yes,' Swe Swe nods, 'that's true. There are many stories of fraud or corruption among businesses in Myanmar and South East Asia. It seems that power does indeed corrupt. Those wielding it regularly come to see themselves as above the law.'

'Right, and while you can't lay all the blame with business schools, it does make you wonder what we are doing to improve the quality and integrity of leadership. I just hope that these partnerships between Myanmar and Western colleges keep business ethics on the syllabus.'

Some young people are being shown the teaching rooms by Sule. As these would-be students file past, we are struck by their bright-eyed enthusiasm and also by the assortment of ethnicities they represent. 'You know,' says Swe Swe, reading our thoughts, 'when I was a student in the UK, and when I was lecturing, you could go through a whole course, a whole degree and there'd be no mention of what you believed, of your home community's customs and values. Even when the class was full of non-Western international students. I always found it so strange. All these things are naturally part and parcel of who we are.'

I couldn't agree with her more. It's as if these aspects of what we bring from the heritage of our home countries remain invisible and irrelevant. Even in international business schools, we remain so monocultural. I wonder whether it's the Cartesian mindset of Western academia. Our minds get divorced from our bodies, our emotions, our spirits. There is this false division between the sacred and the secular.

April is interested in how Swe Swe looks back on her time in the UK having returned to Myanmar a few years ago. 'Have your thoughts on HRM changed?'

'Well, it's very much in its infancy here in Yangon. Of course, it's needed . . . you need to treat your staff fairly and consistently, whichever country you're in. And training is vital. We badly need skills in the workforce. For the first time, some Labour Laws were passed recently here in Myanmar. The contrast with the UK is stark. HRM is very established and important in the UK and the West generally.'

'It seems to be a very popular university course,' April says.

'It's also become very sophisticated in the West, with a strong emphasis on jumping through the hoops of accreditation. It's like HRM has become an industry of its own' I add.

Swe Swe is called away. Through the dust outside we observe the bustle of construction as new office blocks stretch into the sky. I wonder how HRM will fare in this emerging economy. Most employees I talk to in the UK have an ambivalent attitude to HR professionals in their organizations. At best see them as key players in the business, partnering the senior team as they seek to manage change. But a more common view is that the HR department is constantly introducing new initiatives and loading line managers down with time-consuming paper exercises.

Swe Swe returns, issues a few instructions and we move swiftly towards the shiny new lift.

'Sorry,' she says, 'U Thein is not available after all. Let's go for lunch.'

A car meets us at the entrance and whisks us away. As we chat about Swe Swe's plans for the training centre, she is interrupted by a call on her mobile. With her driver battling through the late-morning traffic, there follows a twenty-five-minute dialogue with one of her clients. I gather it's the HR manager of a bank who is fretting about a performance management system that she's introducing to managers. This whole approach is new to the staff and she is hitting resistance. Glad of the air-con as we crawl past overcrowded buses, hooting taxis and kami-kazi cyclists, we half-listen to Swe Swe 'at work'.

April picks up some of the conversation in Burmese but I am more interested in *how* she is saying it. Swe Swe listens carefully, calmly encourages her client, deals with her anxieties and once some shared understanding is reached, she suggests some next steps. It reminds me of an earlier episode at the training centre, where Mo and Sule were having problems with their respective roles and responsibilities for running the new software. We had watched Swe Swe gently build the competence and confidence of her two assistants by clarifying boundaries and drawing out their different skills. All the time resisting the temptation to take over.

I turn to April and whisper: '*This* is empowerment in action. HRM on-the-hoof. If Swe Swe can model and train these skills on her training courses, she will be doing Myanmar businesses a great service.'

I think of elaborate competency frameworks, appraisal systems and 360-degree feedback programmes, so beloved of multinationals. How much better to weave an ethos of responsible leadership into the fabric of the organization! Lightness of touch rather than time-consuming training courses. Modelling skill-sets like coaching, active listening, mindful practices, giving and receiving feedback effectively. Relatively simple behaviours and respectful attitudes that can make a profound impact on the culture of a company.

As we are shown to our lunch table, Swe Swe turns off her phone, introduces her sister Mi Mi to April and me and she is finally able to relax. In between menu choices, the conversation about education continues. Mi Mi mentions one of her heroes Rabindranath Tagore.

'In the early twentieth century, he was a big influence in introducing Indian culture to the West.' She says.

'As well as in the other direction,' adds Swe Swe with a twinkle in her eye.

'Yes, in 1913 he became the first non-European to receive the Nobel Prize for Literature. One of his fables is the poignant story of a caged bird.'

April and I are keen to hear it, so with a shy smile, Mi Mi obliges:

'Once upon a time, there was a bird. It was ignorant. It sang all right, but never recited scriptures. It hopped pretty frequently but lacked manners. Said the Raja to himself: "Ignorance is costly in the long run. For fools consume as much food as their betters, and yet give nothing in return." He called his nephews to his presence and told them that the bird must have sound schooling. The pundits were summoned, and at once went to the root of the matter. They decided that the ignorance of birds was due to their natural habit of living in poor nests. Therefore, according to the pundits, the first thing necessary for this bird's education was a suitable cage.

The pundits had their rewards and went home happy. A golden cage was built with gorgeous decorations. Crowds came to see it from all parts of the world. 'Culture, captured and caged!' exclaimed some, in a rapture of ecstasy, and burst into tears. But while a succession of pundits, goldsmiths and numerous nephews benefit from an elaboration of the cage, the bird inside is neglected and finally breathes its last. Guarded by the kotwal and the sepoys and the sowars, the bird is brought to the Raja and, in a poignant ending: he poked its body with his finger. Only its inner stuffing of book-leaves rustled. As for any complaint from the bird itself, that simply could not be expected. Its throat was so completely choked with the leaves from the books that it could neither whistle nor whisper.'

We are moved to silence. No one is eating.

'That is so profound,' I say at last. 'It sums up what we were discussing earlier. What education and training can so easily become. Whether it's located in London, Mumbai or Yangon.'

'The risk is that organizations overcomplicate their learning programmes. They get preoccupied by the syllabus, the methodology, the certification,' says Swe Swe.

'Losing sight of the learners themselves.' April says with a meaningful nod, having had her own encounters with the mini-industry of counselling courses, supervision and accreditation in the UK.

'It's as if schools and universities,' I add, 'become like the jewel-encrusted cage.'

'In Myanmar right now, good quality higher education is currently in short supply,' Mi Mi declares in a rather exasperated tone, 'which is why we are so excited about Swe Swe's centre.'

'By contrast, in the West, I have to say there is sometimes a spirit of entitlement. We tend to take education for granted, to become preoccupied with the building, the administration, the status of the institution. All that is to miss the point.'

'Mmmm . . . ' Swe Swe goes quiet for a moment. 'I suppose whichever country you're in when it comes to training and education the question is the same. Are we managing to stir the minds of students . . . are we provoking them, inspiring them? I hope our training centre will create a safe place to discuss issues of diversity, to get people questioning things. Even to think about why there are cultural, even political, divisions?'

'Yes, it's all a question of how much attention is being paid to the development of the parrot.' April gives me a quizzical sideways glance. I think she's reproving me for stating the obvious.

'How do you know it's a parrot?' Swe Swe says, raising her eyebrows in mock surprise.

'Well, I don't actually . . . I,' stalling briefly to buy time, ' . . . perhaps that *is* the wrong bird because parrots are known for simply mimicking and that's the opposite of what we are talking about. However, I do see the bird as colourful, full of potential and curiosity.'

'But still sadly lacking from neglect,' Swe Swe adds in a serious tone.

'Isn't it crazy,' I say, slightly changing direction, 'how far political correctness has gone. In the West we are in danger of forgetting what universities are there for. We are becoming so paranoid about free speech, so indignant of any expression of views contrary to what is deemed acceptable. Do you know there's a university in the USA where official notices in the students' restrooms state: "If a professor says something that makes you feel uncomfortable, this is the number to call."'

'Well,' says Swe Swe, 'if you think that's sinister you should spend more time in Yangon. It's informers for the regime *we* have to be concerned about.' She pauses and a smile flickers across her face, 'But I've got an answer to that.'

'Oh, you have?' I say, intrigued.

'Yes, once my training centre gets going, I intend to offer subsidised places on my HRM courses to members of the military.'

I splutter into my drink. After a few moments, I catch her smile and the wisdom of Swe Swe's strategy begins to dawn on me. How to change an oppressive regime? Answer: one soldier at a time.

'That's a good way of giving attention to the bird,' I say.

Perhaps it is a good omen for Swe Swe and a signal of hope for Myanmar, that on the first day of their New Year, it's a Burmese custom to set free captured fish into the lakes and to release caged birds into the air.

CHAPTER TWENTY

(2018) BEING SET FREE

At last, the classroom has glass in the windows although the first floor doorways still open into mid-air. Birds occasionally flutter through the rafters and Buddhist chants float through from loudspeakers at the village temple. For all the distractions, we are sitting in the fulfilment of a dream. Back in 2010, we stood near this spot in stifling heat and surrounded by dense undergrowth as Lincoln and Leah shared their hope and prayer for a new Bible college building. Now, eight years later, it's on the way to fruition. Thanks to the generous support of a church in Newcastle, Australia, and other individual donors in the UK and USA, the building is almost complete; it's just the two wings of classrooms that remain on the drawing board. Washing hangs from lines behind the dormitory blocks, cooking aromas drift from the bamboo kitchen area, and chickens strut between rows of vegetables and flowers.

I am taking a breather from teaching as April is at the front trying to get across the meaning of empathy to around twenty students. No mean feat in a country like Myanmar which politically has experienced a complete deficit of empathy for 50 years or more. Naomi is Lincoln's niece and one of the faculty. Petite and pretty, in her late thirties, she is animated and energetic, combining several roles. At different times of the day and week, she is matron and counsellor to the girl students, housekeeper for the college, disciplinarian, tutor in Old Testament studies. She is also an excellent interpreter, and here she is translating for April, as the young men and women, attractive in their brightly patterned longyis, write notes in their mother dialects. The educational background of the young students—who come from several ethnic groups—is threadbare. They are bright-eyed but lack learning skills and are desperately short on self-esteem. Not for the first time, as I allow the scene to wash over me, I find myself wondering what we are doing here, teaching leadership and listening skills at a small Bible college on the outskirts of Yangon.

April has many relatives in Yangon and on each trip, we take the opportunity to drop by for a chat over a curry. We enjoy the natural beauty of the country, the crimson sun rising over a buzzing, steamy city of pagodas, high rise, and palm trees. The good humour of friends, family, and passers-by. But the main draw is the challenge of teaching in a very different environment where the student 'fees' are a dollar a day. We know Lincoln and his small team appreciates external input. His vision has stayed rock solid. That a better understanding of the bible will help these young people navigate a Godless, animistic environment; and that leadership training will give them the confidence to teach in schools, serve in hospitals, and kick-start businesses. Alongside this, a belief that friendships forged at the college will provide a valued mentoring network in future years.

One way or another I have been leading—and training others to lead—for most of my adult life, but what, I wonder, have we got to offer these students? The gulf between them and us seems so huge, the difference in education, upbringing, culture and life chances. Even for April who shares their language and heritage, her path has diverged so drastically since she left Burma at the age of thirteen. For all this, my mind turns to some common denominators, certain needs shared by all people—whatever their cultural background—but accentuated perhaps for leaders. One is the basic longing to be loved and affirmed, the need for intimacy; then there is the desire to influence the world around us, the need we all have to do something significant. Finally, we have to be able to access the resources to do so, so we need power.

For a while now, in a Western context, I've noticed the training of leaders has become preoccupied with exhibiting specified behaviours, the learning of techniques, collecting 'tickets' of accreditation. Nothing wrong with these things, but they have a tendency to overlook the spiritual essence of leadership: feeling secure, being free, and having agency. Without these essentials being in place, our leadership can so easily become a matter of reaching into a wardrobe of standard clothes that we try on—with varying degrees of success. Or at worst, it descends into an egoistic power trip which oppresses others, and ultimately, destroys ourselves.

If this is true of organizations in 'developed countries', it surely also applies to places like Myanmar where the fall out of failed leadership is all too apparent. A regime obsessed with its desire to retain control, with precious few positive leader role models and where the average person has limited choice and no voice. For this reason, although I continue to explain the story of Nehemiah in the Old Testament as an exemplar of excellent leadership, I am starting to rethink the way we communicate leadership to the Bible school students.

Leadership can be a lonely business. We yearn for some 'golden bullet' that will transform the situation. A decisive move that will prove our leader credentials. What's more, we find ourselves out of reach from other's counsel, unable to confide or admit mistakes because to do so looks weak. At these times of inadequacy, we want to fill the gaps with something tangible. The business shelves of bookshops are full of advice on how to attain this transformational or 'messiah' style of leadership. What most miss is that going for the quick fix distracts us from the longer-term goal. Sustainable change.

This desire for immediate success and legitimacy also disguises a deeper need. In a word: intimacy. What an isolated leader needs is the nourishment of his/her soul, a reminder of the good cause that they originally signed up for. I wonder whether this is true of the military junta in Yangon. They started in the early 1960s intending to restore order to a nation in an era of political free fall. But very soon self-preservation and nepotism took over, with a succession of self-serving administrations creaming off the profits from opium production, sapphire, ruby and jade mining, and teak exports. Lining their own pockets and increasingly blind to poverty on the streets. And surely this is simply a more naked version of what happens in the so-called 'developed world'? Greedy bankers, phone-tapping journalists, corrupt politicians all in search of fleeting fame, chasing the story, the next big hit.

The common ground here is believing themselves to be above the law. Leaders rationalize unethical behaviour, lose sight of their noble vocation, and ignore the deeply buried cry of their conscience, for what they know to be fair and just. I recognize it in myself: my private life not always matching up to my public persona, failing to walk the talk. So what is the antidote? Might it be that the source of a leader's strength arises from the quality of their relationships—including constructive feedback and mutual accountability? How different things might have been for Burma if the ruling generals had listened to men and women of integrity, if they had the humility to take counsel from constructive critics.

Here at the Bible college, this is what Lincoln and his team are putting in place. A wonderful platform of selfless love, through their daily involvement with the students by cooking meals together, sharing their lives, and—when necessary—exerting tough-love discipline. By coming for a few weeks each year, April and I are simply building on this by helping the students to develop an intimate companionship with God and others and, in so doing, to nurture an ethical core to their lives. Together with the faculty, we believe that from this will come the capacity to live as free men or women. And when we are free, we are authentic. Because authenticity is attractive, others will follow. As others follow, mountains will be moved.

Alongside a basic need for intimacy, is an intrinsic desire to be influential. Again, conventional approaches to leadership tend to get this all wrong. An emphasis is placed on getting a following

One of the faculty outside the nearly completed Bible School Building: 'Miracles Happen'

and achieving celebrity status. So many tools are available to assist this mood-bending hubris: arresting graphics, case studies of turnarounds, ted talks, publicity campaigns, discrediting the opposition, emotive appeals. This is all part of the wizardry of the charismatic leader, building their social media platform. Although using less sophisticated props, the grandstanding of uniformed generals addressing serried ranks of officials, to be splashed across tomorrow's issue of *Myanmar Times*, is not far removed.

However, admirers are notoriously fickle. The human need for significance: to be recognized and affirmed by those we value is not found by crowd-pleasing. At least not in the longrun. Jesus himself did not need to be the showman because he was relaxed enough in his own skin. He was aware of, and grateful for, what he already had. With this, he reached out to others with compassion, rather than compiling a CV of success stories. I believe that this was the appeal of Aung San Suu Kyi, certainly in her house arrest days. She displayed a composure and an affinity with ordinary Burmese people based on their shared Buddhist beliefs.

Knowing we are loved begins to address our need for intimacy, having something important to say starts to fulfil our need for significance, then comes the need for agency; the opportunity to speak, the discretion to act. Most of us start with a laudable intention to impact the world for good. But as we build a reputation, the temptation is to believe our own PR, to get carried away with the prestige, and our ego elbows its way in. Herein lies the seduction of power. That, by dint of our position in some hierarchy, our superior competence or persuasiveness, or our political dominance, we somehow have the right to assert our will and exert control over others.

Nobody likes to think that they have no voice, that they can make no difference to the world around them. As we discussed the ingredients of effective leadership, it wasn't long before April and I sensed that the students were struggling. They were in the room, but somehow disengaged. They remained tight lipped and unwilling to ask questions.

'I'm just not getting through,' April said after one particularly tough session. 'The students are dutifully writing in their notebooks as Naomi translates. But I sense a heaviness in the classroom.'

It was becoming clear that most of the Bible college students in front of us were suffering from low self-image and a chronic lack of agency. The next day we decide to change tack and take some individual time with the young men and women. As we do so, horrific stories tumble out through the tears. April tells me it's very difficult for Burmese to express their feelings to anybody except their closest, especially when shame plays a part. Yet, in an environment of trust and devoid of censure, one after another, irrespective of their ethnic group or gender, the students speak of bullying and humiliation that they suffered as they were growing up in their villages—even from family members. In particular, fathers were often distant figures. Most were on the receiving end of power in its most corrosive form.

They did not feel valued, they felt they had to repress their anger. It wasn't just their culture dictating that they shouldn't ask questions of their teachers, it was an internal wall locking in some of their deepest longings and emotions. A place they dared not go.

No wonder there seems to be a fog in the teaching room. They are seeing and hearing about a model of leadership that threatens to break that wall down. We do our best to show them that Jesus knows and cares about each of them; that unlike some they'd met earlier in their young lives, his leadership does not push its way to a place of influence by seeking to manipulate and control.

In more recent years, I had come to recognize that wall in myself. A hidden place that I did not trust, because it was too emotive, too risky to handle. As a result, I had increasingly devalued my heart and lived in my head. It didn't help that in my younger days when I had tried to lead from my heart I had sometimes looked foolish or was misunderstood. My schooling and academic training also succeeded in relegating my passion and I became adept at cool analysis, rational argument, and theorising. This arena felt relatively safe. Contrary to what was promised on the packet however, this route to gaining power was paradoxically *dis*empowering because it slowly but surely cut me off from a whole pool of spiritual resources. Creative and energizing resources that were unique to me.

Our conversations with the students are bringing this all back to me. A right relationship with God had brought me a measure of inner healing. So we try to take them to that place where they also feel secure with their potential to be influential, to speak and act with authority; where they are not left out in the cold as slaves but gathered in as heirs.

It is not easy to explain these things in another language, but Lincoln and Naomi know what we are talking about and do a great job. Gradually, the students are able to express their hurt. As they find the grace to forgive those who had withheld love and release their bitterness and shame, slowly they open up like tender flowers to spring sunshine.

For the first time, our youngest daughter Mala Su is with us at the college. A professional dancer, she is able to discuss with the students the liberating role of dance in worship and praise and how this is a thread running through the Judeo–Christian scriptures. They could and did dance in a rather stiff and formalized manner already, but they were fascinated to see Mala demonstrate different styles like modern jazz in the context of worship.

One morning she takes a bold step. She encourages them to prayerfully attune their hearts and bodies to God's spirit. The students love this and twelve of the group sign up to some sessions to experiment with dance. On the last day, they dance during a time of corporate worship, one more funky and the other to a slower, melodic Burmese song. As they lose themselves in praise, their faces glowing and their bodies moving without inhibition, it seems that deep healing is taking place. It is our turn to shed tears. I realize I am learning much from these young students about leadership. The very subject that I'd come to teach:

> Leadership is not a label or position,
> it is demonstrated by those who follow . . .
> > I am voiceless unless others sing.

> Leadership is not something I possess,
> it is love shared between those around me . . .
> > I am earthbound without others' wings.

As we ride back to the hotel, April, Mala, and I are in positive spirits. Lincoln is beaming and asks about our next visit. Heartened by the students' response, we tentatively diarize the following year. Maybe by then, the college building will have 'wings' and Leah's pre-school will be established on the same site. Sadly, if there are any lessons of leadership to be taken from this ostracized rogue state, they tend to be examples of how *not* to do things. Government ministers who remain unimaginative and intransigent. One phalanx of generals replacing another like shuffling the same deck of cards. An education system so decimated it is sabotaging would-be leaders at an early age. A record of human rights which is among the world's worst. Even that icon of democratic leadership, Aung San Suu Kyi, seemingly powerless to exert political influence. As we say farewell again to the handful of students, the leadership challenge facing them indeed feels immense. It will be a while before they finally find their voice and play their part in shaping their nation. But, we trust that day will come.

CHAPTER TWENTY-ONE

(2018) LIMINAL SPACE

It is a cloudless day in January 2018, and with teaching over, we want to make the most of our last day in Yangon. We arrange to meet up with Khin Khin who wants to take us to her favourite eatery, one of several that boasts a lakeside view not far from the centre of Yangon. The restaurants have a slightly makeshift feel but what they lack in appearance is compensated by gorgeous ethnic food. This one, the *Koe Kant Kou Fu*, is run by friendly staff from the Kokhine district of the Shan state and consists of several thatched-roof huts. In one, a group of students lie languidly or sit cross-legged on the floor, sampling dishes from low tables. Our hut has tables and chairs. We take in the aroma and tastes of several Kokhine specials. Khin Khin and her mother help us choose from the menu: mashed potato with crushed garlic, eggplant salad, yellow Chinese bean with asparagus, bamboo shoots. All this plus a generous helping of chicken and spicy noodles.

Khin Khin is April's second cousin, she is twenty-six and lives in downtown Yangon. We first knew her as a shy four-year-old, hiding behind her parents' legs when we visited from the UK in 1995. She now speaks fluent English, is socially at ease, and regularly registers her latest exploits—which often involves trying new dishes—on Facebook. Her grandmother's home is simple: a timber-built house in several sections, one for each branch of the family, down a rather dimly lit side street. But, as she says, it was filled with warmth as she grew up:

'The most enjoyable childhood memory I had was being surrounded by a lot of relatives, my aunts, my cousins, and they played an important role in bringing me up. I believe in Buddha not in spiritual influences but I accept the existence. We have a small shrine in our house.'

As April lapses into Burmese to chat with Khin Khin, I reflect on the gap of more than twenty years since we last saw her. There is a moment, between sleeping and waking when the ghosts of my dreams dance with the guardians of my day. It's vivid yet momentary. Sometimes weird, sometimes creative, and not easy to pin down. The unconscious and the conscious holding hands, as it were, through a gossamer curtain. I've heard this referred to as liminal space. It's as though Khin Khin is in that place which is betwixt and between, a kind of threshold. Like many of her generation in Myanmar, she is no longer in the innocence of youth, but her future is not yet formed. It happens to individuals and, according to anthropologists, it happens to societies: described as a state of suspense, a moment of freedom between two structured world views or institutional arrangements, where reality itself can be moulded and carried in different directions.

As I consider my limited exposure to Burma and to Burmese folk, I wonder whether part of the enigma of this country is because it is in this in-between space. This thought gathered momentum when I discovered that one facet of liminal thinking is non-violent resistance. The idea, developed by Marshall Rosenberg, is that all human beings have the capacity for compassion and only resort to violence or behaviour that harms themselves and others when they have exhausted more effective strategies for meeting needs. Well-known proponents of this approach include Mahatma Gandhi in India, Martin Luther King in the USA, Nelson Mandela in South Africa, and Aung San Suu Kyi in Burma.

Interestingly, each of these figures was or is propelled by a different faith tradition: Hinduism, Buddhism, and, in the case of King and Mandela, Christian faith. They arose to prominence because they

April's cousin Khin Khin in Yangon

actively but non-violently opposed the social, psychological, or physical injustice around them.

For each of these leaders, they worked and lived in that ambiguous state where, at least in their view, the past had been discredited and the contours of the new normality had yet to be defined. For Gandhi, discrimination against Indians in South Africa and the domination of India under British rule were unacceptable. Such arrangements no longer had legitimacy, if they ever did in the first place. On the fundamental values of truth, nonviolence, and service, he had a simple yet profound message. He asked his followers to reject not only physical violence but violence to the spirit.

For Mandela, apartheid was a brutal and outmoded anathema. Similarly, for Martin Luther King, racism was an abuse of power and the mistreatment of black people had gone on for too long and could no longer be tolerated:

' . . . one of the great problems of history is that the concepts of love and power have usually been contrasted as opposites—polar opposites—so that love is identified with the resignation of power, and power with the denial of love. Now we've got to get this thing right. What [we need to realize is] that power without love is reckless and abusive, and love without power is sentimental and anaemic . . . It is precisely this collision of immoral power with powerless morality which constitutes the major crisis of our time.'

These thought-leaders worked tirelessly in that uncomfortable and previously uncharted liminal space to usher in what was yet to be. Each saw, to differing degrees in their lifetimes, the emergence of what they and their many followers struggled for. To us, looking back, the fulfilment of their respective dreams now seems inevitable, almost taken for granted. Yet for them, it must have sometimes felt like an unreachable fantasy.

Drifting back into the conversation, I ask Khin Khin about her education. Her face lights up as she, rather quaintly addresses me as 'Uncle Chris':

'After I passed high school, I got a chance to attend psycho-social training given by an organization called Salusworld. Back at that time, I was a reserved and lowself-esteem girl. In that training I met a lot of people including a professional trainer. We shared individual' weaknesses and gave advices on how to overcome these barriers. Since from that time, I have become a confident and optimistic person.'

Career-wise she is doing well for herself. She tells us about her current job which involves administering international development for the humanitarian assistance section of the United States Embassy. Like other young Burmese nationals we have met, I gather that she has taken extracurricular steps to broaden her horizons.

'I did some volunteer work organized by the British Council Library in Yangon. I did this for four years.'

I glance across at her mother, who is less fluent in English, and think how proud she must be of her daughter.

'This involved teaching English at an orphanage,' Khin Khin explains as she deftly rearranges her noodles with chopsticks, ' . . . planting trees, and giving contributions to old people in rural districts. It changed my views about my country, it made my eyes wide open. Ten years from now, I would love to be doing a small–medium enterprise that can also benefit my country.'

As we chat, I gaze over Khin Khin's shoulder towards Kandawgyi Lake. What I am hearing and seeing sort of sums up the best and worst of Yangon and Myanmar. It's the weekend and courting couples with earphones take selfies under parasols against the stunning backdrop. There is palpably more freedom here than even five years ago. The working week may be a relentless and poorly remunerated grind for most families, but on public holidays there is almost a carefree atmosphere. For all this, the park area is surrounded by a moat of manic traffic, clapped-out lorries belching fumes, hooters blaring, mopeds and cycles weaving perilously across lanes. Catching my thoughts, Khin Khin says:

'Most people are now blaming the NLD for not improving the environment. People are disappointed with the NLD in government. There has been no improvement. The state of the buses, the traffic, crime in the city . . . they're all worse now.'

'So what's going wrong?' I say.

'People ignore the rules, like traffic rules. They just ignore them—the car drivers, the taxi drivers—because they are so upset. The NLD has good intentions and pass laws, but they have no idea how to implement them. The police are happy for the chaos to happen.'

'Because?'

'Because they know the NLD will lose favour and that plays into their hands.'

What I pick up as Khin Khin talks, is that for all the surface improvements, a vast gulf remains between those who run the country and the rest. A country that for the overwhelming majority is broken. But despite this daily struggle, like so many of her generation, she is spirited, media-savvy, and energetic. She is seeking to improve herself. I discover she has started her MBA course, which takes up most of the weekend, and in the time left over, she is dedicated to improving the lot of those worse off in her country. This is mirrored in what I see. On the far side of the lake, the iconic golden dome of the Shwedagon shimmers in the afternoon heat. That symbol of Buddhism and compassion unchanged for 600 years, a space of spiritual stillness, transcending the noise of the city. Look in the other direction and I see the flashy hotels, the high-rise, get-rich-quick businesses, the unbridled clamour for the new. It feels as if we are at the margins of two worlds. Standing at a threshold, is Burma leaving behind the tried and tested, and, if so, what will replace it?

And what of Aung San Suu Kyi in all this? Justin Wintle reports on a conversation between her and Alan Clements, later published in *The Voice of Hope* in 1997. Here is the heart of someone who is potentially pivotal in shaping Burma's uncertain future:

'We are still prisoners in our own country,' Suu Kyi tells him. The solution—at odds with received notions of Buddhism as a fatalistic faith—is for people to adopt "self-responsibility". Again "Engaged Buddhism is active compassion". As always, she emphasizes the importance of *metta*, "loving-kindness". All dictatorships must collapse sooner or later, and non-violence is one way to hasten, not delay their end. Compassion should be extended even to the perpetrators of violence. "I've always thought that if I really started hating my captors, hating the SLORC and the Army, I would have defeated myself." But it is not just a matter of replacing military with civilian rule. Maintaining one's own dignity and mental equilibrium is of equal importance. "My highest ambition," Suu Kyi says, "is very much a spiritual one: purity of mind". And this involves humility. "If you contemplate your own death it means you accept how unimportant you are". That, however, is not the same as resignation. In Aung San Suu Kyi's view, Buddhist precepts, rightly understood, demand selflessness, even self-sacrifice.'

Since the time of this interview, there have been small shifts in the political landscape. The NLD has finally taken up the seats in government that they originally won in 1990. Aung San Suu Kyi, after further spells of house arrest and plots on her life, has been appointed State Counsellor—the equivalent of the Prime Minister of Burma. Yet the political stalemate continues. Not only that, but there has also been widespread reporting of the ethnic cleansing of the Rohingya in the Rakhine district, with more than 700,000 Muslims being forcibly expelled into Bangladesh. Less well known but equally appalling is the brutal treatment of other minority peoples perpetrated for decades since the Second World War. Atrocities which, publicly at least, Suu Kyi has refused to acknowledge. Indeed, it has been observed by some critics that her resolve is driven less by any political ideology and more by a 'dynastic determination to continue the legacy of her father, General Aung San, known as the "father" of modern-day Myanmar.' Bill Richardson, a USA diplomat, and friend for twenty-five years has lost patience, complaining:

'There is no space for dialogue on Rakhine. She views anyone who offers criticism that does not fit her narrative as disloyal.'

This plays into another unsavoury reality: the nascent sense of racial superiority held by the Bamar people who orchestrate the military machine and dominate Burmese social and political affairs in the Irrawaddy basin and beyond. Yet, I have heard it said that, if pressed, most Burmese whatever their ethnicity, will admit to a deep-seated antipathy towards the Rohingya people. Partly because they are Muslim, but mainly driven by a belief that they do not belong in Burma.

What does seem clear is that quite apart from her family privations, State Counsellor Aung San Suu Kyi has become a somewhat isolated figure. Much of the admiration and goodwill she previously enjoyed outside Myanmar, has for the above reasons, ebbed away. While she and her National League for Democracy party still command respect and support internally, there is a groundswell of impatience concerning their capacity to improve the conditions of daily life for the general populace. There is also a nationalist perception that Suu Kyi and the NLD have a generally Western liberal outlook that privileges minority rights and diversity—including religious diversity—over the protection of the Buddhist faith. Meanwhile, many minorities feel that the government is not taking account of their concerns. In some ways, the 'Lady' cannot win.

Before we write off Suu Kyi, it is worth remembering that those who are pouring scorn on her inaction—the international media— were those who ascribed her celebrity status in the first place. Not something she sought or was comfortable with. To this, we might add scepticism about the capacity of any individual, no matter how noble, to single-handedly 'turn round' a nation. For all her heroic and sacrificial championing of democracy in the face of an unswerving junta, she has failed to build an effective party of opposition. Over the years, Aung San Suu Kyi has been variously portrayed as the figurehead of the NLD, poster girl of Burma, perfect hostage, an icon of democracy, Buddhist exemplar of non-violent opposition, the Lady, pariah Prime Minister. Roughly in that order. But might it be unfair to expect her to carry the future hopes of Burma on her shoulders alone?

It may be more reasonable to look to a wider vanguard of activists who have vision and expertise. The NLD comprises many who have loyally committed themselves to the cause of democracy since the late 1980s and been tortured and imprisoned for their trouble. In her book *Letters from Burma*, Aung San Suu Kyi recalls the unstinting work of those lesser-known figures who have stood faithfully by her including U Kyi Maung, U Aung Shwe, U Win Tin, and U Lwin. It will take time for these old hands alongside recently elected NLD colleagues to become influential members of the parliament, given that they have been excluded from the political process for so long. With an eye to the future, we might also need to look to a younger generation. Rather than being hamstrung by the iron grip of government, many have eschewed politics and chosen to influence their country's destiny via local community development, health interventions, and improving education. In our travels, April and I have met many such individuals. Young people with big ideals like Kamaylar, Dr Sasa, Aung Zaw Moe, Mary and Swe Swe.

Where I believe Aung San Suu Kyi does show prescience, as exemplified in the interview quoted above, is in her insistence that active compassion operates on two levels. First, there is the need for personal spiritual discipline, what she calls 'purity of mind'. Then alongside this is the recognition that things, especially institutions, need to change *systemically*. Both are essential to reverse decades of what has been referred to as *failed state building*. As we have discovered in Yangon and beyond, this can be traced back to the unravelling of the Burmese royal dynasty and the dismantling of a long and revered tradition of monastic learning. Then came the imposition of an alien rule under the British Raj, followed by the relentless growth of a military machine under a succession of unimaginative generals. Personal, value-driven devotion to a cause is necessary to promote national well-being. It is necessary but not sufficient. Also required is rigorous state-craft, the ability to turn values into sociopolitical action. But this will descend into partisan politicking if there is no transcending vision to galvanize different interest groups. According to Thant Myint-U:

'There is . . . a strong utopian streak, going back to the Student Union days of the 1930s, a proclivity for abstract debates, on communism, socialism, democracy, endless conversations about diverse constitutional models and long-term political schemes which never see the light of the day. What is altogether missing is a history of pragmatic and rigorous policy debate, on economics, finance, healthcare, or education as well as a more imaginative and empathic discussion of minority rights and shared identities in modern Burmese society.'

I find it telling that much of this indictment of his own country's failings could equally be applied to the constitutional crisis and lack of respectful and informed debate which is currently afflicting Britain and other Western nations.

Fortunately, if what April and I have found in various conversations with Burmese millennials is anything to go by, there are shafts of hope for the future. The afternoon spent with Khin Khin epitomizes this optimism. The mix of faith-inspired fervour and pragmatic intervention is what we have encountered in fields as diverse as telecoms and health, ecology, and education. It has been both unexpected and enthralling. Long gone is my misty-eyed romantic vision of Burma. It didn't take many visits for a different version of reality to sink in. Sometimes baffling, often hard-hitting, invariably worrying. But alongside this deep unease at what we were witnessing and hearing, a strand of sunshine begins to pierce the gloomy sky. Backed up by freshly acquired skills and qualifications, invariably gained outside Burma, we encountered a younger generation who are already making an impact at a grassroots level. Closing the gap, as it were, between Myanmar's slumber and wakefulness.

Not only is Myanmar in a liminal space, I sense I also have become more aware of my own liminality. Starting with my early exposure to April's family, some of the certainties I held in the past have been found wanting, and whatever is to come is still ill-defined. It is not a bad place to be. It took encounters with ordinary Burmese folk the wrong side of the line between entitled and deprived, between those of faith and no faith, between the welcomed and the exiled, to show me that . . . actually, there is no line. Yes, there are rigged elections that deny access to political power and gated communities that keep the privileged and poor apart. There is religious hate speech which keeps minorities oppressed, and denial of land rights that pushes ethnic groups to the margins.

These dividing lines are very real and demarcate daily existence for most of the population. Yet I wonder whether these are lines drawn by those who want to keep others out because they are afraid. They get underscored by repeated, bullying acts because those who draw them are insecure. They become institutionalized by laws and prohibitions because those lawmakers know they are weak. Maybe in God's economy at least, there is no line, no dividing wall of hostility. It is a fabrication borne of fear and *perfect love casts out fear*. So I end up hopeful about the future of Myanmar because we have encountered enough love to overcome that fear, to eventually erase those lines. Some in the corridors of power like the State Counsellor Aung San Suu Kyi and Anna Sui Hluan, the wife of Myanmar's Vice President, but most in the form of less conspicuous millennials working diligently to restore their communities dotted around Myanmar.

Although she has long since been naturalized, had a British passport and called England her home, April's identity is rooted in Burma: 'I am still a child of the East,' she told me recently. 'I detest the military, the way they have stripped the country of its riches—the precious gems, the teak, the oil—selling out to the Chinese. But I love my people. No amount of greed, self-interest, torture and imprisonment by the army can take away the resilience and character of ordinary Burmese.'

'And what of your beliefs, have they changed over time?' I ask.

'I am made in the image of God, and He will always be there, whether in this country, Burma or anywhere else in the world. If anything, my faith in God has enhanced my culture. Love of family, interest in food, creativity . . . it's great to see the talent of Mala and Seth in dance. I'm sure that comes from the Burmese side of the family.'

As for me, I have begun to shed some of my cultural skin, some of the piety of my religion. But unchanged, indeed reinvigorated, is a truth that I have always felt, nearly lost, and only now been able to articulate. God has made everything beautiful in its time and he has set eternity in our hearts. Or to put it another way, God's Spirit is like a homing device placed inside all of us, and all creation too. Coming closer to the mystical, the enigmatic, the maddening heart of Burma, has, in the end, affirmed rather than diminished this belief. So for all my mistakes and misconceptions of the past, for all my restlessness in the present, for all my unanswered questions about what is to come, I am—strangely—already home. To return to where we started with a plane crash over Africa which is now widely reckoned to have been shot down. In his journal Dag Hammarskjold wrote: 'At some moment I did answer Yes to Someone—or Something— and from that hour I was certain that existence is meaningful and that, therefore, my life in self-surrender had a goal.'

In my early conversations with April's mother and father, it was only ever my intention to fathom a little more fully the past of the family I married into. From this came a tentative foray into the last century of Burmese history alongside some journal reflections on our frequent visits to Yangon and the interior. All this peppered by conversations with locals. The cumulative impact has given me more than I bargained for.

In each passing episode, provocative insights have sidled into my thinking, long-held assumptions have been scrutinized. I have been humbled by the generosity of April's family, both those who exited in the 1960s and those who stayed behind. I am in awe at the self-sacrifice of Burmese nationals as they seek to remedy decades of neglect in their country. I had originally set out to discover some of the hidden beauty of April, her country and her people, and felt I had done so with some success. Less anticipated was that, in the process, I found my spiritual centre of gravity shifting and my emotions churned. I was discovering as much about myself as the country I sought to understand.

AFTERWORD

It is 2018, exactly seventy years on from Austin's romantic match with Margaret in Calcutta and wedding in Rangoon—and a century from the year that April's father was born. One of his granddaughters is about to celebrate her wedding. I am in the process of drafting a speech for the marriage of the last of our four lovely daughters, Mala Su. It's a bit of a struggle. Not the memories and the anecdotes, they come quite easily and there's plenty to choose from her thirty-six years. It's more about what the whole thing signifies. When she walks down the aisle, arm in arm with me next week, it's as if I am saying goodbye. Much like Margaret and Austin on another continent a couple of generations ago, Mala and Rupe had been blithely living their lives, unaware of each other, forging their own paths. Now after a year of tentative meals out, speculative walks in the woods, refashioned wardrobes, occasional arguments and make-ups, they are on the verge of committing themselves to a lifelong partnership. How can this be?

I ponder the words of the marriage service they have chosen and it all begins to make sense:

> Marriage is a gift of God in creation that brings husband and wife together in a joyful commitment to the end of their lives. It is given as the foundation of family life in which children are born and nurtured and in which each member of the family, in good

times and in bad, may find strength, companionship and comfort,
and grow to maturity in love.

It's easy for these semi-familiar words to slip off the tongue, but
I am struck by their depth. They are mystical in their profundity.
This union of two people is to set aside selfish agendas, to love each
other unconditionally. And these words help me see that marriage
is not a cultural convenience, not simply a legalizing device, not an
afterthought following extravagant stag-do's and hen nights, nor
even a religious ritual. It is a gift, a sacrament. Yet these words crackle
with realism too. Love doesn't stand still, it grows. Love rides the
rough times. It doesn't make 'giving away' my daughter any easier,
but it does put the whole thing into a broader, eternal perspective.

Next week marriage vows will be made. Rings will be exchanged
and bells will toll at the small medieval village church in Manas,
deep among the lavender fields of Drome Provence. As with her
grandparents, I marvel at how two independent spirits can come
together and fall in love. Two souls crossing an unseen threshhold as
independent travellers and finding companionship for life. Whether
random collisions or divine destiny, I do not doubt the legacy of the
reluctant emigres, Austin and Margaret. Like her older sisters and
cousins before her, our daughter and her spouse will continue the
great Burmese tradition of her grandfather and grandmother. Their
new home will be a place where friends and strangers alike will feel
part of the family.

I have, of course, another reason to be thankful to Austin and
Margaret. Were it not for their momentous decision to come to
these shores with their young family I would never have met April
on the lower deck of the school bus. She may have lost her jewelled
rings in the English Channel but we found in each other lasting
love. Were it not for her, my fascination with far-off Burma would
have remained naïve curiosity, an untested romance. It is unlikely I
would have visited the land of smiling people and golden pagodas.
Nor had I discovered what was behind those smiles and what those

April and me collecting stones from a field of lavender

pagodas signified. Even now, I am still discovering new mysteries about April and her native country. An intensely private individual, she is the reluctant voice behind this book. It's not that April didn't want this story to be told, she is just more comfortable without the exposure, the limelight. A conversation a few months back went like this:

> A: Where's my magazine?
> C: It's upstairs.
> A: What's up there?
> C: Your magazine.
> A: I know.
> C: Well, if you knew, why did you ask me?
> A: I didn't ask you, I was talking to myself.

(Long pause)

> C: Can you tell me more about Burma?
> A: No.
> C: Why not?

A: It's not something you can write or talk about.

C: I just want to understand better.

A: You have to read between the lines.

(Another pause)

C: What lines? . . . You're not giving me any lines to read between.

Today, April and I still live the joys and frustrations of traversing the border controls of cultural allegiance. Daily we negotiate the no man's land of personal defences. As well as discovering a family so different from my own and a country I had barely heard of as a teenager, I have found out a lot about myself. To my impatience to make things happen, April brings stillness. To my thriftiness, borne of my parents' post-war ration books, she brings unhesitating generosity. To my readiness to 'make do' she brings an unstinting pursuit of quality, of the best. To my weird Western obsession with being punctual, she brings oriental timelessness. To my hastening on to the next thing, she brings the beauty of this moment. While I was steadily 'building a career' throughout my working life, April just seemed to let her life experiences naturally unfold. She studied at the London College of Fashion, worked for a charity, raised four delightful daughters and dabbled in various design projects.

'What are you going to do with it?' I said when she completed her mid-life degree in Psychology.

'I don't know,' she replied as if it was an irrelevant question. 'I did it because I enjoyed it.'

As it happens she went on to train as a counsellor. If there is a golden thread of continuity through April's life, it is about beautifying. As a mother, as a gardener, as a fashion and home designer, as a wedding planner, as a friend and confidante, she brings her gracious and generous gaze wherever she goes.

Sometimes West collides with East. On occasions, it is predatory and closes an era. As in 1885 when Thibaw, the last king of Burma, was deposed by a single British gunboat sailing into the muddy waters off Mandalay. At other times, as in our case, the collision is positive and life-affirming. To slightly alter the last line of a poem by that arch-colonialist, Rudyard Kipling:

'Oh, East is East and West is West, and never the twain shall meet,
Till Earth and Sky stand presently at God's great Judgment Seat;
But there is neither East nor West, Border, nor Breed, nor Birth,
When boy and girl stand face to face, though they come from the ends of
    the Earth!'

As I reflect on my relationship with April, which has withstood buffeting for four and a half decades, I conclude that one may not have to be in love to learn a new language but maybe one has to learn a new 'language' to fall in love.

We sit in contented silence at the breakfast table.

'Why do they do that?' April says randomly, not actually specifying what she is referring to. She is looking into the middle distance in a dreamy but concentrated sort of way. This is one of her specialities.

'Do what?' I ask, slightly curious and searching for a visual clue.

No answer comes and I return to scanning the newspaper. Many of April's best conversations are in her head. Possibly, one legacy of Mount Hermon and the broken schooling that followed—the fracture of teenage friendships, the turmoil of switching countries— is going to a safe place where others do not intrude. It's from that place that she seems to gather strength and determine what is important. Sir George Scott, an unsung Victorian adventurer in colonial Burma, once observed: 'A Burmese woman really in earnest about her business is more than a match for any man.'

ADDENDUM

For a while, it seemed Myanmar was inching towards a more democratic rule. But in recent days, history has repeated itself with tragic consequences. In November 2020, the National League for Democracy (NLD) party, led by Aung San Suu Kyi, won new elections by a landslide. As they had done originally in 1988 and again in 2015.

On 1 February , the day the new parliament was due to open, the generals, backed by the armed forces, seized control and demanded a rerun of the vote, claiming widespread fraud. The NLD's refusal to account for 'no-name' votes particularly riled the junta. Military commander-in-chief Min Aung Hlaing announced a year-long state of emergency after which it would hold 'free and fair elections.' Ms Suu Kyi has been held at an unknown location since the coup. NLD MPs who managed to escape arrest formed a new group in hiding. Their leader has urged protesters to defend themselves against the crackdown (Alice Cuddy, BBC News, 1 April 2021).

Since the seizure of power, protest on the streets has been escalating by the day, the largest since the so-called Saffron Revolution in 2007, when thousands of monks rose up against the military regime. At the time of writing, more than 700 deaths have been reported with thousands injured on the streets of Yangon, Mandalay, Nay Pyi Daw, Bago, and many other towns and cities across the country. Protesters, who include teachers, lawyers, students, bank officers, and government workers, are enraged by the actions of the military who have arbitrarily imposed restrictions, including curfews and limits to gatherings. In the plaintive words of one Burmese youth in a newsfeed from the capital: 'We were just learning to fly, and now they have broken our wings'.

Armed with no more than handmade weapons, protestors have faced security forces using water canon, rubber bullets, and live ammunition and, in recent days, air attacks against the Karen in eastern Myanmar. Some soldiers, with no stomach for firing on their own people, have deserted across the border to India and Thailand. It has been reported that the military is now forcefully conscripting boys in their teens to swell their ranks.

Southeast Asian countries have been pursuing diplomatic efforts to end the crisis. However, the ten-member Association of Southeast Asian Nations (ASEAN) will not unanimously sign up for sanctions and condemnation of the junta. Thailand, Vietnam, Cambodia, and initially even the Philippines, once the most liberal member state on human rights and democracy, have all refused to criticize the coup, describing it as an internal matter. Singapore, the biggest foreign investor in Myanmar, has been stronger in its statements, expressing 'grave concern' and describing the use of lethal force against protesters as 'inexcusable' (Jonathan Head, BBC News, South East Asia correspondent, 26 February).

US Secretary of State Antony Blinken has accused the security forces of a 'reign of terror'. The US, UK, and European Union have all responded with sanctions on military officials. Sasa, who is mentioned in this book, has petitioned the United Nations as an envoy from Myanmar, but the veto from two member states, China and Russia, stymies any meaningful UN sanctions. Unusually China has backed calls for the release of Ms Suu Kyi and a return to democratic norms. But this needs to be tempered with a subtext of economic self-interest.

It looks highly unlikely that the intransigence of the military regime will soften soon. Perhaps we need to look to a younger generation of millennials, some of whom I interviewed for this book, for a brighter future. For sure, each of them is inspired by a higher purpose, forged by their Christian or Buddhist upbringing and values. All are operating outside the myopic bubble of central government at Naypyidaw and choosing to return to their home communities to pass on their experience and invest these skills for the next generation. For much-needed improvement in war-torn Myanmar, it is perhaps on these grassroots activists that we should pin our hopes.

Chris Mabey
16 April 2021

SOURCES

Suu Kyi, Aung San. 1991. *Freedom from Fear*. London: Penguin Books.

Suu Kyi, Aung San. 1997. *The Voice of Hope*. London: Penguin Books.

Than, Ba. 2003. *Myanmar's Attractions and Delights*. Yangon: Today Publishing House.

Bhatia, V (ed). 1994. *Rabindranath Tagore: Pioneer in Education*. New Delhi: Sahitya Chayan.

Chin Human Rights Organization. 2012. *Threats to Our Existence: Persecution of Ethnic Chin Christians in Burma*, 2 September

CSW (May 2019) *Burma's Identity crisis: how ethno-religious nationalism has led to religious intolerance, crimes against humanity and genocide* https://www.csw.org.uk/2019/05/21/report/4339/article.htm, accessed 30 May 2019

Human Rights Watch. 2009. *Myanmar Report* https://www.hrw.org/asia/myanmar-burma, 27 January

International Crisis Group. 2017. *Buddhism and State Power in Myanmar*, Report 290 (Asia) 5 September

Keane, David *https://www.mdxminds.com/2017/05/24/towards-universal-ratification-of-the-international-convention-on-the-elimination-of-all-forms-of-racial-discrimination-the-case-of-myanmar/* accessed 15 January 2019

Keane, David. 2018. Towards the Ratification of the International
    Convention on the Elimination of Racial Discrimination by
    Myanmar. Middlesex University. Working paper

King, Martin Luther (1967) https://kinginstitute.stanford.edu/king-
    papers/documents/where-do-we-go-here-address-delivered-
    eleventh-annual-sclc-convention accessed 4 December 2018

Larkin, Emma. 2004. *Secret Histories*. London: John Murray.

Lukianoff, Greg, and Jonathan Haidt. 2018. *The Coddling of the
    American Mind*. New York: Penguin Press.

Mabey, C, and D. Knights. 2018. (eds) *Leadership Matters? Finding
    Voice, Connection and Meaning in the 21st Century*. New York:
    Routledge.

Mabey, C, and W. Mayrhofer. 2015. (eds) *Developing Leadership:
    Questions Business Schools Don't Ask*. London: Sage.

MacLean, Rory. 2008. *Under the Dragon: A Journey through Burma*.
    London: Tauris Parke Paperbacks.

Mang, Pum Za. 2016. Buddhist Nationalism and Burmese
    Christianity. *Studies in World Christianity. 22 (2): 148–167*.

McPhedran, Colin, 2002. *White Butterflies*. Canberra: Pandanus
    Books.

Mineo, Liz. 2018. Back to Myanmar with fresh insights. *Harvard
    Gazette*. 19 November.

Naimark, Jared. 2018. https://www.irrawaddy.com/election/
    opinion/fukuyamas-flawed-take-on-burma *Fellow at Stanford
    University* accessed on 7 November

Nair, Keshavan. 1997. *A Higher Standard of Leadership: Lessons from
    the Life of Ghandi*. San Francisco: Berrett-Koehler.

Orwell, George. 1974. *Burmese Days*. London: Mariner Books.

Physicians for Human Rights (January 2011) *Life under the Junta:
    Evidence of Crimes Against Humanity in Burma's Chin State*
    https://s3.amazonaws.com/PHR_Reports/lifeunder-the-junta-
    burma-chin-state.pdf accessed 30 May: 2019

Popham, Peter. 2014. Burma's Wild, Wild West. *The Independent
    Magazine*. Saturday 3 May, 28–31.

Popham, Peter. 2012. *The Lady and the Peacock: The Life of Aung San Suu Kyi*. New York: The Experiment.

Prospect Burma https://prospectburma.org/success-stories/ accessed 10 July 2018

Sargent, Inge. 1994. *Twilight over Burma: My Life as a Shan Princess.* Hawaii: University of Hawaii Press.

Smith, A.W. 1930. Working Teak in Burma Forests. *The National Geographic Magazine.* August, LVIII No 2, 239–56.

Thant Myint-U. 2007. *The River of Lost Footsteps*. London: Faber and Faber.

The 2014 Myanmar Population and Housing Census (2017) *Thematic Report on Education Census Report*, Volume 4-H – Education

The Burma Star Association https://www.burmastar.org.uk/burma-campaign/battle-histories/the-battle-of-kohima/ accessed 22 May 2020

Ellis-Peterson, Hannah.2018. From Peace Icon to Pariah: Aung San Suu Kyi's fall from grace. *The Guardian.* Saturday 24 November.

Transnational Institute (2018) *From War to Peace in Kayah (Karenni) State: A Land at the Crossroads in Myanmar,* July

U Thant's Memoirs (1978) *View from the UN*, posthumously published, initially by Doubleday, p 24

U Thant House (2015) *U Thant: His Life and Legacy,* Exhibition on the life and legacy of former United Nations Secretary-General U Thant, 31 Panwa Street, Windermere Crescent, Yangon.

Unigwe, Chita. 2019. Beyond the West, there are many Gretas. *The Guardian*, October 5, p 5.

Williams, Rowan. 2012. Archbishop's address to the Synod of Rome, Stanford University https://kinginstitute.stanford.edu/king-papers/documents/where-do-we-go-here-address-delivered-eleventh-annual-sclc-convention accessed 4th December 2018

Wintle, Justin. 2007. *Perfect Hostage: A Life of Aung San Suu Kyi*. London: Faber and Faber. p 428.

FURTHER READING

Reports

CSW (21ˢᵗ May 2019) *Burma's identity crisis: How ethno-religious nationalism has led to religious intolerance, crimes against humanity and genocide.* This Report provides a comprehensive picture of violations of freedom of religion or belief throughout Myanmar. It examines the sources of intolerance, the role of legislation, the impact on Muslims and Christians across the country, the response of the international community and proposes future action. https://www.csw.org.uk/2019/05/21/report/4339/article.htm, accessed 30 May 2019

Transnational Institute (2018) *From War to Peace in Kayah (Karenni) State: A Land at the Crossroads in Myanmar.* I have drawn extensively on, and commend, this research report by Martin Smith and colleagues. *'Aid in itself does not solve conflict. Indeed, it can result in the paradox in many conflict-divided countries of "aid rich, people poor", often furthering the centralisation rather than reform of government.'*

Physicians for Human Rights (2011) *'Life under the Junta: Evidence of Crimes Against Humanity in Burma's Chin State'*, January https://s3.amazonaws.com/PHR_Reports/lifeunder-the-junta-burma-chin-state.pdf accessed 30 May 2019

The United Nations Office of the High Commissioner for Human Rights, *UN Special Rapporteur report on the situation of human rights in Myanmar, A/73/332,* August 2018 with reference to the number of churches destroyed or damaged in Kachin and Shan States.

Books

Craig, Charmaine. 2018. *Miss Burma.* London: Grove Press. (A novel, based on the author's own family, depicting the shifting fortunes of a Karen family in post-War Burma.)

Fink, Christina. 2001. *Living Silence: Burma under Military Rule.* London: Zed Books. (A searching analysis of the psychological effects of sustained military rule on a wide diversity of people in Burma.)

Larkin, Emma. 2004. *Secret Histories.* London: John Murray Publishers.

(The author takes a year-long journey through Burma, writing in reference to the places George Orwell worked and wrote.)

Maclean, Rory. 1998. *Under the Dragon.* London: Harper Collins. (In this classic literary travel novel, Maclean traces his journey through Myanmar in search of a traditional Burmese woven basket.)

Marshall, Andrew. 2002. *The Trouser People: A Story of Burma in the Shadow of the Empire.* London: Penguin Books Ltd. (An engaging account of Sir George Scott, a Victorian adventurer who, among other things, introduced football into deepest Burma.)

Mason, Daniel. 2002. *The Piano Tuner: A Novel.* London: Picador. (A fictional story about a piano tuner who travels to the jungles of Burma in the years following its colonisation by the British.)

Maung Maung, (ed). 2011. *Aung San of Burma.* Yangon: Unity Publishing House. (A revealing account of Major-General Aung San through the eyes of those who knew him well.)

MiMi, Aye. 2019. *Mandalay: Recipes and Tales from a Burmese Kitchen.* London: Bloomsbury Publishing. (A family story and stunning photographs woven around traditional Burmese cuisine.)

Mullen, Matthew. 2014. *Pathways that Changed Myanmar.* London: Zed Books. (A thorough analysis of the victimisation of the Rohingya Muslims.)

Popham, Peter. 2012. *The Lady and the Peacock.* New York: The Experiment. (An exhaustive biography of Aung San Suu Kyi, rigorously sourced and engagingly written.)

Rogers, Benedict. 2012. *Burma: Nation at the Crossroads.* London: Rider (Penguin Random House) Publishing. (A comprehensive account of Burma's struggle for freedom, informed by a moral framework and well-researched sources.)

Rogers, Benedict. 2010. *Than Shwe*. Chiang Mai: Silkworm Books. (A unique story of the rise to power of the tyrannical general who led the ruling military junta in Myanmar from 1992 to 2011)

Myint-U, Thant. 2007. *The River of Lost Footsteps*. London: Faber and Faber.

(A highly informative and thorough account of the histories of Burma from the third century to the present day. It's author is Burmese, the grandson of U.N. Secretary General U-Thant)

Winn, Patrick. 2018. *Hello Shadowlands: Inside the Meth Fiefdoms, Rebel Hideouts and Bomb-scarred Party Towns of Southeast Asia*. London: Icon Books. (One telling comment: 'On paper, Burma's top exports are gas, precious gems and legumes . . . but this is a joke . . . The real top exports are meth, jade and heroin - all derived from the war-racked hinterlands.')

Wintle, Justin. 2007. *The Perfect Hostage*. London: Hutchinson. (A scholarly account of the life of Aung San Suu Kyi, starting with her father General Aung San, based on first-hand sources.)

Phan, Zoya and D. Lewis. 2009. *Little Daughter: a Memoir of Survival in Burma and the West*. London: Simon & Schuster. (Brought up an animist in the jungle, this book tells the story of Zoya Phan and the ongoing oppression and human rights abuses in Burma, especially among the Karen.)

Enjoyed this book?
Interested in hearing more about Myanmar?
Want to know more about the author?

Visit my website **www.chrismabey.co.uk**.
I will be glad to hear from you.

ACKNOWLEDGEMENT

I am indebted to April's family. It was casual conversations with her mother Margaret, father Austin and Aunt Jessie that first sparked my interest in their homeland, usually laced with delicious Burmese meals. Their vivid memories brought twentieth century Burma alive for me. In the other direction, I'm grateful to my daughters Zoe and husband Matt, Sundy, Louisa and Mala Su and her husband Rupe, for checking the book at various drafts.

A group of friends, some writers themselves, have also provided invaluable feedback along the way: John and Eileen, Andy, Jane, Daniel, Christine, Phil, Jean, Clare, Martin, Bob and Celia, Steve, Siew Lin and Edmund, and Paul. A special thanks to Lawrence and Marj who travelled and taught with us on six of our seven visits to Yangon and to Ewen who joined us twice.

For their timely, editorial input, my thanks to Anastasia Parkes and Amanda Saint, both from Jericho Writers, and to Amberdawn Manaois from Penguin Random House.

The staff of Prospect Burma have been enormously helpful by putting me in touch with scholarship students. I am indebted to all the Burmese millennials who whisper hope for their forsaken but beautiful country, and cousin Monty, who faithfully acted as our guide on so many occasions. I must also mention Lincoln and Leah, the Chin couple who run the small Bible college and pre-school in Yangon. Their compassion and dedication over the years has been heart-warming. They and their family have become good friends.